Information and IT literacy

Enabling learning in the 21st century

Information and IT literacy

Enabling learning in the 21st century

Edited by
Allan Martin and Hannelore Rader

facet publishing

Published by
Facet Publishing
7 Ridgmount Street
London WC1E 7AE

Facet Publishing (formerly Library Association Publishing) is wholly owned by
CILIP: the Chartered Institute of Library and Information Professionals.

First published 2003
Reprinted 2003

British Library Cataloguing in Publication Data
A catalogue record for this book is available from the British Library.

ISBN 1-85604-463-7

Typeset from editors' disks by Facet Publishing in 11/13 Elegant Garamond
and Humanist 521.
Printed and made in Great Britain by MPG Books Ltd, Bodmin, Cornwall.

Contents

Contributors

Carl Alphonce, University of Buffalo, State University of New York, USA
Kirsty Baker, The Open University, UK
Susan Beatty, University of Calgary, Canada
Deborah Bragan-Turner, University of Nottingham, UK
Debra Burhans, University of Buffalo, State University of New York, USA
Caitriona Curran, Queen's University Belfast, UK
Chris Dillon, The Open University, UK
Nigel Ford, University of Sheffield, UK
Peter Godwin, South Bank University, UK
Tessa Griffiths, King's College London, UK
Helen Hathaway, University of Reading, UK
Mark Hepworth, Loughborough University, UK
Susanne Hodges, University of York, UK
Linda Hodgkinson, The Open University, UK
Hilary Johnson, University College Northampton, UK, and SCONUL Task Force on Information Skills, UK
Gareth J. Johnson, University of York, UK
Bill Johnston, University of Strathclyde, UK
Helene Kershner, University of Buffalo, State University of New York, USA
Philippa Levy, University of Sheffield, UK
Claire McGuinness, University College Dublin, Republic of Ireland
Catherine McKeown, Queen's University Belfast, UK
Alison McNab, University of Nottingham, UK
Sarah McNicol, University of Central England, UK
Andrew Madden, University of Sheffield, UK

Louise Makin, Manchester Metropolitan University, UK
Allan Martin, University of Glasgow, UK
Lindsey Martin, Edge Hill College of Higher Education, UK
David Miller, University of Sheffield, UK
Nader Naghshineh, University of Tehran, Iran
Gill Needham, The Open University, UK
Jo Parker, The Open University, UK
Juliette Pavey, University of Durham, UK
Janet Peters, University of Wales College, Newport, UK
Emma Place, University of Bristol, UK
Simon Price, University of Bristol, UK
Hannelore Rader, University of Louisville, Kentucky, USA
Peter Reffell, University of Leeds, UK
Kate Sharp, University of Bristol, UK
Barbara Sherman, University of Buffalo, State University of New York, USA
Paul Smith, University of Bristol, UK
Caroline Stern, Ferris State University, USA
Ruth Stubbings, Loughborough University, UK
Audrey Sutton, Kilmarnock, UK
J. Stephen Town, Cranfield University, UK
Deborah Walters, University of Buffalo, State University of New York, USA
Sheila Webber, University of Sheffield, UK
Sylvia Williamson, Edge Hill College of Higher Education, UK

Editors' introduction

The creation of this volume was stimulated by a sense which both of us had, on each side of the Atlantic, of being personally involved in immensely significant educational change. This change is part of the response made by higher education to the challenge presented by the emergence of IT- and information-rich learning environments. One of us, as a librarian, was faced with the challenge of giving students meaningful access to an almost infinite, and endlessly growing, quantity of information available through online sources. The other was faced with the challenge of developing a university-wide programme that would enable students to use the IT tools that are offered to them, tools that enable them to access information, to analyse it, to organize and present it, and to communicate with their tutors and their peers. It soon became clear to both of us that we stood on converging tracks, that the sorts of skills necessary to handle information could not be separated from those necessary to use IT.

We are far from unique in this respect. In many institutions IT and library services have been brought together. Often this is a marriage of convenience, or an organisational dodge, a neat scooping together of 'services that support the student'; in such cases the two may continue to exist independently side by side, their cultures not even overlapping. Sometimes, however, the attempt is made to make the merger real, to restructure completely the way in which IT and library services serve the learner; in these cases the real difficulties emerge – long-evolving and deep-rooted occupational cultures, involving apprenticeship and professional qualification, expertise and the language used to express it, perceptions of the customer, and assumptions about what is worthwhile. Add to this the perceived threat to one's own job security implied by structural change (especially if presented as 'opportunity for rationalization'), and there may be a recipe for inaction and even resistance. Organizational convergence can seem like worlds on course for collision. Successful mergers have more often been the result of a reaching out from both sides, each drawing in the other in order to provide a better service for students, for researchers and for teachers (and presented as 'opportunity for service enhancement').

All too often those whose responsibility it is to enable learners to make best use of their learning environment resolutely persist in ploughing their own furrow, not taking their eyes, as it were, from the soil. 'User education' or 'bibliographic instruction' remains focused on the library stock, and the library's own online links, while 'IT training' concentrates on the delivery of routines for using applications software, including web browsers.

Yet there is a growing number of educators who realize that these two tracks are both different sides of the same coin, that using IT tools and using information are fundamental and interlocking aspects of empowering the learner to learn successfully in an environment that is well provided with both. IT skills are fundamental to gaining access to and finding one's way around online information sources, while thoughtful deployment of IT tools is necessary to use the information gained effectively, and to present the results of study.

This convergence is more easily recognized by those who realize that low-level skills are only the beginning of enlightenment, and that learners are given more power to learn if they can take a thoughtful attitude towards the appropriate use of IT and information tools, and of information, and a critical attitude towards the results of using such tools. Successfully achieving study tasks is about thinking as well as pressing buttons. Knowing how to use a browser to navigate the web is a key skill, but it is also necessary to choose the appropriate pathway to access information that is likely to be relevant, and to be able to critically evaluate the quality and relevance of information located to the study task. Knowing how to edit text in a word-processor is a key skill, but it is also necessary to select the appropriate applications for the task, and to use the facilities they offer to convey effectively one's understanding of the material and the argument that is being presented. Information and IT facilities are tools for thinking, not substitutes for it. Developing a programme that delivers critical and evaluative skills is challenging, partly because more justification is required and more time and resource to deliver courses and support, and partly because the more high level the skills become the more there is another convergence, with what the academics do.

In this respect accreditation and certification can be a mirror of our ambitions to serve our students. Basic skills certification is a useful threshold marker, but only a beginning, and the challenge here is to see the critical and evaluative use of IT and information tools developed at higher levels of accreditation. This means working closely with teachers to tease out the role of higher-level information and IT skills in achieving learning outcomes for subject courses, and to explore the ways in which these skills can be delivered at the right point, either through central provision or by subject teachers themselves. There is no reason why higher-level information and IT skills should not be incorporated into the learning outcomes of the course or module. Who delivers the skills is less important than that delivery is integrated with subject teaching, so that the skills can be consolidated in relevant practice as soon as they have been learned, and that IT and information skills providers work closely with subject teachers.

Notions of key skills and employability underline the linkage between what is learned in educational contexts and the use to which it is put in employment or in everyday life. What we give to our students is not just intended to make them better students, but to make them more effective employees, and to enable them to live more fulfilling lives. Thus we should be considering how information and IT skills link with the delivery of other identified key or core transferable skills. In this work we need to be sensitive to employers' recruitment practices; for instance, since many employers of graduates now assume them to possess basic IT literacy, we should not waste energy or resources agonizing over which basic IT certification is provided. Since employers generally prefer graduates to have higher-level synthesizing and teamwork skills, we need to consider how work with information and IT tools can contribute to development of such skills.

One of the main challenges we face is to develop a theoretical context for the discussion of issues concerning information and IT literacy. There is often in this area a gulf between theory and practice, with practitioners working very hard to deliver information or IT training to students, focusing very hard on delivery issues, but with little time to consider the broader context in which they are active. We should aspire to a theoretical context which allows for critical examination of the whole range of issues surrounding information and IT literacy: definition of the nature of information and IT literacy, and justifications for provision to deliver these skills. Part of achieving this is having the confidence to believe that 'service providers' can take an analytical and critical view of what they do, and can seek theoretical models to underpin what they do.

The book is a snapshot taken in the midst of change. As such, it captures the thinking and experience of some of those who are implementing change, some of those who are looking back on it, and some of those who are looking forward to the next evolution. It also includes input from those who are viewing the change process from a research perspective. Although the collection is predominantly from higher education, there is also some consideration of the school and further education sectors. And although the largest number of chapters come from England and Scotland, this is nevertheless an international collection, for it reflects changes that are happening globally. The convergence of information and IT literacies is a change still happening, and this collection will not be the last word on it.

The opportunity to put this volume together was furnished by the IT&ILit2002 conference, held at the University of Glasgow in March 2002. This was the first time that those involved in education were able to come together, from many parts of the world, to focus on the convergence of information and IT literacies. Most of the chapters in this book began life as presentations to that conference, and have benefited from the quality and the intensity of the debate which took place there. For the 2003 conference, the rather cumbersome 'IT&ILit' name has been replaced simply by 'eLit'; and eLit2003 will take place at Glasgow Caledonian University, 11–13 June 2003 (see www.eLit2003.com). All we know of eLit2004 at the time of writing (May 2003) is that it will not be in Glasgow (see www.elit2004.com); but we do know that the debate for which the eLit conference offers a forum is one which is central to the success of the educational enterprise in an information-rich and participatory global society.

The book is organized into four parts. Part 1 sets out the context in which current developments are taking place. Part 2 takes one particular model, the 'Seven Pillars' model of information literacy proposed by SCONUL (Society of College, National and University Libraries), and highlights a number of activities taking place in the UK based upon this model. Part 3 looks at the range of issues raised in implementation of information and IT literacy programmes. Part 4 provides a flavour of the current research being pursued in this area.

Part 1, Contexts, is intended to set out the landscape in which the developments discussed in the rest of the book are taking place. Allan Martin outlines the changes that have taken place in learning style and in the use of new technology in education. He goes on to examine the evolution of concepts of computer/IT literacy and information literacy, and suggests that these be synthesized within a concept of e-literacy. Finally he identifies some of the challenges raised by the adoption of e-literacy as an encompassing concept for information and IT literacies. Hannelore Rader focuses on the emergence of information literacy as an educational priority. She examines the development of several national standards of information literacy, offering examples from around the world on how these standards can be integrated into curriculum and practice. She emphasizes the development of creative partnerships between librarians and academics, and considers the outcomes of successful information literacy programmes.

Part 2, Exploring the Seven Pillars Model, shows how one particular information literacy model, in this case the 'Seven Pillars' framework devised in the UK by SCONUL, can be developed into the implementation stage. The examples presented show that the framework allows a range of practical implementation strategies and directions. Hilary Johnson outlines the work of the SCONUL Task Force on Information Skills, of which she is convenor, and in particular the 'Seven Pillars' model which has been the most significant output of the group. Other members of the Task Force are involved in writing each of the other four chapters in this section. Stephen Town provides further context to the Task Force's work, and focuses on the achievements, through the series of workshops across the UK, in identifying critical success factors for information literacy programmes. Chris Dillon and colleagues present an account of developmental work in information literacy at the UK Open University, focusing on three initiatives: SAFARI, a generic web-based resource designed to be used by students to meet a broad range of information skills outcomes, and designed to be integrated into the curriculum; MOSAIC, a standalone information literacy course, based on the Seven Pillars model, and developed out of experience with SAFARI; and work in the key skills area, resulting in the production specification of an information literacy key skill specification. Janet Peters and her colleagues report on an investigation of information skills delivery in UK higher education institutions within three subject areas, Theology, Chemistry and Education; they find that there are no major differences in the way in which information skills are delivered in these subjects, nor in the learning outcomes, from the perspectives of both librarians and academics, and conclude that a generic approach in delivering information literacy to first-year students could be successful. Peter Godwin describes the work carried out at South Bank University to set up a series of detailed information skills benchmarks at five levels, as part of its Core Skills framework, and considers the likely impact of the framework.

Part 3, Challenges to Implementation, explores the range of issues raised in implementation of information and IT literacy programmes. Sheila Webber and Bill Johnston offer a vision of the information-literate student and the information-literate university, in the context of which they examine issues surrounding the assessment of information literacy, and identify the factors and modes of assessment that form a framework for progress, as well as the problems that need to be faced. Caroline Stern considers the challenges facing the designer of an information literacy course, placing this alongside the results of a survey of incoming students' information literacy competencies.

The next six chapters focus on experience at particular institutions, in the UK and Canada. Peter Reffell presents an account of the way in which delivering IT literacy was addressed at the University of Leeds, challenging the assumption that IT skills training packages are suitable for students in higher education, and arguing that a more sophisticated approach which is sensitive to student diversity and the needs of higher education is necessary. Catherine McKeown and Caitriona Curran report a comparable process from Queen's

University Belfast, in which a number of initiatives were carried out, which enabled a proposal for an institution-wide IT training strategy to be developed. They conclude, like Reffell, that a more complex and developmental framework is required than that assumed by skills training packages, and outline the student and skills development model that they propose. Lindsey Martin and Sylvia Williamson discuss the development of IT and information skills modules in different subject areas at Edge Hill College, and show how these are embedded within subject curricula. Susan Beatty describes a different approach to integration of information and IT literacy with learning activity, encapsulated in a vision that was carried through to the creation of the Information Commons at the University of Calgary, and that involved genuine convergence of the attitudes and activities of library and IT staff. Susanne Hodges and Gareth Johnson discuss the experience of Iliad, the IT and information literacy programme of the University of York, which has been running since 1995; successes of the programme so far are identified, and the challenges that it now faces are confronted. Ruth Stubbings and Alison McNab outline the issues surrounding delivery of information skills at Loughborough University, and the experience with the DotM (Database of the Month) sessions, one-off highly focused sessions intended to be of direct practical relevance to students.

The remaining chapters in Part 3 consider IT and information literacy from a range of directions. Emma Place and her colleagues discuss the structure, value and application of the RDN (Resource Discovery Network) Virtual Training Suite, a public-funded free educational resource designed to help students in UK further and higher education to develop internet information literacy. Results are available from early evaluation of the RDN, showing a positive attitude to it from users, and suggesting that it is an important resource worth developing further. Juliette Pavey offers the results of an IT skills audit of staff and students at the University of Durham, and discusses the outcomes of the audit. Deborah Walters and her colleagues at the State University of New York at Buffalo describe how a computer fluency course (including both computing concepts and skills) was redesigned to offer fewer lectures and more hands-on time; as a result students were more satisfied with the experience, they seemed to have learned more, and, because of a shift to the use of undergraduates instead of graduates as support staffing, the course cost less to deliver.

In Part 4, Research Perspectives, contributors describe a variety of research activities involving secondary and tertiary education students and faculty in England, Ireland, Scotland, Singapore and Iran. Sarah McNicol describes the work of a project investigating children's IT and information literacy development, and looking in particular at the help they are given by others, especially parents and friends. The work suggests that children develop a sophisticated ability to identify other people who can assist them in dealing with IT and information literacy challenges, a social aspect of learning often overlooked by their teachers. Mark Hepworth provides information on one aspect of information literacy, searching electronic information, and suggests how literacy in this arena can be taught based on an in-depth study of search sessions using web search engines and public access catalogues. Results indicate the use of electronic information skills should be taught within the context of teaching and learning a new subject. Andrew Madden and his colleagues report on a project to determine what teachers require of school children in terms of effective internet information seeking and critical evaluative information skills. Results suggested that children need clear guidelines, that they learn more from peer groups than searching the internet, that internet use appeals to students more than using books, that students are often more skilled in using the internet than teachers and that various teaching mandates prevent teachers from making the best use of the internet in teaching. Claire McGuinness discusses how information literacy is often viewed as an extra and not a regular, required component of post-secondary undergraduate education in the Irish Republic. Interviews with academic lecturers from the Social Sciences in five universities were analysed and show that information literacy plays a relatively insignificant role in their teaching. Louise Makin discusses the 'Big Blue' project, which examined information skills training in the UK, Australia and the USA, developed a model of information skills development, and created, from the various outputs of the project, an Information Skills Toolkit intended to assist institutions that are planning an information skills programme. Audrey Sutton describes a study aimed at finding ways of improving the way in which teachers and librarians can improve children's learning through utilizing information resources. The research suggests that the use of a clear framework of information skills against which to evaluate children's development and give teachers a greater understanding of pupils' information-related activities could improve learning. Finally, Nader Naghshineh considers information-seeking behaviour in terms of cultural environments, addressing a range of issues including knowledge generation, identification and dissemination of information, social, psychological and communication issues and technology and management.

Taking all the contributions to this book together, it is clear that they represent a ferment of ideas and activity. We see the creation, utilization and modification of different models of information or IT literacy, the development of new environments for learning and experimental courses, the exploration of information-related behaviour, and lots of thought about the significance of it all. In all this diversity of activity, we nevertheless see the emergence of a new community of practice, the e-literacy community. The IT&ILit2002 conference was perhaps the first gathering of that community; and the succeeding eLit conferences will maintain the opportunity for face-to-face meetings. A growing community, although it can keep in touch by e-mail and post information through the web, still needs to meet face to face; it is about people as well as ideas. The community will also create a literature, and this collection is part of that process. We hope that readers of this volume will be able to take an active parts in the evolution of e-literacy as a crucial enabling factor in lifelong learning for the 21st century.

Note on terminology

There is some terminological duplication in the *IT* (information technology) area, with the abbreviations *ICT* (information and communications technologies) and *C&IT* (communications and information technologies) also used in Europe or the UK. *C&IT* has become a semi-official term in the UK, but is not used elsewhere. *ICT* has been adopted by the organs of the European Commission and is the term most widely used by the educational bodies of EU Member States; it is also used by some UK agencies. *IT* however is still the preferred term in the USA and the rest of the world. In the UK further education sector *ILT* (information and learning technology) has become the accepted term. These terms tend to be used with the same meanings in discussions of the provision of services for students and staff. To avoid confusion, in this book we have compromised on IT, since it is the term most widely used across the world. This is not to suggest that it is any better, or any worse, than other approximately equivalent acronyms. Sometimes the other acronyms will, however, appear in particular chapters. Do not be put off by this.

Acknowledgements

We are grateful for the help of the following group of international colleagues, who reviewed the contributions and offered many constructive suggestions:

Patricia Breivik, San José State University, California, USA
Alex Byrne, University of Technology, Sydney, Australia
Alix Hayden, University of Calgary, Canada
Jesus Lau, Universidad Autonoma de Juarez, Mexico
Derek Law, University of Strathclyde, Glasgow, Scotland
Bozena Mannova, Czech Technical University, Prague, Czech Republic
Klaus Merle, Johannes-Gutenberg University, Mainz, Germany
Ola Pilerot, University of Skovde, Sweden
Alex Reid, University of Western Australia
Paul Thomson, Jordanhill School, Glasgow, Scotland
Les Watson, Glasgow Caledonian University, Scotland

The members of the IT&ILit2002 Steering Committee, of which Allan Martin was the convenor, also contributed to the review process. They are Susan Ashworth and Irene Brown of the University of Glasgow, Karen Barton and Margaret McCann from Glasgow Caledonian University, and Shona Cameron and Nick Joint of the University of Strathclyde.

David Gentles at the IT Education Unit, University of Glasgow, played a major part in formatting the files, preparing the manuscript and compiling the index, and Rebecca Casey at Facet Publishing put up with the delays and did not give up on us.

Allan Martin
Hannelore Rader

Part 1
Contexts

1

Towards e-literacy

Allan Martin

Introduction

Over the past few decades, the view of teaching and learning has changed dramatically. The emergence of student-focused learning models has led to re-examination of the activities of learning. At the same time, information technology (IT) has enabled new ways of setting up learning activities. In the IT-rich learning environment, students' achievement of IT (information technology) and information literacy becomes essential to their success as learners. This chapter considers these changes, and identifies some of the challenges facing the institution, and the protagonists of IT and information literacy.

Learning styles

There has been, during the last three decades, a major shift in the way in which teaching and learning in higher education are perceived. Up to the 1960s the notion of teaching as the imparting of academic knowledge was largely taken for granted in the university, with the traditional methods of the lecture (for delivery of knowledge), the tutorial (for discussion of knowledge), and the essay (for demonstration of knowledge inculcation). During the 1960s and 1970s student-centred theories began to be adopted, drawing upon the work of psychologists such as Vygotsky, Piaget and Bruner, who emphasized the role of the learner and the centrality of learning as a participatory and interactive process. The placing of the student at the centre of discussions of learning was implied by the growing popularity of constructivist theories of learning. According to Perkins (1992, 49), 'Central to the vision of constructivism is the notion of the organism as "active" – not just responding to stimuli, as in the behaviourist rubric, but engaging, grappling, and seeking to make sense of things.' Scott, Dyson and Gater (1987, 7–8, following Driver and Bell, 1986) summarize the key elements of a constructivist view of learning in science:

1   Learning outcomes depend not only on the learning environment but also on the prior knowledge, attitudes and goals of the learner.

2   Learning involves the construction of knowledge through experience with the physical environment and through social interaction.

3   Constructing links with prior knowledge is an active process involving the generation, checking and restructuring of ideas or hypotheses.

4   Learning science is not simply a matter of adding to and extending existing concepts, but may involve their radical re-organisation.

5   Meanings, once constructed, can be accepted or rejected.

6   Learning is not passive. Individuals are purposive beings who set their own goals and control their own learning.

7   Students frequently bring similar ideas, about natural phenomena, to the classroom. This is hardly surprising when one considers the extent of their shared experiences.

Central to the constructivist model is interaction as a learning catalyst, with the subject material, with the student's own experience, and with other individuals (tutors, students, etc.). The significance of intellectual interaction and feedback is captured in Pask's Conversation Theory (Pask, 1976), and in Laurillard's 'conversational framework' (Laurillard, 1993, 1997). In Laurillard's model, four types of activity make up the learning process in higher education: discursive (dialogue between tutor and student), interactive (engagement with and feedback from the subject domain), adaptation (of descriptions given and tasks set, by tutor and by student), and reflection (on experience and performance). Mayes emphasises the cyclical, and therefore maturational, nature of the process by proposing a recurring sequence of three stages, conceptualization (interaction between student's existing knowledge structures and new information), construction (application and testing of new conceptualizations through carrying out of relevant tasks) and dialogue (elaboration and testing of new conceptualizations through interaction with tutors and colleagues and personal reflection) (UHI, 1999, 24).

Learning is also recognized as a sequential process, the character of which may change over time. Cognitive theories such as those of Piaget posit a set of stages which the cognitive system will pass through as it becomes more mature and complex, moving from processes focusing upon concrete stimuli towards those with an increasingly conceptual element. It is suggested that a sequence of learning maturation can be observed in many students in higher education: a learning of what are the appropriate learning processes for a higher education context. Perry (1970) observed a movement from a *dualistic* perspective, through which problems were viewed as essentially simple and having right and wrong answers, towards a *relativistic* perspective, viewing problems as complex and not necessarily possessing 'correct' or even clear solutions.

Perception of the learner

The change in perspective in learning is changing the way in which teaching is perceived. In the context of theories of learning which focus on the active involvement of the learner in the construction of meaning, teaching becomes a process of facilitation of student learning, rather than one of supplying knowledge to passive receivers. Teaching is still an essential element in the educational process, since education is at base a process of cultural induction, with the educators as the bearers of the culture. New forms, such as resource-based learning, encourage the active participation of the student in the learning process. Thus, Cresswell (1998) discusses a first-year biology course in which the traditional lecture format was replaced with a resource-based learning structure, in which students were divided into groups of six or seven, each group being assigned a postgraduate demonstrator as 'mentor' and set ten tasks leading to the preparation of a scientific paper; and argues that the change led to increases in both staff efficiency and 'educational value', as well as fostering personal transferable skills, such as teamwork, time management and IT skills. A development of resource-based learning is PBL (problem-based learning), which seeks to move beyond bounded and structured tasks focused on 'academic' resources to a real-life dimension, requiring difficult questions of judgement to be addressed. Problem-based learning has been the basis of reconstructed curricula in a number of medical schools.

As theories of learning have developed, so has the model of the learner, from a model of an empty pot to be filled with knowledge or a *tabula rasa* to be inscribed upon by the teacher, through a behaviourist one of the learner as enthusiastic rat to be rewarded for displaying remembered behaviour or knowledge, to a constructivist model of an individual creating and re-creating his/her map of existence and planning/re-planning the way through it. For the first model, the lecture and tutorial were the appropriate activity, for the second, the cumulative delivery and testing of small units of knowledge or practice. For the constructivist model, student-focused modes of delivery are appropriate, which allow students to develop their own models of knowledge and practice, and processes of assessment which offer continuous feedback from self, colleagues and teachers.

Yet with the move to centrality of the learner, there has also come a recognition of the learner as more than merely a learner, as an individual who happens to be, on some specific occasion, also a learner. Learning is a situated activity, inseparable from the learner's life-world; meaning is constructed by the learner as an intentional act in a social context. Thus the psycho-social model of the learner becomes more complex, as each not only addresses the mastery of competencies, but also has expectations of the educational process, which may be social and vocational as well as academic, and intentions or goals that are focused and reformulated as education proceeds, but that also extend beyond the academic. Indeed, for many students, the mastery of academic knowledge and practice may only be part of the baggage taken on board on entering higher education, and can be jettisoned with relief immediately on leaving it. Beaty, Gibbs and Morgan (1997) point to 'learning orientation' as a key construct in understanding the relationship between students and their learning: orientations may be *vocational* (with an employment objective), *academic* (demonstrating a subject interest), *personal* (focused on some personal development goal) or *social* (aimed at social gain), and focus on different purposes for learning. 'Approaches to learning' characterize both intentionalities in learning and processes adopted: Entwistle (1997, 19) defines three types of learner: *deep* learners seek understanding of structures, *surface* learners memorize elements of knowledge such as names, facts and procedures, while *strategic* learners strive to do whatever will deliver success.

With the recognition of the breadth of learner goals and expectations has also come the recognition that learners have a right to such goals and expectations, and the view that the providers of education are accountable to the learner. The expectation of 'value for money' or 'value-addedness' on the part of the student, and the additional expectation that HEIs (higher education institutions) should be able to explain how they satisfy such expectations is recognized as a valid aspect of educational provision. In this way psychological models of students as learners are being merged with sociological models of students as goal-oriented individual decision makers acting upon their own perception of the world (à la Max Weber) and economic models of students as choosers and consumers of educational products. The student is now accepted as a cultural being, one who lives in a cultural milieu, and the cultural background and assumptions of the student become significant elements of the learning process. At a time when political and economic exigencies dictate that higher education be extended far beyond a hitherto privileged fragment of the population, HEIs come face to face with cultures beyond those with which they have been wont to engage.

New technologies

As views of the learning process, and of the roles within it of the teacher and the student, have evolved, technological developments have, felicitously, offered means by which student-centred learning methodologies can be more effectively implemented, and a major phenomenon of higher education from the 1980s onwards has been the massive influx of new technology into higher education. There is no doubt that increasing use of IT has been an assumption in policy development, sometimes under the impression that deployment of IT solutions will reduce costs, usually in the belief that it will somehow improve the quality of the educational process. Langlois (1997), reporting to UNESCO (United Nations Educational, Scientific and Cultural Organization), argues that for both economic, political and social reasons universities must adopt IT: in economic terms, universities should adopt IT to be efficient and competitive; in political terms, governments are pressing universities to reduce costs, and IT represents a route for doing this; and in social terms, students' demand must be taken into account, and students demand IT provision.

> A new type of student, computer-literate, will expect that his university and its teaching staff are equally familiar and equipped with new technologies. As a service to their students, universities have to enhance Information Technologies as, in future years, it will be widely spread in all areas of the labour market. Information literacy will be essential for all future employees. Modern students are now looking for more flexible learning patterns and universities must commit themselves to creating new learning environments.   (Langlois, 1997, 2)

Langlois (4–5) identifies six ways in which teaching and learning will benefit from ICT: expansion and increased efficiency of the instructional process; the development of new teaching materials and distance learning modules; increased cost-effectiveness; changes in the role of the teacher to that of facilitator and guide rather than provider of knowledge; changes in learning styles towards more student-focused modes; and improvements in communication largely due to use of e-mail. However, she also identifies the following major problems (5–7):

* Adaptive difficulties: a traditionalist outlook may evoke resistance to IT adoption; IT literacy of staff may be limited; and IT activities by teachers may be unrecognized, providing little incentive to innovators.
* Cost factors: IT needs high investment; IT-involved courses are expensive to develop; and students have further cost burdens if they wish to acquire their own computers.

- Telecommunications support structures in some countries are not well developed and will take time to be built up.
- Technical support staff are often in short supply in universities.
- There is fear that use of IT and individualisation of the learning process will lead to isolation of students and the loss of social dimensions of learning.
- There is a fear that use of IT will promote the world's dominant languages and discourage use of lesser-used languages.
- The internet can be slow; information may be too abundant, but also unreliable or outdated; and search systems do not keep up with the volume of content.

Collis and van der Wende (1999), however, in a major comparative study focusing on the USA, UK, Australia, Finland and Belgium, report positively on the current situation, finding that: the use of basic IT tools in higher education is widespread; the world wide web is becoming the major support tool for IT-involved learning, superseding standalone products; there is support within institutions for ongoing and innovative instructional activities; often integration of the best features of face-to-face and online instruction is taking place; and active student participation is being encouraged, and group-interaction modes, such as discussion groups, are widespread. They also identify problems: at the institutional level, IT strategies are often lacking, with the result that while interesting innovations proliferate, they do not necessarily lead to institutional adoption or lead to institutional change; there is a lack of incentives for staff using IT (echoing Langlois); and there is often poor understanding of IT and the possibilities it offers by senior management, leading to opportunities being missed. Significantly, they point out (111–12) that 'although improving the quality of education is generally cited as a reason for decision making about ICT in a higher education institution, reasons that drive decisions are more related to strategy, in terms of increasing the number of students, or economic, doing the same or more with less expenditure on instructors and facilities, or both'.

There is no doubt, however, that IT has enabled student-focused learning approaches to be successfully implemented. As an obvious example, IT has added to the potentiality of resource-based learning, since the range of resources that can be made available to the student has been greatly enhanced through electronic means of access. Another example of a learning activity that has come into its own through the adoption of constructivist views of the learning process and through developments in ICT is the use of simulation. Simulations of physical processes are already a well established element in computer-based learning, and advances in technology allow the (virtual) realism to become greater and the user interface to become easier to use and more transparent. Although simulation and academic gaming in the humanities and social sciences have a respectable history since the 1970s (see, for example, Abt, 1970; Greenblat and Duke, 1981; Craig and Martin, 1986), it is only the advent of desktop computing that has allowed them to approach their potential (see, for example, Barton and McKellar, 1998).

This convergence of learning practice and technological enablement is not altogether accidental. Although the facilitation of student-centred pedagogy has been far from the main driver of technological development, many of the individuals who drove technology forward came out of educational environments in which empowerment rather than reception was becoming a dominant culture.

IT and the learning environment

Of major significance for the approach to IT taken by higher education in the UK was the MacFarlane Report (COSUP, 1992), which despite its Scottish origin and focus, was seen throughout the UK as pointing the way forward. MacFarlane insisted that for higher education to move on, a holistic view on the nature of the learning environment must be maintained, with more student-focused learning approaches matched by a suffusion of IT across curriculum and pedagogy. This would have profound effects upon students:

> Students will have to be taught how to manage their own learning processes to an unprecedented degree. They will have to learn how to swim in a sea of information, to use the rich resources of a supportive learning environment, to self-pace and self-structure their programmes of learning. They will have to choose from a spectrum of learning styles ranging from virtual self-instruction under support to group working of various types. The effectiveness of each individual student's learning process will have to be efficiently monitored, and appropriate arrangements devised for each individual student to interact effectively with supervisors and tutors. The supportive environment will offer the student a powerful and continuous means for self-assessment and for planning the development of their learning processes and skills generation. There will be a continuing need for academic counsellors and tutors, and for collaborative inputs in areas like study skills. (COSUP, 1992, 32)

The key role of IT in an holistic and student-centred learning environment was once again underlined by the UK Dearing Report (NCIHE, 1997), which stated that, 'The aim of higher education should be to sustain a learning society.' (*Summary Report* §23) The 'learning society' reflects the notion of a society in which knowledge is a key commodity, flexibility is a characteristic of the workforce, and leisure is a characteristic of social life. This has implications for the way education is organized and offered: it is organized into identifiable units that can be taken individually or joined together in combinations, and are offered through a variety of teaching methodologies, including distance and resource-based modes. 'New technology is changing the way information is stored and transmitted. This has implications both for the skills which higher education needs to develop in students, and for the way in which it is delivered' (§20). A significant element in Dearing is the flagging of 'key skills' as part of the higher education agenda for the learning society. All students need to have key skills: communication, numeracy, use of IT, and learning how to learn. 'We see these as necessary outcomes of all higher education programmes.' (§38)

Dearing stimulated the perception of the learning environment as central to the learning process, and this hastened a number of UK developments in terms of the IT-related facilities made available to students. There has been increased focus on the 'hybrid library', in which access to IT-based resources is as important as access to traditional paper-based stock. Technical developments have enabled serious consideration of VLEs (virtual learning environments) through which students are given access to a range of online resources, tools and interactive facilities specific to themselves, and MLEs (managed learning environments), in which a VLE is located within the institution's administrative data structure. The introduction of VLEs in higher education is now seen by institutions as a priority issue, and a number of institutions have already adopted one proprietary system to be used across the institution. There is a growing trend for traditionally distinct library and computing or IT services in higher education institutions to merge into single 'information services'. Such mergers have, however, not been easy, because of the tension between different cultures within the merged services. The result of such mergers may be the creation of integrated learning support centres, where computing, library and other student support facilities are offered. Finally, the setting up of co-ordinated key skills programmes has been undertaken by many institutions.

But this convergence has presented two key challenges to educator and student alike. The first challenge is that of conceiving of and effectively using an IT-rich learning environment. Although it seemed during the 1970s and 1980s that computer-based learning would be the main route through which IT would support learning, in fact the use of generic IT tools, for accessing information, for analysing it, for organizing it, for presenting it and for communicating it, and for interacting with teachers, students and peers has become central to the learning process. This development is symbolized by the appearance of the virtual learning environment, a software suite which, theoretically, offers students access to all of the information and the tools relevant to their own learning situation, through an IT interface. While existing instantiations of this concept do not yet meet up to expectations, there is wide and insistent demand that the notion of the virtual learning environment is realized to a degree which patently empowers all those involved in the learning enterprise.

The second challenge is that of re-conceiving the role of the educator. Some of the claims for IT-based distance learning may suggest that the role of face-to-face education is over. But in practice, teachers and learners admit that there is no substitute for the face-to-face encounter as an educational experience. IT-supported learning environments in most institutions do not seek to replace the face-to-face encounter, but to enable teachers and learners to make the most of it. Distance courses that seek to replicate the face-to-face encounter through video-conferencing, discussion fora, chat rooms or plain e-mail, offer a second best to the personal encounter but one that is justified by the exigencies of geography or circumstances; and often seek to set up as part of the course brief opportunities for real face-to-face encounters. Teachers should therefore view these facilities as enhancements rather than threats. But it is also necessary to ask who is an educator, for the holistic conception of the learning environment has underlined the relevance to the educational process of those who enable access to key skills and tools, including those related to IT and information.

For the student confronted by an ICT-rich learner-focused environment in which learning is expected to take place, the ability to make use of the tools and facilities that make up such an environment is crucial to success. Hence the emphasis placed upon the acquisition of IT and, latterly, information skills.

Concepts of computer literacy

Almost from its first appearance in the 1940s, the computer has been perceived as something whose impact upon the world and its inhabitants will be profound. It rapidly entered popular culture, as both the deliverer of a utopian future, and as a potential threat to humanity. Kurt Vonnegut's *Player Piano* of 1952 presented a not-so-distant US society run as a technocracy with, at its heart, the giant computer EPICAC XIV. A revolution succeeds in overthrowing the ruling group, and wrecks the computer; but at the end the people cannot resist beginning to tinker with the pieces again. The computer has never lost its power as an image, and that image has been nurtured by literature and the media, but it has also changed, over the last half-century, from that of a semi-secret wonder, to a tool for the expert, to a taken-for-granted part of everyday life. It will not be surprising that attitudes and practices regarding the way students use IT have developed over time.

Concepts of computer literacy can be seen as passing through three phases, the *Mastery* phase (up to the mid-1980s), the *Application* phase (mid-1980s to late 1990s) and the *Reflective* phase (late 1990s on). This schema should not suggest an organized and systematic development, but rather a gradual change of emphasis, to which not all participants necessarily subscribe.

Mastery phase

In the Mastery phase the computer was perceived as arcane and powerful, and emphasis was placed on gaining knowledge and skill to master it. 'Computer Basics', whatever they may be called, consist of how the computer works (simple computer science), and how to program it (using whatever languages were current at the time), often with additional input on the social and economic effects of computers. During this phase the term 'computer literacy' was proposed by John Nevison (1976), writing in the magazine *Science* that:

> Because of the widespread use of elementary computing skill, there should be an appropriate term for this skill. It should suggest an acquaintance with the rudiments of computer programming, much as the term literacy connotes a familiarity with the fundamentals of reading and writing, and it should have a precise definition that all can agree on.

> It is reasonable to suggest that a person who has written a computer program should be called *literate in computing*. This is an extremely elementary definition. Literacy is not fluency.   (Nevison, 1976, 401, italics original)

This approach is taken by major reports of the time. In the UK, the Barnard Report (UGC/CBURC, 1970), in considering those students to whom computing experience should be made available, offered several arguments, familiar today but at the time very forward-looking:

- Computing is an all-purpose tool.
- Computers will impact on the whole curriculum: 'Computers will usurp the traditional functions of libraries and will be regarded as essential aids to any form of scholarly activity. Thus, we may even expect to find computers in regular use in arts departments as well as in science and engineering' (p. 5).
- The power of this tool should be available to all graduates as the elite of tomorrow.
- Practical computing skills will be valuable in employment.
- The application of the computer to subject skills should be 'strongly encouraged' at undergraduate level.

The Report recommended emphatically that: 'We have no hesitation . . . in advising that all undergraduates should be taught computing' (p. 5). The main focus of computer skill was to be upon programming, with a small admixture of information about the computer and its impact. Programming skills were seen as enabling students of all subjects to make use of the computer. Alas, the target set by Barnard would stretch the credibility as well as the purses of most universities. McDonough (1986, 113) suggested some of the reasons:

> The main reason was lack of finance, though there were other important causes. Mainframe computing was not ideally suited to undergraduate use with its demand for large numbers of simultaneously active terminals. The lack of educational software was a major disincentive in humanities departments in the University. The lack of experience of many members of staff in these departments in using computers was also a major obstacle.

The same approach is visible at the school level. The report of the Computers and the Schools Committee of the Scottish Education Department (SED 1969, 1972) took the view that 'a broad base of knowledge about and interest in the computer' needed to be developed in schools, and proposed an 'Introductory Course in Computer Studies' to achieve it. This one-year course was to be provided for the great majority of school pupils, and consist of applications of computers, components and functioning of the computer, introductory programming, and history and current developments. Detailed suggestions are provided on the topics in the course, and in these the emphasis on programming as the key to understanding and using computers is even clearer. However, the lack of practical application for most of the Introductory Course would make much of it look like a specialist subject, and, despite the Committee's recommendation, 'Computing' was soon a specialist subject leading to an O-Grade qualification (at age 16), and it was later to be developed as a Higher examination subject (at age 17).

Similar events were taking place in the USA. Braun, writing in 1981, reported that:

> Almost a decade ago, a dozen pioneers in educational uses of computers met at Dartmouth College to discuss the concept of computer literacy. The group decided that every citizen of the United States *must* have an understanding of computers at some level. They recommended to the Federal Government that a required computer literacy course be developed for presentation at the junior high school level. That recommendation was not considered very seriously at the time because there was not a widespread perception of the impact of computers in our society and because computers were too expensive to make available to every student in junior high school (part of the recommendation was that computer programming, which requires access to a computer, be an important component of the proposed course).
> (Braun, 1981, 227)

Towards the end of the 1970s the desktop PC (personal computer) appeared; this development led ultimately to a mass market in computing and offered every individual the possibility of access to computing power. However, the emphasis of computer literacy did not change, because the lack of user-friendly applications meant that the computer remained a specialist tool or hobby vehicle. Despite the increasing home ownership of microcomputers (as the desktop computers came to be called), the main usage was, in the early 1980s, programming and game playing.

A popular view held that programming was educationally important as a useful meta-skill. In much the same way as learning Latin was once recommended as a stimulator of orderly thinking, programming was seen as important for the transferable thinking skills that it would engender. These lay in the areas of logical and systematic thinking (for example, by preparing flowcharts students develop the ability to think through sequences of events logically), problem-solving (students analyse the problem as a whole system, and develop a solution through a 'top-down' planning process) and 'debugging'(students do not see a solution as 'right' or 'wrong' but work over the task several times to achieve the best product). This argument was deployed in the case of the computer language Logo, which, between the late 1970s and mid-1980s was championed as a powerful 'tool for thinking' by enthusiasts such as Seymour Papert (Papert, 1980). Logo was taken up widely in schools in the USA and the UK, especially in the primary sector (see Martin, 1986, for an indication of the range of areas in which it was considered for use). Unfortunately, asserting that 'Logo is good for the brain' was easier than proving it, and Logo champions found it difficult to move beyond anecdote as evidence. The widespread claims for Logo did not survive these debates and, while Logo still remains on the school curriculum, it is limited to some aspects of mathematics and control technology.

Application phase

The demands of the market led during the 1980s to the development of simple user interfaces and easy-to-use mass market applications, which revolutionized computer usage and stimulated a move into the Application phase of computer literacy. In this phase an intuitive graphical user interface (such as Windows) is taken for granted, and the computer is perceived as an everyday tool which can be applied to a wide range of activities in education, work, leisure and the home. Applications software is powerful and simple to use. 'Information Technology' or 'IT' becomes the normal term of reference to computing activities, although the perceived need to acknowledge the contribution of communications technology leads to terms like ICT (Information and Communications Technology) and C&IT (Communication and Information Technology). How to use com-

puter applications becomes the focus of computer literacy activity, and definitions of 'computer literacy' or 'IT literacy' focus on lists of practical competences
rather than specialist computing knowledge. This is reflected in the volume of
training materials produced and the appearance of mass certification schemes
focusing on basic levels of ICT competence. It is also now feasible to build IT
literacy requirements into curricula at school and post-school levels. The development of the internet happens during this phase, and another major change in
perception is stimulated when simple tools for e-mail and for navigating the
world wide web appear in the latter half of the 1990s.

The major emphasis in higher education during the 1990s was still on computer-based learning, but by the mid-1990s UK HEIs were increasingly
recognizing that student IT literacy was an important objective. In many universities Computing/IT Services developed self-teach materials focused on
particular applications. This activity had been going on for many years, at first
focusing on specialist applications for limited numbers of users, then including
more generic applications and being directed towards any student. Meanwhile,
individual departments in many institutions continued to develop their own
courses on 'Basic IT' or 'Introduction to the Computer', with an emphasis on
the applications required for study within the department. In a few institutions
(e.g. Durham, York, Glasgow) co-ordinated programmes were organized specifically focused on the delivery of basic IT skills. These usually originated within
the Computing Service (as in Durham and York), but could originate elsewhere
(as in Glasgow). In some universities (e.g. Luton) IT skills were included in programmes covering a wider range of 'key' or 'core' skills considered necessary for
the student or for the graduate. In others (e.g. Cheltenham and Gloucester
College of Higher Education) the context was more specifically that of the skills
required to study at undergraduate level.

During this period curricula and qualifications developed focusing on levels
of achievement of 'information technology' competences. Qualifications seeking
to map IT competences, such as the CLAIT (Computer Literacy and
Information Technology) scheme (developed by the RSA) and the Cambridge
IT Certificate (developed by the University of Cambridge Schools Examination
Board) became widely used in British schools and further education. The
ECDL (European Computer Driving Licence) was developed as a Europe-wide
ICT skills certification scheme. While some UK higher education institutions
have taken up ECDL, others developed their own ICT certification schemes or
developed ICT skills modules as elements of degree programmes.

Reflective phase

The transition to the Reflective phase is more gradual, and stimulated by the need for students to be autonomous learners, and by the 'evaluation imperative' called forth by the vast and uncontrolled mass of information now confronting the learner. In this phase the facility with IT tools is taken for granted, or regarded as something straightforwardly acquired either as early as possible (preferably in childhood) for generic competence, or wherever needed for more specific competence. The emphasis moves towards reflective and evaluative aspects of usage: deciding upon appropriate usage of applications, evaluating the data that they give access to, interpreting the information they generate, and deciding upon appropriate use of the resulting document or product. In this phase the notion of 'information literacy' which has been developing in the user education areas of the library since the 1980s converges with changing ideas of IT literacy. Terminology is still unsettled, with claims on the one hand that 'information literacy' now encompasses IT, and on the other suggestions that 'literacy' should be superseded by a term such as 'fluency' connoting a more sophisticated and situationally relevant approach.

The term 'fluency' is proposed by an influential US National Research Council report (NRC, 1999), which comments that:

> Generally, 'computer literacy' has acquired a 'skills' connotation, implying competency with a few of today's computer applications, such as word processing and e-mail. Literacy is too modest a goal in the presence of rapid change, because it lacks the necessary 'staying power.' As the technology changes by leaps and bounds, existing skills become antiquated and there is no migration path to new skills. A better solution is for the individual to plan to adapt to changes in the technology.
>
> (NRC, 1999, 2)

'FITness' (Fluency in Information Technology) covers three types of knowledge:

- *contemporary skills*: 'the ability to use particular (and contemporary) hardware or software resources to accomplish information processing tasks' (NRC, 1999, 18). This covers most of the applications-focused student IT training currently being carried out. Naturally these skills will change over time as hardware and software evolve.
- *foundational concepts*: 'the basic principles and ideas of computers, networks, and information' (NRC, 1999, 2–3). These include computer structure, information systems, networks, modelling, algorithmic thinking and programming, the limitations of IT and its social impact.

- *intellectual capabilities*, which 'integrate knowledge specific to information technology with problem domains of personal interest to individuals' (NRC, 1999, 20). These are general thinking skills which might be recognizable in many disciplines, and include sustained reasoning, managing complexity, testing solutions, evaluating information, collaboration, anticipating change and expecting the unexpected.

However, it is not clear yet how widely this approach will be adopted. While thinking skills can be seem as a valuable complement to familiarity with applications, the need for an elementary grounding in computer science may be difficult to understand. In the end IT fluency may be seen as a computer scientists' vision of a reflective IT literacy.

Information literacy

Information literacy is seen by librarians as a key requirement in accessing and making appropriate use of the vast amounts of information which are now available to students, particularly through the internet. 'Information literacy' has developed in the USA since the late 1980s as a refocusing of 'bibliographic instruction' (the equivalent UK term is 'user education') in academic libraries. The refocusing arose from awareness of changes in the practice of teaching and learning. An influential 1987 symposium recommended that 'Reports on undergraduate education identify the need for more active learning whereby students become self-directed independent learners who are prepared for lifelong learning. To accomplish this, students need to become information literate' (Breivik and Wedgeworth, 1988, 187–8). The notion was soon backed up by the report of an American Library Association committee (reprinted in Breivik, 1998, 121–37), which defined the information-literate person as one who 'must be able to recognize when information is needed and have the ability to locate, evaluate, and use effectively the needed information' (121–2). A recent report from the Association of College and Research Libraries focuses on higher education (ACRL, 2000), and presents a set of performance indicators based on five 'standards'. The information-literate student:

- determines the nature and extent of the information needed
- accesses needed information effectively and efficiently
- evaluates information and its sources critically and incorporates selected information into their knowledge base and value system
- uses information effectively to accomplish a specific purpose

- understands many of the economic, legal and social issues surrounding the use of information and accesses and uses information ethically and legally (ACRL, 2000, 8–13, passim).

In the UK, SCONUL has offered the 'Seven Pillars' model, where IT skills and basic library skills support seven 'information skills', increasing competence in all of which leads to achievement of information literacy. The seven are as follows:

- recognizing an information need
- identifying what information will fulfil the need
- constructing strategies for locating information
- locating and accessing the information sought
- comparing and evaluating information obtained from different sources
- organizing, applying and communicating information
- synthesizing and building upon information.

(adapted from Town, 2000, 17–18)

In this model, basic IT skills are seen as a key element underpinning information skills. The Seven Pillars model is now being implemented in some UK higher education institutions. (See Chapter 2 for a further development of information literacy themes.)

Refocusing on e-literacy

In the context of current developments, I would suggest that a synthesizing concept is that of *e-literacy*. By e-literacy I mean the awarenesses, skills, understandings and reflective-evaluative approaches that are necessary for an individual to operate comfortably in information-rich and IT-supported environments. An individual is e-literate to the extent that they have acquired these awarenesses, skills and approaches. There are many environments in which the achievement of e-literacy is important. The most significant are the learning environment, the work environment, and the leisure and personal development environment. For the individual, e-literacy consists of:

- awareness of the IT and information environment
- confidence in using generic IT and information tools
- evaluation of information-handling operations and products
- reflection on one's own e-literacy development
- adaptability and willingness to meet e-literacy challenges.

The awarenesses, skills and approaches which constitute e-literacy will vary from one environment to another. However, to the extent that environments share common features, such as the type of tasks required of individuals within that environment, or the user interface or applications normally used, e-literacy definitions will overlap. e-literacy is a dynamic property, in two ways: as each environment changes, its particular e-literacy requirements will need to be redefined at regular intervals; and, as far as the individual is concerned, e-literacy is acquired through a cumulative educative and/or experiential process. e-literacy cannot be expressed in binary terms – as either present or not present. In broad summative terms, it could be possible to talk about the achievement of particular defined levels of e-literacy, but a more precise and, for the individual student, more productive approach would be to consider individual e-literacy in more formative terms, as the match of an individual profile with a needs matrix of the particular environment. These two approaches are not however contradictory, and can both be developed, since both have value.

The e-literacy challenges

In approaching e-literacy, a number of challenges face the institution, and the people in it who can take e-literacy forward.

The Strategic Challenge: e-literacy development needs to be adopted fully into the strategic plans of the institution. This means making clear commitments rather than vague suggestions. It means conceiving e-literacy as a broad and integrated characteristic which extends throughout a student's academic career. It also means integrating e-literacy plans with those for learning environment development, key skills and employability strategies.

The Resource Challenge: Plans need to be backed up with adequate resource, appropriately located. e-literacy provision, whether centrally provided or devolved to faculties or departments, cannot be enabled for nothing. It does not have to be grossly expensive, but it does need dedicated resource. Integration with related provision, such as VLE rollout or staff development, and collaboration with other institutions may enable best use to be made of existing resources.

The Cultural Challenge: Drawing together e-literacy providers from cultural milieux which are significantly different (as are often those of the library and the computing service) may be a major difficulty. Such cultural differences are not easily surmounted, and apparently positive measures such as setting up integrated teams may be subverted by pre-existing loyalties and assumptions. There is also a cultural challenge in developing collaborative actions with academic staff, who may have preconceptions of librarians or of computer support staff.

The Political Challenge: When new units are formed, noses are inevitably put out of joint, sensitivities ruffled and structures of power threatened. While at the top this may lead to Machiavellian manoeuvring, at the bottom there may develop a bunker mentality as a response to the perceived uncertainty of the situation.

The Pedagogical Challenge: e-literacy is about making learning more effective, and protagonists of e-literacy need to be able to consider how students can employ e-literacy in specific pedagogical situations. Pedagogy is closely linked to assessment, and there is also a need to consider how assessment can capture e-literacy achievements. In this respect, personal development planning offers a particularly useful option.

The Staff Development Challenge: e-literacy affects staff, of all types, as well as students, and it is important that provision is made for staff in addition to students. Staff have different e-literacy needs from students, and a picture needs to be formed of the intersecting and overlapping e-literacy needs of all those involved in the business of the institution.

The Collaboration Challenge: Delivering e-literacy effectively is often enhanced by collaborative action, either within the institution (e.g. with academic departments), or with other institutions.

The Theoretical Challenge: It is important to develop an effective theory of e-literacy. All too often e-literacy developers are very busy, updating materials and delivering courses, setting up programmes, talking to staff or students, and there is no time left to be reflective. Yet without theoretical resource, in the form of models that link e-literacy to the learning process and to the other processes of the institution, and hypotheses that seek to take forward understanding of the nature of e-literacy, the case that can be made for e-literacy will rest on anecdote, and there will be no vision within which the routes forward can be charted.

The Complexity Challenge: e-literacy is multi-levelled, and involves at most levels evaluative and reflective activity. It should not be regarded as a simple set of 'basic skills' which can be addressed by simple remedies or off-the-peg syllabuses that are not focused on the specific needs of students at different levels of education. e-literacy itself demands respect as a complex and changing target.

Conclusion

We have seen that a number of trends have converged in the areas of information-using in education. These include the rapid development of information technology, changes in the theory and practice of learning, the evolution of conceptions of computer and later IT literacy, the rise of information literacy as an imperative, the emergence of electronic learning environments, and the increasing importance given to the acquisition of transferable skills which will be relevant to lifelong learning. These convergences can be viewed best through the concept of e-literacy. We have identified a number of challenges which confront the concept and the practical development of e-literacy. These challenges are not easy to address. They will require determined action at more than one level. But the reward for success is great: the full empowerment of students as lifelong learners in the information- and IT-rich learning environment.

References

Abt, C. C. (1970) *Serious Games,* New York, Viking Press.

ACRL (2000) *Information Literacy Competency Standards for Higher Education: standards, performance indicators and outcomes,* Chicago, Association of College and Research Libraries.

Barton, K. and McKellar, P. (1998) The Virtual Court Action: procedural facilitation in law, *ALT-J,* **6**, 87–94.

Beaty, L., Gibbs, G. and Morgan, A. (1997) Learning Orientations and Study Contracts. In Marton, F., Hounsell, D. and Entwistle, N. (eds), *The Experience of Learning*, 2nd edn, Edinburgh, Scottish Academic Press, 72–86.

Braun, L. (1981) Computer-Aided Learning and the Microcomputer Revolution, *Programmed Learning and Educational Technology,* **18**, 223–9.

Breivik, P. S. (1998) *Student Learning in the Information Age,* Phoenix, Oryx Press.

Breivik, P. S. and Wedgeworth, R. (eds) (1988) *Libraries and the Search for Academic Excellence,* Metuchen, NJ, Scarecrow Press.

Collis, B. and van der Wende, M. (eds) (1999) *The Use of Information and Communication Technology in Higher Education,* Twente, Netherlands, Center for Higher Education Policy Studies, Universiteit Twente.

COSUP (1992) *Teaching and Learning in an Expanding Higher Education System,* Edinburgh, Committee of Scottish University Principals [MacFarlane Report].

Craig, D. and Martin, A. (eds) (1986) *Gaming and Simulation for Capability*, Loughborough, SAGSET.

Cresswell, J. E. (1998) Back to the Future: team-centred, resource-based learning as the antecedent of computer-based learning, *ALT-J,* **6**, 64–9.

Driver, R. and Bell, B. (1986) Students' Thinking and the Learning of Science: a constructivist view, *School Science Review*, (March), 443–56.

Entwistle, N. (1997) Contrasting Perspectives on Learning. In Marton, F., Hounsell, D. and Entwistle, N. (eds), *The Experience of Learning*, 2nd edn, Edinburgh, Scottish Academic Press, 3–22.

Greenblat, C. S. and Duke, R. D. (1981), *Principles and Practices of Gaming-Simulation,* Beverley Hills/London, Sage Publications.

Langlois, C. (1997) *Universities and New Information Technologies: issues and strategies*, IAU/UNESCO Information Centre on Higher Education. Available at www.unesco.org/iau/tfit_paper.html.

Laurillard, D. (1993) *Rethinking University Teaching: a framework for the effective use of educational technology,* London, Routledge.

Laurillard, D. (1997) Learning Formal Representations through Multimedia. In Marton, F., Hounsell, D. and Entwistle, N. (eds), *The Experience of Learning*, 2nd edn, Edinburgh, Scottish Academic Press, 172–83.

McDonough, W. R. (1986) The Aeneas Project – implementing the Nelson Report at Queen's University, Belfast, *University Computing*, 8, 113–15.

Martin, A. (1986) *Teaching and Learning with Logo,* London, Croom Helm.

NCIHE (National Committee of Inquiry into Higher Education) (1997) *Higher Education in the Learning Society: report of the National Committee,* HMSO, [Dearing Report].

Nevison, J. M. (1976) Computing in the Liberal Arts College, *Science*, (22 October), 396–402.

NRC, Committee on Information Technology Literacy, Computer Science and Telecommunications Board, Commission on Physical Sciences, Mathematics and Applications, National Research Council (1999) *Being Fluent with Information Technology*, Washington DC, National Academy Press.

Papert, S. (1980) *Mindstorms,* Brighton, Harvester Press.

Pask, G. (1976) Styles and Strategies of Learning, *British Journal of Educational Psychology,* 46, 4–11.

Perkins, D. (1992) Technology Meets Constructivism: do they make a marriage? in Duffy, T. and Jonassen, D. (eds) *Constructivism and the Technology of Instruction*, Mahwah, NJ, Lawrence Erlbaum, 45–57.

Perry, W. G. (1970) *Forms of Intellectual and Ethical Development in the College Years,* New York, Holt, Rinehart and Winston.

Scott, P., Dyson, T. and Gater, S. (1987) *A Constructivist View of Learning and Teaching in Science,* Leeds, Children's Learning in Science Project, University of Leeds.

SED (Scottish Education Department), Consultative Committee on the Curriculum (1969) *Computers and the Schools: an interim report,* Curriculum Paper 6, Edinburgh, HMSO.

SED (Scottish Education Department), Consultative Committee on the Curriculum (1972) *Computers and the Schools: final report,* Curriculum Paper 11, Edinburgh, HMSO.

Town, J. S. (2000) Wisdom or Welfare? The Seven Pillars model. In Corrall, S. and Hathaway, H. (eds), *Seven Pillars of Wisdom? Good practice in information skills development. Proceedings of a conference held at the University of Warwick, 6–7 July 2000,* SCONUL, London, 11–21.

UGC/CBURC (1970) *Teaching Computing in Universities,* London, HMSO [Barnard Report].

UHI (University of the Highlands and Islands Project) (1999) *Towards a Learning Strategy for the University of the Highlands and Islands,* Inverness, University of the Highlands and Islands Project.

Vonnegut, K. (1952) *Player Piano,* London, Macmillan.

2

Information literacy – a global perspective

Hannelore Rader

Introduction

This chapter explains what is meant by an information-literate society, provides a short history of the development of several national standards of information literacy, and describes examples from around the world of how these standards can be integrated into an academic curriculum to ensure that students in higher education become information literate and productive workers in the knowledge society of the 21st century. Also addressed are current challenges in higher education, lifelong learning skills, successful learning environments in the technology environment and collaborations for learning and teaching. Emphasis is on the development of creative partnerships between librarians and faculty to ensure that students are prepared for successful careers in the 21st century. Strategies are provided for academic librarians to develop successful partnerships. These strategies include understanding the curriculum, becoming involved in faculty development and acquiring instructional skills. This chapter emphasizes information literacy developments in the USA and provides examples from other countries. Ideas related to the assessment of learning outcomes for information skills are summarized to help document students' fluency in information use.

Education environment in the 21st century

At the beginning of the 21st century enormous changes are occurring in higher education throughout the world as a result of new information and technological developments. These changes are affecting every segment of society and all levels of education. Faculty and teachers need to acquire new sets of technology and electronic information skills in order to effectively prepare and teach students the knowledge base in all disciplines as well as relevant information skills. New learning communities are evolving based on the necessity that learning must be continuous at all levels and at all ages, and must include resource-based learning. Schools and universities need to teach their students to integrate learning opportunities into everything they do in order to become successful in the constantly changing work environment and in society. Educators need to create partnerships with business to take advantage of organizational information needs related to evolving technology, the internet, the global marketplace and the new economy.

Students need to obtain high levels of literacy during every phase of their education. They have to achieve excellent skills in reading, writing, mathematics and critical thinking to be successful in the new millennium. Given the complex technology environment and increasing global interactions, students must attain excellent communication and information skills to function productively in the workforce of the future.

Higher education is undergoing major changes throughout the world. Legislators, funding agencies and consumers of higher education are demanding appropriate learning outcomes and graduates prepared to function successfully within the global economy. New university models are slowly emerging to address financial needs and competition. Some models are for-profit, such as the University of Phoenix, based in Arizona, with a major stock portfolio on Wall Street. The University of Phoenix has a somewhat competitive and controversial presence in many states. Other institutions are trying to become virtual universities, offering distance education programmes using the internet throughout the USA and the world. The virtual university model offers students educational opportunities to learn across distance and independent of time schedules, something many people desire (Stallings, 1997).

Libraries and the digital environment

The effect of technology on libraries has been especially noteworthy during the past decade. Many people have begun to consider libraries less important than in the past because they believe that the internet is the world's library. Likewise books and other printed information are now often considered less valuable and less important than electronic information. Yet libraries are one of the most important components of the information age and librarians are dealing successfully with new technological advances. Libraries are becoming agile, learning-oriented information centres. Librarians are working on helping society understand the value and contributions of libraries, particularly in the areas of organizing, preserving and providing access to information. As academic librarians prepare for a growing sophisticated technology environment they are facing many challenges as well as many opportunities.

Most academic libraries are technologically in better shape than other educational entities because during the past decade academic librarians have been in the forefront of technological developments and related changes on their campuses. They were usually one of the first campus groups to computerize their information environment through library system software, hardware, networking, web page development and assistance to users. They partner with their campus information technology department to accomplish numerous technological tasks. Academic librarians have developed diverse technology skills and specialized expertise to ensure that they become leaders in higher education and in this new information environment.

Academic librarians play a major role in the educational changes taking place in teaching, learning and research in higher education by providing an appropriate information environment and the most efficient and effective user access to all types of information resources. They provide successful information services to help and guide their users in their information searching. They provide practical and effective instruction in the use of information for teaching, learning and research by integrating such instruction throughout the curriculum. Librarians are building partnerships on campus for faculty development, distance education, information technology, student support and assessment of learning outcomes. They are making the library the centre for teaching, learning and research on campus by providing the most inviting and accessible information environment. Above all, they ensure that all students learn appropriate information skills and fluency so that after they graduate they become productive members of the information society. Academic librarians are building partnerships with the teaching faculty to integrate information skills instruction throughout the undergraduate and graduate curricula.

Information literacy defined

Information as a concept originates from scholastic training: to instruct, to teach and to train. Critical thinking requires that information, regardless of type of media, must be analysed critically in reading and thinking. People need to continually evaluate information and apply it to new ideas, which then change the organization of work, the value of knowledge in the economy and cultural values (Dowler, 1997).

Information literacy has been defined as a set of abilities to 'recognize when information is needed and have the ability to locate, evaluate, and use needed information effectively' (ACRL, 2000). In the information age of the 21st century information-literate citizens will be the building blocks for a society that is equitable and possesses economic growth potential. People will need information skills for their professional, personal and even entertainment activities. Librarians, teachers, technologists and some policy makers have recently begun to address the need for information skills training and teaching at all levels of education. The issue of training members of the existing workforce in effective information handling still needs to be addressed in a major way, hopefully very soon. Ultimately, people of all ages need to be prepared for lifelong learning, and teaching individuals appropriate information skills will be a major step in that direction. Libraries can provide key access points to electronic and print information and can offer appropriate training programmes to assist citizens in gaining necessary information skills. Unfortunately, libraries and librarians have been largely ignored in the vital debate regarding the preparation of citizens for the information age. However, they can still be effective resources for information access and teach people information handling skills to continue their learning. Information literacy endeavours are just at the beginning and more work is needed to understand the complexity, long-term effects and importance of preparing people for the effective use of information.

In the last decade information literacy has become a global issue and many information literacy initiatives have been documented throughout the world, with particularly strong efforts and examples in North America, Australia, South Africa and Northern Europe (Bruce and Candy, 2000). These programmes address many concerns relative to technology and information skills. In education, teachers, librarians and others are working to integrate information skills instruction within the curricula to achieve relevant learning outcomes. Other initiatives involve distance education, research and publication activities related to information literacy. More recently, employers and policy makers have addressed the need for workforce development to ensure that workers develop appropriate technology and information skills to handle their job responsibilities effectively.

More specifically, information literacy can be defined as a set of abilities to:

- determine the extent of information needed
- locate and evaluate information
- incorporate selected information into one's knowledge base
- use information ethically, legally and with an understanding of economic and social issues.

Information literacy includes library literacy, media literacy, computer literacy, internet literacy, research literacy and critical thinking skills.

National standards for information literacy
Association of College and Research Libraries (ACRL)

Several countries have developed standards for teaching and even assessing information skills. One of the first countries to work on these standards was the USA. In particular, the ALA (American Library Association) and one of its divisions, the ACRL (Association of College and Research Libraries) have a 30-year history of developing definitions and standards for information literacy. After various meetings, discussions and publications ACRL issued their document *Information Literacy Competency Standards for Higher Education* (ACRL, 2000). This document was endorsed by the AAHE (American Association of Higher Education) (Breivik, 2002). ACRL is working with other professional associations to procure endorsements to integrate the need for information skills into accreditation requirements. At the same time, ACRL and ALA are preparing translations of the standards, which are to date available in Spanish, Greek, German and Chinese. The document describes five standards, 22 performance indicators and 87 outcome measures, which are summarized below.

The ACRL Information Literacy Competency Standards for Higher Education (ACRL, 2000) have been adopted for use in a number of countries such as Mexico, Spain, Australia, Europe, and South Africa. Available at www.ala.org/acrl/il, the five standards are:

I   The information-literate student determines the nature and extent of the information needed.

II The information-literate student assesses needed information effectively and efficiently.

III The information-literate student evaluates information and its sources critically and incorporates selected information into his or her knowledge base and value system.

IV The information-literate student, individually or as a member of a group, uses information effectively to accomplish a specific purpose.

V   The information-literate student understands many of the economic, legal and social issues surrounding the use of information, and accesses and uses information ethically and legally.

In addition, there are 20 performance indicators and 87 outcome measures, of which some examples are listed in Table 2.1.

Table 2.1   *Sample ACRL performance indicators and outcome measures*

Standard	Sample performance indicator	Sample outcome
I	The information-literate student defines and articulates the need for information.	The student explores general information sources to increase familiarity with the topic.
II	The student selects the most appropriate investigative methods or information retrieval system for accessing the needed information.	The student investigates benefits and applicability of various investigative methods.
III	The student summarizes the main ideas to be extracted from the information gathered.	The student reads the text and selects main ideas.
IV	The student applies new and prior information to the planning and creation of a particular product or performance.	The student organizes the content in a manner that supports the purposes and format of the product or performance.
V	The student acknowledges the use of information sources in communicating the product or performance.	The student posts permission granted notices, as needed for copyrighted material.

Using these standards librarians and faculty can collaborate to integrate the teaching of information skills into the undergraduate and graduate curricula. Faculty and librarians can plan teaching modules together, both for classroom use and online. Then using the criteria for outcome measurements provided in the ACRL document they can measure whether or not the students have learned the appropriate information skills.

In 2001 ACRL published the *Objectives for Information Literacy Instruction: a model statement for academic librarians* (ACRL, 2001), designed to provide guidance in the development of objectives for the five information literacy competency standards. ACRL has also developed the Standards Tool Kit consisting of instructional tools, web pages and other resources that will help anyone to use the standards (ACRL, 2003a).

Teaching information skills involves much preparatory work, including such activities as developing teaching modules for undergraduates, subject majors, graduate and professional programmes. It also involves the customizing of teaching to appropriate student levels and students' existing knowledge bases.

To help academic librarians become well-trained instructors of information skills and to create productive partnerships with teaching faculty ACRL has created the Institute for Information Literacy (ACRL, 2003a):

- To prepare librarians to become effective teachers in information literacy programmes.
- To support librarians, other educators and administrators in playing a leadership role in the development and implementation of information literacy programmes.
- To forge new relationships throughout the educational community to work towards information literacy curriculum development.

Programme initiatives include:

- *Annual Immersion Programmes.* Four and-a-half-day programmes that provide intensive information literacy training and education for instruction librarians.
- *Institutional Strategies: Best Practices.* A programme that assists individual institutions in developing strategies for developing and implementing effective information literacy programmes.
- *Community Partnerships.* A programme that provides opportunities for a combination of community partners (e.g. academic and K-12; academic, K-12, and public, etc.) to work toward instituting 'community-based' information literacy programmes.
- *Web Resources.* Links to a wide variety of information literacy issues including best practices, assessment, and links to other information on information literacy resources. Available online at www.ala.org/acrl/nili/nilihp.html.

ALA American Association of School Librarians (AASL) and Association for Educational Communication and Technology (AECT)

In 1998 the ALA AASL (American Association of School Librarians) and the AECT (Association for Educational Communication and Technology) developed nine information literacy standards for learning for students in primary and secondary education, called *Information Power: building partnerships for learning* (AASL, 1998).

- *Standard 1.* The student who is information literate accesses information efficiently and effectively.

- *Standard 2.* The student who is information literate evaluates information critically and competently.
- *Standard 3.* The student who is information literate uses information accurately and creatively.

Information skills for independent learning
- *Standard 4.* The student who is an independent learner is information literate and pursues information related to personal interests.
- *Standard 5.* The student who is an independent learner is information literate and appreciates literature and other creative expressions of information.
- *Standard 6.* The student who is an independent learner is information literate and strives for excellence in information seeking and knowledge generation.

Information skills for social responsibility
- *Standard 7.* The student who contributes positively to the learning community and to society is information literate and recognizes the importance of information to a democratic society.
- *Standard 8.* The student who contributes positively to the learning community and to society is information literate and practises ethical behaviour in regard to information and information technology.
- *Standard 9.* The student who contributes positively to the learning community and to society is information literate and participates effectively in groups to pursue and generate information.

Information Power: building partnerships for learning is designed to help students become skilful producers and consumers of information. It is built on the following guidelines to help teachers incorporate information skills throughout the curriculum:

- Helping students flourish in a learning community not limited by time, place, age, occupation or disciplinary borders.
- Joining teachers and others to identify links in student information needs, curricular content, learning outcomes, and a variety of print and non-print resources.
- Designing authentic learning tasks and assessments.
- Defining your role in student learning.

Other educational initiatives

Based on the information summarized above regarding information skills standards for elementary and secondary education many education departments throughout the USA have made information skills instruction a requirement, and the NCATE (National Council for Accreditation of Teacher Education) has made information literacy education an accreditation requirement.

AASL and ACRL are also collaborating in various ways to ensure that information literacy education throughout the USA becomes sequential throughout the education requirements from kindergarten through university education.

In the USA the National Forum for Information Literacy was established in 1990 to promote information literacy as a means of individual empowerment within the current information society, to support and encourage grassroots initiatives and to bring together national leaders from education and business to address information literacy concerns and effective lifelong learning. The Forum is based in Washington, DC and includes more than 70 educational, governmental and non-profit organizations (National Forum for Information Literacy, 1990).

LOEX, the clearinghouse for library instruction, was founded in 1971 by librarians at Eastern Michigan University in Ypsilanti, Michigan (LOEX, 1971). The purpose of this clearinghouse is to collect and distribute materials related to library instruction and eventually information literacy. To date there have been more than 30 annual national conferences and several LOEX-of-the-West conferences to address many aspects of instructing people in information skills in the academic environment.

Many regional and state conferences on user instruction and information literacy have been held as well. More than 5000 publications relating to information use instruction and information literacy have been published in English since 1973. Most of them were published in the USA but many articles and books have been published in other languages around the world.

Similar efforts to address information literacy education in university settings have been made in such countries as Australia, China, South Africa, England, Sweden, Botswana and Mexico. Resource-based learning ultimately enables students to assume responsibility for their own learning and prepares them for the information-based society. Teaching students to become independent learners is quickly becoming a major goal for higher education (Farmer and Mech, 1992).

Creating a successful learning environment is also crucial for success. This includes such things as a user-friendly physical environment, diverse electronic information access, appropriate state-of-the-art technology classrooms and librarian–faculty co-operation and interaction. Additionally, librarians must ensure that students receive guidance and assistance at the time of need, in a collaborative learning and problem-solving learning environment.

Effects of teaching information skills

Various accrediting agencies in the USA have recognized the importance of information literacy in the curricula of colleges and universities and the important role librarians should assume in the teaching–learning environment, by including appropriate criteria for outcome measures with regard to information literacy in the accreditation requirements. Most noteworthy for its work in the area of information literacy in higher education is the Commission on Higher Education, Middle States Association of Colleges and Schools. Working with the Association of College and Research Libraries and the National Forum on Information Literacy, the Commission has surveyed 830 institutions nationwide to explore the status of initiatives regarding information literacy in the USA. They found that educational institutions in the middle states are leading the nation in applying information literacy strategies on campuses. Several of these institutions have developed formal assessment strategies for measuring information literacy outcomes (Ratteray and Simmons, 1995).

The Commission on Higher Education, Middle States Association of Colleges and Schools, developed the following standard on information literacy in 1994:

> Each institution should foster optimal use of its learning resources through strategies designed to help students develop information literacy – the ability to locate, evaluate, and use information in order to become independent learners. It should encourage the use of a wide range of non-classroom resources for teaching and learning. It is essential to have an active and continuing program of library orientation and instruction in accessing information, developed collaboratively and supported actively by faculty, librarians, academic deans, and other information providers.
> (Middle States, 1995)

In 1995 the Commission on Learning Resources and Instructional Technology of the California State Universities issued a report entitled *Information Competence in the CSU* which recommends policy guidelines for the effective use of learning resources and instructional technology. Information competency is one major area identified for which recommendations are provided. Among many possibilities considered are co-operative ventures between the universities, community colleges, primary and secondary schools to help all students become information literate. Also recommended is a close collaboration between faculty and librarians. The report provides a number of useful suggestions to establish effective information competence programmes within California State Universities:

- Undertake a systematic assessment of student information competence to develop benchmarks.
- Develop model list of information competence skills for students entering the university and graduating from the university. Establish agreement with K-14 on these skills.
- Develop pilot information competence programmes or courses on several campuses.
- Develop a 'teaching the teachers' programme so that faculty development in information competence can occur.
- Develop computer software that enables the teaching of information competence.
- Develop faculty workbooks and checklists for K-16 to assist faculty with the teaching of information competence.
- Work with the California Superintendent of Schools to ensure that information competence is on the agenda for K-12.
- Work with the community colleges and support their ongoing information competence initiative.
- Collaborate with textbook publishers to help with the integration of the concepts of information competence into textbooks.
- Pilot a distance-learning effort with information competence. (Commission on Learning Resources and Instructional Technology, 1995)

To assist with advocacy for information literacy the California State Universities System thus established a new system-wide position.

These examples from higher education document concerns related to educating students to become effective in the information age by helping them gain information and critical thinking skills. Nationwide accrediting groups, state education departments and academic librarians have realized the importance of training students in the use of information, and that such training must become integrated into the higher education curriculum. Academic librarians are actively becoming involved in curriculum development on their campuses and countless examples of such endeavours can be found in the literature and on the web. Academic librarians are working with faculty to rethink their teaching styles from lecture mode to interactive, resource-based and collaborative instruction. In many academic institutions, centres for teaching excellence are being created to help faculty update their teaching styles in terms of the electronic environment and student learning needs. Often these centres are rightly located in the library, providing opportunities for librarians to form partnerships with teaching faculty for curriculum development and new teaching initiatives. The environment now offers opportunities as never before for academic librarians to demonstrate their expertise in information handling and user training while involving themselves in the teaching–learning environment on the campuses.

Surveys of the literature and interaction with international colleagues indicate that concerns with preparing students for success in the information age are definitely shared worldwide among librarians and educators (Rader, 1996). The emergence and rapid growth of the internet have created much interest and need on the part of students to gain access to electronic information and to become information literate. The need to find, organize, assess and apply information to problem solving is an international concern. Given the ease and speed with which information can now be shared, it is advisable that librarians and educators cooperate and share their expertise and experiences not only locally and nationally but also internationally. To prepare both librarians and teachers for educating students in the information age the following factors should be considered:

* Information changes continually.
* Learning and teaching must be interactive and recognize diversity in learning styles.
* Teaching and training must be a process of facilitating and sharing rather than dispensing.
* Information work is becoming more and more competitive.
* Librarians and teachers must market themselves aggressively as information experts.
* Information is a commodity and must be handled like a valuable product.
* Teachers and trainers must be continuous learners.
* Effective teaching utilizes learning outcomes and behavioural goals.
* Good teaching is based on student need.
* Information skills must be integrated into the curriculum and taught incrementally.
* Teachers and librarians must work with accrediting and education agencies and curriculum planners to ensure that information skills become a required component of the curriculum.

International efforts to develop an information-literate society
(see p. 42 for associated websites)

In the USA and in Australia some professional organizations related to education, law, nursing and medicine are already beginning to address lifelong educational needs for their professionals and include information literacy as an important factor (Proceedings, 1997). In Australia, Christine Bruce has expertly defined information literacy as seven distinct areas: information technology, information sources, information process, information control, information construction, information extension and wisdom experience (Proceedings, 1997).

Librarians on every continent have been working on teaching people a variety of library and information skills. This can certainly be demonstrated through a review of the literature related to this topic (Rader, 2000). It can also be seen that each year since 1973 the number of publications related to user instruction and information literacy has continued to increase. During the past decade many librarians have been sharing their experiences and their expertise related to information skills instruction at national conferences as well as the annual conferences of IFLA (International Federation of Library Associations), which meets in a different country each year. IFLA members have focused their concerns regarding the teaching of library and information skills through the establishment of a Roundtable on User Instruction, recently changed to the User Instruction Section. During the past five years a number of programmes sponsored by the Roundtable and the University and Research Libraries Division have focused on information literacy.

Africa

Academic librarians in several African countries have been working on preparing their students for the global information environment by teaching them information skills. At the University of Botswana librarians have integrated information skills instruction throughout the curriculum. In South Africa in recent years academicians and librarians have co-operated to improve the learning process for all populations, and information literacy instruction has been used as part of the preparation for lifelong learning. A noteworthy project with help from the Ford Foundation and Readers Digest Foundation has helped the Western Cape librarians develop curriculum-integrated information literacy programmes in academic institutions. School and public librarians have been exploring the teaching of information skills in public school settings. At UNISA (University of South Africa) in Pretoria and at the University of Pretoria several initiatives related to information literacy have been in place during the last decade.

China

Since the early 1980s the Chinese government has supported and encouraged the teaching of library and information skills in academic institutions and several national conferences have been held in the country. Although many Chinese universities (39%) offer user instruction, only a small percentage of the students enrolled in higher education are able to participate in this. As the network and technology environment in China grows, the need for information skills instruction is growing as well. The information skills instruction programme at Tsinghua University, a highly technological institution, serves as a good model for the future. China has just held the first National Conference on Information Literacy in January 2002 at Heilongjiang University in Harbin City. They translated the ACRL Information Literacy Competency Standards into Chinese and are distributing them throughout the academic Chinese library community. The conference was attended by more than 170 librarians and much interest was expressed in working with the ACRL standards to help students gain information skills.

Australia and New Zealand

Academic librarians in Australia and New Zealand have been actively pursuing the connection between lifelong learning and information literacy. They have held four successful national conferences on information literacy organized by the University of South Australia Library, the ALIA (Australian Library and Information Association) and the Information Literacy Special Interest Group. Proceedings have been published for each of these challenging conferences (Booker, 2000). Australian librarians have also developed strategies to advance information literacy as a profound educational issue for society. Librarians at the University of South Australia have a mandate to ensure that students achieve information literacy. At the University of Technology in Sydney students receive information skills instruction on a regular basis. At the Queensland University of Technology, the librarians teach an intensive, advanced course on information retrieval skills to graduate students. It is particularly noteworthy that Australian librarians have been especially concerned with information skills training within the workforce and the profession. The country's emphasis on lifelong learning is leading to new partnerships between faculty and librarians, transforming teaching and learning.

UK

During the past three decades academic and school librarians in the UK have been actively involved in developing theories and programmes related to user instruction and information literacy. The ex-polytechnic universities and schools in particular have experimented with and set up a variety of information skills instruction programmes. Among the various methodologies used have been mediated instruction packages and computer-assisted instruction modules. Information skills programmes have also been focused on in open learning and adult education courses. In 1998, SCONUL (Society of College, National and

University Libraries) (www.sconul.ac.uk) created a task force to prepare a statement on information skills for higher education. SCONUL proposed seven sets of skills developed from a basic competence in library and information technology skills (Corrall and Hathaway, 2000). The majority of academic librarians are engaged in some type of teaching of information skills. In March 2002, Scotland hosted an international conference on Information Technology and Information Literacy addressing a variety of topics related to information literacy teaching and information technology concerns. (Available at www.iteu.gla.ac.uk/elit/itilit2002/.)

Germany

In the former German Democratic Republic user education was a major component of education. During the 1970s many German academic librarians began to open their library stacks to users and realized that user instruction would be needed. However, it was not until the 1990s when German librarians began to address user instruction in a more practical and systematic manner using information literacy concepts developed in the USA, online teaching and learner-centred techniques. A good example of current curricular-integrated information skills teaching can be found at the University of Heidelberg.

Netherlands

In the Netherlands information technology is part of the general secondary education curricula and information literacy courses are often included in the high school curricula. The emphasis in education is on problem-solving skills through efficient information-handling skills. Tilburg University holds several week-long workshops for librarians and technologists addressing the topic of information technology and education including modules on information literacy.

Sweden

Academic librarians in Sweden have been involved in user education for more than 20 years, particularly in the areas of engineering, medicine and economics. They have utilized information technology to provide more efficient instruction to students at the beginning of their courses so that librarians can develop advanced electronic information skills instruction for upper-level and graduate students. Librarians at Malmo University, established in 1998, are working on integrating information literacy into the curriculum to meet the many diverse information needs of their students. Three national conferences on information literacy have been held.

Canada

The information policy of the Canadian government among many other information concerns promotes an information-literate population. During the past three decades Canadian academic librarians have been concerned with teaching students library and information skills. An annual national conference has been addressing information skills concerns for more than 30 years. Instructional librarians in academic libraries are continuing to address the challenge of integrating information skills instruction into the total curriculum. Although some progress has been made during the past five years, much more is needed compared with efforts in the USA and Australia.

Mexico

Collaboration between librarians and faculty is a relative new trend in Mexican academic libraries and few examples have as yet been documented. Librarians are trying to assume the role of user information educators but they face more challenges in doing this than their counterparts in the USA and in countries with more advanced economies. However, an excellent example of a user education programme can be found at Juarez University. Three national conferences on user education have been held in Mexico, sponsored by the Universidad Autonoma in Juarez, Mexico.

South America

Information regarding user instruction and information literacy from countries in South America has been difficult to find. Details are not available as yet but librarians in Argentina, Brazil and Colombia are working on information skills initiatives.

Expected outcomes of teaching information skills

During the past three decades it has been documented through workshops and publications that the teaching of information skills to students ensures that:

- students become lifelong learners
- students acquire critical thinking skills
- students become effective and efficient users of all types of information
- students use information responsibly
- students become effective in doing research
- students become productive members of the workforce.

Conclusion

It is apparent that in this century information literacy is becoming an important global initiative in education. This fits in well with the new education initiatives in higher education and the emergence of a new learning environment, especially in the electronic environment. Librarians and faculty are collaborating like never before to train students in information and technology work as part of their total education so that ultimately they can be successful in the electronic information environment. In developing counties such as South Africa and Mexico information literacy initiatives are helping formerly uneducated people to gain important information and literacy skills so they can succeed in the 21st century.

In developed countries in Europe, North America and Australia information literacy efforts have been documented and indicate that teachers and librarians are co-operating in teaching information skills in various configurations. Research related to information literacy is in progress in various countries. The European Community is initiating several co-operative ventures related to information literacy, standards have been developed and are utilized in teaching information skills, and the assessment of information literacy is now an important goal for everyone.

Ultimately, citizens in every country will need training in effective information use to be productive in society. Teacher training institutions as well as library/information schools must update education programmes to address information skills instruction. Teachers and librarians will be challenged not only by the training of future citizens and members of the workforce to become productive information workers, but especially by working with policy makers to ensure that information literacy becomes a governmental priority. Singapore and Australia are two countries in which the government has instituted such policies.

Most importantly, national and international collaborations are needed to ensure that information literacy becomes part of policy governing education and governmental initiative. New skills are needed in digital education, research and the work environment and lifelong learning will be a requirement for every person.

References

AASL (1998) *Information Power: building partnerships for learning*, American Association of School Librarians (AASL) and Association for Educational Communications and Technology, Chicago, American Library Association.

ACRL (2000) *Information Literacy Competency Standards for Higher Education*, Chicago, Association of College and Research Libraries. Also available at www.ala.org/Content/NavigationMenu/ACRL/Standards_and_Guidelines/ Standards_and_Guidelines_by_Topic.htm [accessed 8 June 2003].

ACRL (2001) *Objectives for Information Literacy Instruction: a model statement for acad-*

emic librarians, Chicago, Association of College and Research Libraries. Also available at www.ala.org/Content/NavigationMenu/ACRL/Standards_and_ Guidelines/Standards_and_Guidelines_by_Topic. htm [accessed 8 June 2003].

ACRL (2003a) *Institute for Information Literacy*. Available at www.ala.org/Content/ Navigation Menu/ACRL/Standards_and_Guidelines/Standards_and_ Guidelines_by_Topic.htm [accessed 8 June 2003].

ACRL (2003b) *Standards Tool Kit*. Available at www.ala.org/Content/Navigation Menu/ACRL/Standards_and_Guidelines/Standards_and_Guidelines_by_Topic. htm [accessed 8 June 2003].

Booker, D. (ed.) (2000) *Concept, Challenge, Conundrum: from library skills to information literacy. Proceedings of the Fourth National Information Literacy Conference conducted by the University of South Australia Library and Australian Library and Information Association Information Literacy Special Interest Group, 3–5 December, 1999, Adelaide*, Adelaide, University of South Australia Library.

Breivik, P. S. (2002) Information Literacy and the Engaged Campus. Giving students and community members the skills to take on (and not be taken in by) the internet, *AAHE (American Association of Higher Education) Bulletin*, **53** (1), 3–6.

Bruce, C. and Candy, P. (2000) *Information Literacy around the World. Advances in programs and research*, Wagga Wagga, New South Wales, Charles Sturt University.

Commission on Learning Resources and Instructional Technology (1995) *Information Competence in the CSU: a report*, California State University, 19–21.

Corrall, S. and Hathaway, H. (eds) (2000) *Seven Pillars of Wisdom? Good practice in information skills development. Proceedings of a conference held at the University of Warwick, 6–7 July 2000*, London, SCONUL.

Dowler, L. (1997) *Gateways to Knowledge: the role of academic libraries in teaching, learning, and research*, London, MIT Press, 140–1.

Farmer, D. W. and Mech, T. F. (1992) Information Literacy: developing students as independent learners, *New Directions for Higher Education*, **78**, 1–124.

LOEX (1971) Available at www.emich.edu/public/loex/loex.html.

Middle States (1995) *Information Literacy: lifelong learning in the Middle States Region*, Philadelphia, Commission on Higher Education, v.

National Forum for Information Literacy (1990) Available at www.infolit.org.

Proceedings (1997) *Information Literacy: the professional issue. Proceedings of the Third National Information Literacy Conference conducted by the University of South Australia Library*, Adelaide, University of South Australia Library.

Rader, H. B. (1996) User Education and Information Literacy for the Next Decade: an international perspective, *Reference Services Review*, **24** (2), 71–4.

Rader, H. B. (2000) Silver Anniversary: 25 years of reviewing the literature related to user instruction, *Reference Services Review*, **28** (3), 290–6.

Ratteray, O. M. T. and Simmons, Howard L. (1995) *Information Literacy in Higher Education*, Philadelphia, Commission on Higher Education, 1.

Stallings, D. (1997) The Virtual University Is Inevitable: but will the model be non-profit or profit? A speculative commentary on the emerging education environment, *Journal of Academic Librarianship*, **23**, 271–80.

Model programmes from the USA

California State University–San Marcos. Available at
    http://library.csusm.edu/departments/ilp/.
University of California–Berkeley. Available at www.lib.berkeley.edu/TeachingLib/.
Florida International University. Available at
    www.fiu.edu/%7Elibrary/ili/ilipropl.html.
University of Louisville. Available at www.louisville.edu/infoliteracy.
University of Washington. Available at http://washington.edu/uwired.
University of Wisconsin–Parkside. Available at
    www.uwp.edu/information.services/ library/.

Model programmes from other countries

Australia/New Zealand
    Queensland. Available at www.lib.qut.edu.au/elearn/tutorial.html.
    Sydney. Available at www.library.usyd.edu.au/skills/.
Canada
    Guelph. Available at www.lib.uoguelph.ca/LibEd/.
China
    Tsinghua University. Available at www.tsinghua.edu.cn/english/service.html.
Germany
    Heidelberg. Available at www.ub.uniheidelberg.de/allg/schulung.html.
Mexico
    Ciudad Juarez. Available at
    www.uacj.mx/bibliotecas/ICS/servicios/referencia/ menu.htm.
Netherlands
    Tilburg. Available at www.tilburguniversity.nl/services/library/courses.html.
South Africa
    Cape Town. Available at www.library.uct.ac.za/infolit.
    Pretoria – University of South Africa. Available at
    www.unisa.ac.za/library/afdeling/client/usered/students/libinfo.html.
Sweden
    Malmo University. Available at www.bit.mah.se/bit.nsf/e-searchview.
United Kingdom
    Glasgow. Available at www.lib.gla.ac.uk/Training/index.
    SCONUL. Available at www.sconul.ac.uk.

Part 2
Exploring the
Seven Pillars model

3

The SCONUL Task Force on Information Skills

Hilary Johnson

Introduction

The SCONUL (Society of College, National and University Libraries) Task Force on Information Skills was first convened in early 1999, as a result of increased awareness of information skills training as an important strategic issue for university and college libraries and information services. A major concern at that time was that the nature and importance of information skills was being overlooked in the rapid build-up of activity in relation to the use of IT (information technology) in HE (higher education). It was felt strongly that, within higher education, information literacy should include the notion of an individual who is able to contribute to the synthesis of existing information, to further develop ideas building on that synthesis, and, ultimately, create new knowledge in a particular subject discipline. Town (2000, 14) argues that the development of information skills 'enables people at universities and in their subsequent careers, to turn knowledge into wisdom through effective application', a prime learning outcome for higher education in all its manifestations.

The initial tasks that the SCONUL Executive Board set the group were to look at: defining what was meant by 'information skills'; articulating why information skills are important for higher education students; assessing the size and scope of current activity in UK higher education; and identifying principles of good practice in this area, within UK higher education, and from other countries. As a result of the Task Force's work, a briefing paper was produced in autumn 1999 (SCONUL, 1999), and the SCONUL autumn meeting of that year took this theme as a major strand. An important part of the briefing paper dealt with the Seven Pillars model of information skills, which has since been drawn upon in a number of curriculum developments. A need identified early on was for there to be a more commonly acknowledged qualification to be available. This was couched in terms of an 'ECDL (European Computer Driving Licence) equivalent'. The Task Force has developed its thinking in this respect and engaged with one major provider, The Open University, in ongoing activity in this aspect. The pros and cons of such an accredited course development are being explored. Another major strand of the Task Force work has been to consider the issues surrounding the measurement of performance for information skills work. These developments are reported in this chapter.

Remit of the Task Force

The SCONUL Task Force on Information Skills was first convened in early 1999, as a result of increased awareness of information skills training as an important strategic issue for higher education libraries and information services. A major concern at that time was that the nature and importance of information skills was being overlooked in the rapid build-up of activity in relation to the use of IT in higher education. The initial brief was to provide answers to the following questions:

- What do we mean by information skills?
- Why do we consider the development of information skills important?
- What is the size and scale of activity in UK higher education libraries relating to information skills?
- Are there identifiable elements of good practice in the sector to be shared?

The focus of the work was to be the UK higher education sector. A concern was that there was undue emphasis being given to students' information technology skills that was overlooking vital broader elements such as critical evaluation and the use of resources across both print and digital environments.

The results of the Task Force's investigations were incorporated into the SCONUL Briefing Paper published in the autumn of 1999 (SCONUL, 1999). The reception accorded to the Briefing Paper, together with the identification of further areas of work by Task Force members, led to the suggestion that the group remain in existence (see Appendix) with a revised action plan. Individual membership has changed over the years but the focus of the group has remained strong, and its achievements are considerable.

The Seven Pillars model

One of the most effective (in terms of stimulating debate) elements of the Briefing Paper has been the Seven Pillars model (see Figure 3.1). This was largely a synthesis of attempts at defining 'what we mean by', which owed a tremendous amount to the work of a number of other workers in the field. It was designed to be a practical working model which would facilitate further development of ideas among practitioners in the field, and would hopefully stimulate debate about the ideas and, in our view more importantly, about how those ideas might be used by library and other staff in higher education concerned with the development of students' skills.

The model combines ideas about the range of skills involved with both the need to clarify and illustrate the relationship between information skills and IT skills, and the idea of progression in higher education embodied in the development of the curriculum through first-year undergraduate up to postgraduate

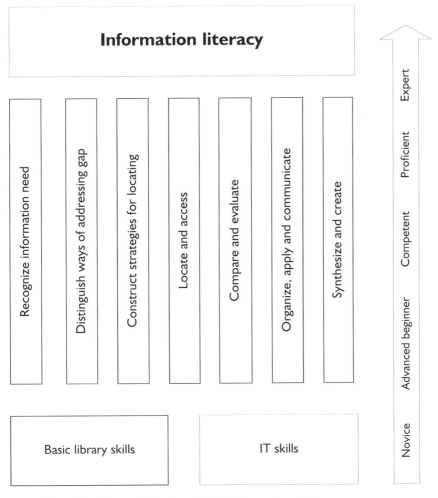

Fig. 3.1 *The 'Seven Pillars' model of information skills*

and research-level scholarship. In a somewhat crude diagram, this enabled the identification of seven 'pillars' (headline skills) but in a context which acknowledged some basic building blocks (basic library and basic IT skills as prerequisites for the development of the headline skills) and incorporated ideas of progression from 'novice' to 'expert' status. Peter Godwin, a current Task Force member, has worked on the development of progression within levels of higher education and begun to map the Seven Pillars skills to the four levels of undergraduate and the M level of postgraduate work (this work is reported in Chapter 7 of this book). The Task Force sees this as a continuum leading to the development of high-level scholarship skills, or information literacy.

The question of terminology featured early on in our work, as we wrestled almost more with the 'what do we call it?' question than anything else. We have continued to use the term 'information skills' for what we are interested in, rather than formulations such as information literacy or information handling. The use of the word 'skills' in certain sections of the UK HE scene is problematic, and we certainly feel that 'skills' is too limiting a concept, because, we feel, real information literacy encompasses a range of cognitive as well as motor skills. However, 'literacy' in some applications has a threshold meaning which we are also anxious to avoid.

Subsequently it has become possible that ideas which relate HE scholarship to the 'reflective practitioner' concept may provide a way out of the terminological dilemma. What we strive to achieve in students is an intelligent and educated approach to establishing a need for, searching for, finding and using information, and (at the highest levels) in turn contributing to that information base within the sphere of higher education which could be regarded as 'information scholarship'. The correct place of information skills is as one of the founding practice areas for the university as an academic community of practice. Diana Laurillard (2001) has outlined the concept of the 'reflective practicum' that is the modern university. Students need to be equipped with the skills needed to be competent learners in the Reflective Practicum. An extra value of this approach is that it establishes a link between the skills that learners need to be learners, and those that they need as members of different kinds of communities of practice after graduation.

Dissemination

In the summer of 2000 the SCONUL Task Force organized a conference taking the Seven Pillars as the theme (Corrall and Hathaway, 2000). The conference was well attended and has had a stimulating effect on activity in this field. The Task Force itself has continued to be active, principally in the areas of awareness raising and stakeholder influence, the question of generic or subject-based information literacy input, the possibility of a syllabus presented in the manner of the ECDL for information skills, and the consideration of performance measures.

A number of areas of activity come under the heading of awareness raising. The 'Big Blue' Project (funded by the UK Joint Information Systems Committee) has systematically audited the current UK situation in both higher and further education, and investigated particular case studies. Although to some extent going over previous ground, this is a larger project than was possible before. Furthermore, the papers presented at the IT&ILit2002 Conference in Glasgow (March 2002), which form the basis for this volume, have been a good way of continuing the dialogue with practitioners. This is also being enabled through links with the Institute for Learning and Teaching, many of the members of which are library or academic-related staff. We have hopes of the fact that the first president of CILIP (Chartered Institute of Library and Information Professionals), Sheila Corrall, has long been an advocate of information literacy development (and has been a recent member of the Task Force itself). The summer of 2002 saw involvement in the IFLA International Conference (again in Glasgow), and the eLit2003 Conference (once again in Glasgow) offered further opportunities (www.elit2003.com).

Information skills and subject disciplines

A second major strand to Task Force activity is to attempt to answer the question 'Does discipline matter?' A major outcome of the Seven Pillars conference was a debate about the extent to which it mattered, in the teaching of information literacy, as to whether the students were studying chemistry, or geology, or English or sociology. To what extent are the skills generic, and to what extent dictated by the subject curricula and norms? The HEFCE (Higher Education Funding Council for England and Wales) had recently begun publishing their Subject Benchmarks, which endeavoured to encapsulate the curriculum expectations for designated subjects. A number of these referred to the kinds of skill we were talking about, and some members of the Task Force conducted an analysis of them. A small project was put in hand which made some first forays into investigating subject differences as perceived by staff involved in subject delivery. Tapping into the views of both academic teaching staff and library staff, questions were put to those working in three disparate subject areas – chemistry, theology and education. Some very rich data has been elicited as a result, and the outcomes are reported in Janet Peters' paper in this volume (Chapter 6).

As another side to this subject versus generic coin, the Task Force welcomed an approach from the OU (Open University) in connection with an intention on their part to develop a standalone Level 1 module on information literacy to be offered to OU students in all subjects. Necessarily a course aimed at inculcating generic information skills among students at the very first level of HE study, the course development is called MOSAIC and ran with its first cohort in May 2002. Task Force members have contributed as external assessors helping with the curriculum development, which has grown out of the Seven Pillars model. We look forward very much to finding out what the student experience with this web-based course is, and we are very grateful to the University of Reading for agreeing to fund a small group of their students to undertake the course, which Helen Hathaway will be evaluating as part of an internal investigation. This will provide invaluable evidence of how such a course may sit alongside curriculum delivery in a different institution from the OU. If successful, we have plans to develop the programme to be offered as a customizable shell to other universities for flexible incorporation into their own study and information skills activities. More information about this development is to be found in Chapter 5 of this volume.

Performance indicators for information skills programmes

The fourth area of current activity for the Task Force has been one in which we have joined forces with the SCONUL Advisory Committee on Performance Indicators. The question of the best way of measuring information skills work in HE libraries has been puzzling us for some time. The SCONUL Statistics series (widely considered to be an invaluable aid to trend analysis over a number of years) has always been sadly lacking in this area of library work. The SCONUL Advisory Committee on Performance Indicators' interest in this problem coincided with the Task Force's thinking that the important measure should be not an input one (how many hours of library staff are being allocated to this?) but rather an outcome one (what difference are we making?). Stephen Town, a Task Force member who is also usefully a member of the Advisory Committee, has led a series of workshops which are at least beginning to develop an answer. By taking a Critical Success Factors approach, the workshops have enabled a wide range of practitioners to consider what is critical to the success of information skills training work. A full report on the work is given in Chapter 4 of this book. An outcome of the work which will, we hope, become embedded in daily practice is the inclusion of measures in the *SCONUL Performance Measures Handbook*, which will be available to all SCONUL members later in the year.

Conclusion

As a result of these projects, and other discussions and activities fuelled by the dynamic and exhilarating debates at the IT&ILit and eLit conferences, the SCONUL Task Force looks forward to working with a wide range of specialists and practitioners from within and outside HE libraries, with the intention of developing an increasingly refined and robust approach to enhancing students' ability to function effectively as members of both the Reflective Practicum and the Information Society.

References

Corrall, S. and Hathaway, H. (eds) (2000) *Seven Pillars of Wisdom? Good practice in information skills development. Proceedings of a conference held at the University of Warwick, 6–7 July 2000*, London, SCONUL.

Laurillard, D. (2001) *Supporting the Development of Scholarship Skills through the Online Digital Library,* presentation at the SCONUL Autumn Conference, November 2001. Available at www.sconul.ac.uk/Conference/Autprog.htm.

SCONUL (1999) *Information Skills in Higher Education: a SCONUL position paper*, London, SCONUL. Available at www.sconul.ac.uk/publications/publications. htm#2.

Town, J. S. (2000) Wisdom or Welfare?: the Seven Pillars model. In Corrall, S. and Hathaway, H. (eds) (2000) *Seven Pillars of Wisdom? Good practice in information skills development. Proceedings of a conference held at the University of Warwick, 6–7 July 2000*, London, SCONUL.

Appendix: Current members of the SCONUL Task Force on Information Skills

Deborah Bragan-Turner, Humanities Librarian, University of Nottingham.

Sheila Corrall, Director of Academic Support Services, University of Southampton.

Peter Godwin, Academic Services Librarian, South Bank University.

Helen Hathaway, Team Manager, Faculty of Science, University of Reading Library.

Hilary Johnson, Chief Librarian, University College Northampton (*Convenor*).

Jo Parker, The Open University.

Janet Peters, Head of Library and Learning Resources, University of Wales College, Newport.

Stephen Town, Director of Information Services, Royal Military College of Science, Cranfield University.

4

Information literacy: definition, measurement, impact

J. Stephen Town

Introduction

This chapter covers three main areas: the context and definition of information literacy; the development of performance measurement for information literacy programmes, reporting on the SCONUL (Society of College, National and University Libraries) Information Skills Task Force's recent series of workshops; and some conclusions in relation to the impact of information literacy programmes on the individual and on the information profession.

Definition and the 'skills' agenda

Measurement is key to the usefulness of information literacy as a concept. The definition of information literacy depends upon an ability to recognize the difference between those who are so literate, and those who are not. Recognition of these differences will help in designing programmes to correct deficiencies. Conversely, recognition of what is successful in existing information skills programmes will feed back to a developing understanding of the concept.

Unfortunately, a number of issues obstruct clarity in the field of information literacy, particularly in the UK. The term 'ICT literacy' is a particularly unfortunate elision. ICT (information and communications technology) literacy appears to imply inclusion of information literacy, but in fact is only a synonym for IT (or computer) literacy. Its use tends to obscure the fact that information literacy is a well developed concept separate from IT (information technology) literacy. As we shall see later, this is not the case in other English-speaking countries. In most contexts preparation for the information age tends to be viewed solely as an issue of skills development, when information literacy clearly also requires a basis of knowledge. A previous paper suggested that the UK's approach to the information age might be seen as one of welfare provision rather than developing wisdom (Town, 2000). The concentration on providing equipment, infrastructure and content alone will not result in the information poor becoming information rich unless they have the capability to make beneficial use of this investment. One suggestion is that the dictionary definition of wisdom is precisely applicable to the concept of information literacy: 'Possession of expert knowledge together with the power of applying it practically' (*Oxford English Dictionary*).

The approach to information literacy in our professional literature might be a cause for concern. The emphasis on research-based models and on extensive internal debates over definition seems to miss the point that in this field meaning cannot be separated from application. What is needed is the development of practical programmes which make a measurable difference.

National drivers towards information literacy

It is not possible here to cover in detail the driving forces arising from individual national contexts towards developing the information society, and in consequence the need for widespread information literacy and associated programmes. There appears to be common ground in three main connected issues which lead to a national needs analysis for progress. Firstly, a nation perceives a need for competitive reasons to be a player in the global knowledge economy. Secondly, this suggests a need for the upskilling of its population to work effectively in this sort of economy, resulting in a national 'learning agenda'. The 'learning agenda' also tends to become explicitly associated with the skills of citizens, the development of these skills within educational programmes, and their subsequent application for lifelong learning, in the workplace, and in personal life. Thirdly, the growth of digital media and communications results in a situation of widespread information overload, leading to the need for both individuals and corporations to have effective information and knowledge management. The sequence tends to run from national concern to process analysis to products for developing information literacy (Bundy, 1998). I shall consider the initial skills analysis very briefly in three specific national contexts below. All are from English-speaking contexts where 'information literacy' appears to be a commonly understood concept.

In the UK the information age was recognized as a key issue by the new Labour government in 1997. Reports outlined and combined the citizen's right to an information infrastructure (Great Britain. DfEE, 1997) with the necessary learning agenda for a successful society in a knowledge-based future global economy (Great Britain. DfEE, 1998). The main contextual driver in the UK was the desire for improved national performance and competitiveness in this global economy, and led to the desire to provide coherent packages for lifelong learning for UK citizens. A defined national set of 'key skills', for learning, for careers, and for personal life, were identified at www.qca.org.uk/nq/ks/. The six skill areas were:

- number application
- communication
- information technology
- working with others
- improving one's own learning and performance
- problem solving.

When this approach was applied to UK higher education, the Dearing Report (NCIHE, 1997) identified a concept of 'graduateness' defined by the following skills:

- communication skills
- numeracy
- use of information technology
- learning how to learn
- subject-specific skills.

Both these analyses failed to explicitly identify information literacy as a requirement, or to separate information skills from technology skills. This differentiates the UK approach from those of the other national examples below.

In the USA, information literacy had been recognized sufficiently as both a concept and a challenge related to the information age for a National Forum to be created in 1989, bringing together a coalition of interested parties, from librarians through educators to politicians (www.infolit.org/). Subsequently an Institute for Information Literacy (www.ala.org/acrl/nili/), and a set of competency standards for higher education (www.ala.org/acrl/ilstndardlo.html) followed. When the national skills debate was in progress, information literacy and its component skills were therefore recognized, with a clear distinction made between information and technology and systems. The Secretary's Commission on Achieving Necessary Skills (SCANS, 1991) produced the following analysis:

Foundation skills	Competencies
Basic	*Resources*
Thinking	*Interpersonal*
Personal	*Information*
	Systems
	Technology

Since then this early recognition of need has led to information literacy programmes at all levels of education in the USA. There has been no real issue of definition, and apparently little divergence of opinion about what practically is sought. A US model was provided at an early stage with outcome measures (Doyle, 1992); and more recently the Big6 model and programmes for Schools (see www.big6.com/) has been created as a commercial venture.

In Australia, the relevant government body (Mayer Committee, 1992) suggested the following 'Competency strands' for citizens:

- collecting, analysing and organizing information
- communicating ideas and information
- planning and organizing activities
- working with others in teams
- using mathematical ideas and techniques
- solving problems
- using technology.

Once again technology skills are clearly separated from information-related skills. There has been much subsequent activity in Australia, particularly in higher education, to which full justice can hardly be done here, but including task forces, conferences, standards and a joint Australia and New Zealand Institute for Information Literacy (see Bundy, 1998). A distinctive model for information literacy has been developed to reflect personal 'conceptions' (Bruce, 1997).

The SCONUL Information Skills Task Force

Despite the lack of explicit national recognition of the importance of information literacy, one sector within the UK has been involved in delivering information skills programmes for some time. Higher education, and particularly HE libraries, have increasingly taken on the challenge of explaining the developing environment of electronic information resources to learners, and of educating them in effective use. That this would assist learners in developing a suite of information-related competencies was recognized:

One distinguishing feature of the competent graduate is the ability to identify appropriate sources of data and information, to be able to collect these in a cogent manner, to deconstruct parcels of information and subsequently reflect on these. The final component is the ability to reconstruct the information, to synthesise these raw materials, and to be in a position to communicate the interpreted information to others.

(*ITATL Report*, 1997)

SCONUL, conscious of the growth of both the importance of and activity in this area in HE libraries, established a Task Force in 1999 to develop a position on information skills. Among its objectives were definition and demonstration of the importance of information skills, the identification of good practice, and an answer to the question of how information skills activity related to institutional and national strategies for information literacy (see Chapter 3).

Performance measures for information skills: what's important

These objectives suggested strongly that performance measurement and evaluation of information skills programmes were issues that needed to be addressed. Defining information literacy depends on identifying what is important about the concept, and about information skills programmes.

The protocol chosen for the performance measures investigation, which was also supported by SCONUL's Advisory Committee on Performance Improvement, was to apply a standard methodology for identifying candidate performance measures. This method used a 'small group' approach to include stakeholders from a diversity of institutions, if necessary repeated around the UK, as the most practical method to achieve a credible national sample. The results from these groups are in the process of collection and analysis in order to create a list of specific measures. Comparison to standard models and frameworks for performance measures will be used to identify any missing measurement areas. These may well arise as the groups consisted mainly of library staff rather than a full range of stakeholders. This reflected the limitations of practicality, and the reality of lack of widespread understanding of information literacy as a concept among these broader stakeholders. The results and recommended measures will be presented in manual form for SCONUL members to choose and use as required.

CSFs (critical success factors) are what must be accomplished for a service or process to be achieved successfully (Oakland, 1993). This method for identifying 'what is important' was the methodology chosen to be used in the small group settings. CSFs are normally expressed as a set of about six short memorable 'must have' or 'need' statements. All should be essential for a an information skills programme to be successful, and together they should encompass everything that is important about it. These six phrases then help define specific measures for information skills. The suggested process for developing CSFs was as follows:

1 Brainstorm to produce a list of all factors which have an impact on your service's information skills programme.
2 Group the impacts into related areas.
3 Create a statement for each area.
4 Agree a set of about six for your group by eliminating duplication and the less important.
5 Suggest practical performance measures relating to each statement.

This method was supplied to facilitators for all the workshops undertaken.

Initially the Task Force itself tested the methodology, albeit in constrained circumstances. This was followed by a workshop at the SCONUL Annual Conference in Glasgow, 2001. Participants were mainly Chief Librarians, providing the perspective of an important group of stakeholders. These results were reported in the SCONUL Newsletter (Town, 2001). A mixed group of staff from the newly converged Academic Support Services at Southampton University also undertook the exercise (Town, 2002). Seven regional workshops were arranged for winter 2001/2, facilitated by Task Force members or by local library staff using the standardized methodology, and advertised to local academic libraries and their staff. These took place at De Montfort University, Manchester Metropolitan University, Reading University, Nottingham University, South Bank University, University of Wales College, Newport, and Glasgow University. In all more than 30 small groups involving well over a hundred participants (mainly library staff involved in information skills programmes) provided results for collation and synthesis into a single list of measures.

Sample critical success factor results are given in Table 4.1 to give a flavour of the variety of expression and content arising from different groups.

Although there were differences in emphasis among the groups, and each group provided something significant to the overall analysis, there was a strong degree of agreement over the important factors.

Synthesis of the group's work suggests the composite list of six critical success factors for information skills programmes shown in Table 4.2. A more detailed commentary will accompany these raw findings in the resulting SCONUL manual. Table 4.3 shows a list of suggested measures arising from these CSFs, or at least those elements that need to be measured in order to judge the success of information skills programmes. Clearly many of the suggestions will not be susceptible to simple quantative measurement; others invite 'yes or no' answers. Participants in the workshops generally found it easier to define what was important than to identify specific measures or indicators.

Table 4.1 *Sample critical success factor results*

Sample Results 1	Sample Results 2	Sample Results 3
We must:		
• Satisfy our users	• A programme for	• Dedicated, well trained
• Make a difference	students	staff to provide IS
• Integrate with	• The right attitude from	• Suitable training venues
academic programmes	academic staff	• Close liaison and
• Achieve wide market	• Management of the	communication with
penetration	programme	teaching staff
• Use staff competent to	• A curriculum and	• Students to recognize
deliver	delivery	their own needs and
• Be properly equipped to	• Resources	know how to fill the gap
deliver		• Appropriate assessment
• Use the best-value		methods to build into the
approach		planning cycle for future
		programmes
		• Results

The next step in the work is to compare these results with standard approaches to performance measurement. This will help to define any areas missing or underdeveloped in the above analysis. At a minimum, comparison will be made with the frameworks suggested by the 'The Effective Academic Library' (HEFCE, 1995), the 'Balanced Scorecard' approach (Kaplan and Norton, 1996), and the European Framework for Quality Management (www.efgm.org). This will help to fill in the gaps inevitably created through the focus on a single group of stakeholders (library staff) throughout the exercises. Mapping the proposed measures against each element of these different frameworks will highlight areas of measurement that may be missing through limitations of perspective on the part of participants in the groups. It would have been valuable to conduct the workshops with different groups of stakeholders, for example students, academic staff, funders and employers. Time, accessibility and understanding of the concepts and issues among these groups ruled this out as a practical proposition, but it remains an aspiration. When this step has been completed, a manual will be produced for SCONUL members as a guide for performance measurement and improvement of information literacy and information skills programmes.

Table 4.2   *Critical success factors*

CSF1	**CSF2**
Staff with:	Resources sufficient to:
• the skills, knowledge, understanding and motivation to teach • awareness of teaching and learning issues • subject understanding • the support of a full staff development cycle.	• deliver and develop information skills education • provide adequate staff • allow time for preparation and assessment as well as delivery • provide suitable environments and materials.
CSF3	**CSF4**
Student Outcomes which:	Partnerships with:
• are clearly identified • are formal course requirements • combine academic knowledge with transferable skills • motivate and engage all students • result in long-term benefit.	• a range of stakeholders • those within and beyond the university • academic departments • other providers • other institutions • professional bodies.
CSF5	**CSF6**
Strategic Framework which:	Sustained Pedagogic Quality through:
• embeds information skills in the curriculum • recognizes the importance of ILit • recognizes the contribution of and involves libraries and their staff • ensures parity of provision and equality of standards alongside other academic elements.	• effective programme designs • learning materials and delivery methods • fitness for purpose • meeting the needs • recognition of a diverse student population.

Table 4.3   *Measures arising from the CSFs*

CSF1: Staff	CSF2: Resources

CSF1: Staff

- ILT membership
- Teaching qualifications
- Peer observation
- Self-assessment
- Student feedback:
  — via library
  — via department
- Staff development and appraisal policy
- Training availability
- Teaching time
- Preparation time

CSF2: Resources

- Demand versus supply
- Staffing levels
- Student/staff ratios
- Staff stress levels
- Currency of materials
- Suitability of delivery
- Courseware quality
- Per capita spending
- Rooms and utilization
- Virtual environments
- IT infrastructure and support
- Cost-effectiveness of methods
- Existing SCONUL measures
- Development funding

CSF3: Students

- Evidence of student progression:
  — Pre-assessment
  — Post-assessment
- Academic feedback
- Course assessment
- Employer and graduate feedback
- Reports from professional bodies
- Student awareness and motivation
- Usage statistics
- Behavioural changes
- Registrations

CSF4: Partners

- Library representation and membership of course teams
- Degree of integration of ISE into courses
- Market penetration
- Generic versus subject
- External initiatives and involvement
- Employer and professional body recognition
- Liaison measurement
- Credits value
- Benchmarking
- Attitudes surveys

continued

Table 4.3 *Measures arising from the CSFs*

CSF5: Strategies	CSF6: Pedagogy and Programmes
• Clear strategy • Incorporation in institutional strategies • Learning and teaching • Overall strategic plan • Widening participation • Incorporation in policies and quality plans • Incorporation in programme plans	• Learning outcomes • Conformance to academic standards • Feedback from academics and students • Peer review • Flexibility • Meeting stakeholder expectations including accreditation • Systematic QA • Teaching methods • Timeliness

Impact and conclusions

One critical and essential area of information skills performance measurement which remains to be resolved is the measurement of outcomes in individual learners. We need to be able to prove that programmes have had an effect on individuals. The key impact of information skills programmes must be on those who participate. Without some effective measure of the difference made to individuals and their capabilities, the value of programmes will remain uncertain and arguable. One suggestion to answer this problem is to use the SCONUL Seven Pillars model (SCONUL, 1999) as the framework for a diagnostic tool for individuals. This requires substantial further work to relate the generic elements of the model, not only to an individual's skill or knowledge levels, but also to the requirements of their particular context.

The impact of this work so far has been to help to define information literacy more precisely, in terms of what is important about it and about how programmes might be successfully constructed to achieve it, at least from a librarian's perspective. As a result, I would contend that information literacy is personal and individual, that it is a corpus of knowledge rather than simply a set of skills, and that it will therefore be achieved through education rather than training. It will be a lifelong endeavour, as information resources continue to change and develop. Information literacy can only currently be created through partnerships because no single professional group has complete enough command of the knowledge or skills suggested by the model to teach the entire corpus effectively. Part of the reason for this is that information literacy is contextual in both subject field and in local service access, and that the absence of knowledge of either negates the benefits of familiarity with the other.

My personal conclusion drawn from this work and the broader analysis and perspective provided by the SCONUL Task Force is that information literacy programmes are about changing people. This is the outcome that will 'make the difference', as the Task Force suggested a successful programme should do. In this sense information literacy activity is different from other library functions, although of course these may result in similar outcomes. This activity is about education rather than mediation, or service or information provision. It implies a change to the focus of a library's work from one of relative isolation and independence to one of collaboration with teachers and others. In so doing librarians will have to share some of our core professional knowledge. 'The need for a … comprehensive information literacy programme is now more acute than at any time in the history of information. The fundamental information concepts that we take for granted are more relevant to more people than they have ever been' (Dale and O'Flynn, 2001).

The fundamentals of information science are now not an esoteric branch of knowledge shared only by a group of professionals, but an intrinsic requirement of anyone negotiating modern information services. Alongside this need to share and educate is a need to demystify our processes; the removal of unnecessary barriers to use or complexity in our existing systems and services will allow us to focus on the more important elements of information literacy. The future of our role and of our profession will depend upon us facing these challenges.

Acknowledgements

I would like to thank all the participants in the workshops, for the benefit of their experience and insight into the process of delivering information literacy programmes.

I would also like to thank SCONUL, its members, the Advisory Committee on Performance Improvement, the Information Skills Task Force, and others for their support for, and organization and facilitation of the workshops.

Feedback request

This work is ongoing, and comments and contributions are actively sought on any aspect. The Task Force is particularly interested in feedback on the Seven Pillars model, and on examples of institutional objectives and measures for information skills education.

References

Bruce, C. (1997) *The Seven Faces of Information Literacy*, Adelaide, Auslib Press.

Bundy, A. (1998) *Information Literacy: the Key Competency for the 21st Century*, University of South Australia. Available at www.library.unisa.edu.au/papers/inlit21.htm.

Dale, A. and O'Flynn, S. (2001) Desperation: information literacy levels falling in Corporania, *Journal of Information Science*, **27** (1), 51–3.

Doyle, C. S. (1992) *Outcome Measures for Information Literacy: final report to the National Forum on Information Literacy*, Syracuse, NY, ERIC Clearinghouse.

Great Britain. DfEE (1997) *Connecting the Learning Society. National Grid for learning: the government's consultation paper*, London, Department for Education and Employment.

Great Britain. DfEE (1998) *The Learning Age: a renaissance for a new Britain*, Cm 3790, London, HMSO.

HEFCE (1995) *The Effective Academic Library: a framework for evaluating the performance of UK academic libraries*, London, HEFCE.

ITATL Report (1997) *Higher Education Funding Council for England, Information Technology Assisted Teaching and Learning (ITATL) in UK Higher Education. Final ITATL report to HEFCE by the Consortium of Telematics for Education, University of Exeter*, London, HEFCE.

Kaplan, R. S. and Norton, D. P. (1996) *The Balanced Scorecard: translating strategy into action*, Boston, MA, Harvard Business School Press.

Mayer Committee (1992) *Employment Related Key Competencies for Post Compulsory Education and Training: a discussion paper*, Melbourne, Australian Education Council.

NCIHE (National Committee of Inquiry into Higher Education) (1997) *Higher Education in the Learning Society: report of the National Committee*, London, HMSO [Dearing Report].

Oakland, J. S. (1993) *Total Quality Management: the route to improving performance*, 2nd edn, Oxford, Butterworth-Heinemann.

SCANS (1991) *What Work Requires of Schools: a SCANS report for America 2000*, Washington DC, US Secretary's Commission on Achieving Necessary Skills.

SCONUL (1999) *Information Skills in Higher Education: a SCONUL position paper*. Available at www.sconul.ac.uk/publications/publications.htm#2.

Town, J. S. (2000) Wisdom or Welfare? The Seven Pillars model. In Corrall, S. and Hathaway, H. (eds), *Seven Pillars of Wisdom? Good practice in information skills development. Proceedings of a conference held at the University of Warwick, 6–7 July 2000*, London, SCONUL, 11–21.

Town, J. S. (2001) Performance Measurement of Information Skills Education: what's important? Report and findings of a workshop held at the SCONUL Conference, Glasgow, April, 2001, *SCONUL Newsletter*, **22**, 21–4.

Town, J. S. (2002) Welfare or Wisdom? Performance measurement for information skills education. In Stein, J., Kyrillidou, M. and Davis, D. (eds) *Proceedings of the 4th Northumbria International Conference on Performance Measurement in Library and Information Services, Washington DC, August 2001*, ARL, 203–8.

5

Information literacy at the Open University: a developmental approach

Chris Dillon, Gill Needham, Linda Hodgkinson, Jo Parker and Kirsty Baker

Introduction

As the availability of information increases, there is a growing need for skills not only in accessing information but also in assessing critically its validity and quality. In the UK the National Committee of Inquiry into Higher Education (NCIHE, 1997, the Dearing Report) had identified information technology as a 'key skill' in the HE curriculum (together with learning how to learn, communication and numeracy) but not the related but distinct set of information-handling or information literacy skills. In 1998 the Standing Conference of National and University Libraries (SCONUL, since 2001 the Society of College, National and University Libraries) set up a Task Force to 'stimulate debate about the place of information skills within the context of current activity surrounding "key skills", "graduate-ness" and lifelong learning' (SCONUL, 1999). The Task Force identified two main strands in its definition of information literacy in higher education. The first relates to the notion of the 'competent student' and the development of skills 'which students will need to call upon in the process of undertaking study at a higher education level – a "tool" for the "job" of being a learner'. The second strand looks towards information skills underpinning life-long learning and contributing to the formation of the 'information-literate' person beyond the immediate demands of HE study.

Increasingly there is agreement that the development of information skills should be a central part of the curriculum in UK higher education. Pioneering work in information literacy has been carried out in many Australian universities and in parts of the USA, but concern was expressed by the SCONUL Task Force that a coherent approach was lacking in the UK. In response, the OU (Open University) Library's ILU (Information Literacy Unit) proposed that the OU's expertise in designing and delivering distance learning materials could be used to offer information skills development to a wider audience at home or in the workplace, as well as to students on formal programmes of study. Concurrently, the OU's COBE (Centre for Outcomes-Based Education) was working on the development and assessment of key skills such as communication, information technology, and improving own learning and performance. There was thus an excellent opportunity for collaboration between ILU, COBE and other colleagues on the development of information literacy skills as part of the ongoing University-wide key skills work.

Information literacy at the OU

Because of the wide range of OU students' backgrounds and skills, and the many different requirements of courses from entry to postgraduate level across a broad spectrum of subjects, a number of strategies are being developed to teach and assess information skills. The approach to skills is developmental so that, as they progress through their studies, students have access to appropriate resources and assessment. The three areas of development are:

- SAFARI (Skills in Accessing, Finding and Reviewing Information): a generic web-based resource
- MOSAIC (Making Sense of Information in the Connected Age): a stand-alone information literacy course
- key skills development and assessment-only options.

SAFARI: a generic web-based resource

SAFARI is a generic web-based resource designed to be used by students to meet a broad range of information skills outcomes. Unlike traditional course-based printed materials, SAFARI can be easily updated to provide new links to resources for a wide range of courses.

There is no formal registration or assessment; students can access SAFARI at any time and use it to suit their needs. They can work through it all section by section, completing the activities as they go along. Alternatively, depending on their needs and experience, students may work through specific sections only – for example, to learn about searching databases, evaluating web resources or how to produce a bibliography. OU-registered students have the facility of saving their work so that they can log on and off at will. Accessibility is also important and SAFARI has been developed so that all content is compatible with screen reading software and users can control the way text is displayed on the screen.

SAFARI is designed to be integrated into the curriculum. Course teams can guide their students to specific parts of SAFARI at appropriate points in a course and use the generic resources to teach information skills and principles. SAFARI includes self-assessment questions with automatically generated hints and feedback to support students' learning. The aim is for students to develop their skills explicitly and to raise awareness about their particular strengths and needs.

MOSAIC: a standalone information literacy course

U120 MOSAIC (Open University, 2002) is a ten-CATS (Credit Accumulation Transfer Scheme)-point course focusing on information skills at HE Level 1. It is web based with some supporting printed material, and grew from experience gained from SAFARI and support from the SCONUL Information Skills Task Force.

The skills developed are closely linked to those identified in the 'Seven Pillars' model proposed by the Task Force. In this model seven 'headline' skills and attributes link a foundation of basic library and IT skills to a higher level concept of information literacy. The skills and attributes are the:

- recognition of an information need
- identification of ways of addressing the knowledge gap
- construction of strategies for locating information
- ability to locate and access information
- ability to compare and evaluate information
- ability to organize, apply and communicate information
- ability to synthesize and create information.

The model assumes an iterative practice that supports the development of the individual as a reflective and critical user of information. MOSAIC builds this approach into its teaching and assessment strategy by guiding the student through a number of different information skills development activities. On completing each activity students are encouraged to tackle an assessment exercise to consolidate their information skills, and to reflect on their approach to learning by identifying what they have learnt, what went well and what went less well. Students may return to these activities and rework them at any time during the course. At the end of the course the student brings together the records of their activities with an overall reflective evaluation of their work and submits the resulting portfolio of evidence for assessment.

The course offers a structured development of core information literacy skills linked to formal assessment and CATS points that can be counted towards a degree. The aim is for MOSAIC to be integrated into programmes of study to support not only subject learning but also the broader intellectual development of the student as an information-literate person.

As with SAFARI the project involved close collaboration within the OU between the Information Literacy Unit, academics, and production and course-support staff. As part of the University's quality assurance procedures, teaching and assessment material generated by the MOSAIC and SAFARI course teams was read by critical readers drawn from OU academic staff and SCONUL Task Force members. A group of OU students acted as developmental testers, working through the teaching and assessment components as the course material went through its draft stages and feeding back comments and suggestions to the course team.

MOSAIC was offered in its first pilot presentation in 2002. The course is delivered over 12 weeks and offered twice each year; telephone and online tutorial support is provided for all registered students.

Key skills: a framework for learning

For a number of years the OU has used the key skills national standards developed by the Qualifications and Curriculum Authority (QCA, 2000) to support curriculum development and change. Hodgkinson (2000) describes the process of using national key skills standards as a set of external reference points for curriculum and assessment design. The national key skills standards cover the following areas. They are:

- improving own learning and performance
- communication
- information technology
- working with others
- problem solving
- application of number.

Information literacy is not identified by QCA as a distinct key skill although there are overlaps with some aspects of information technology, communication and improving own learning and performance.

The national standards key skills are organized into five levels of achievement. Levels One and Two focus on the development of basic skills and are intended to build confidence in applying skills to largely routine situations. Level Three marks a shift from being able to tackle straightforward tasks to being able to deal with more complex situations, and Level Four indicates the standards students should be aiming to achieve towards the end of their undergraduate studies. Level Five is aimed at an individual's continuing personal and professional development and is relevant to postgraduate work and the requirements of professional bodies.

At the higher levels (Four and Five) a common framework for learning and skills development becomes explicit. This three-stage framework emphasizes the activities of strategic planning, critically monitoring progress, and reviewing and evaluating performance as 'metaskills' that support and facilitate learning and application in different contexts. The defining components are:

- *Developing a strategy*: identifying current capabilities and setting targets to improve skills in specific areas; devising strategies and identifying resources and feedback to develop skills.
- *Monitoring progress*: implementing the strategy for improvement, managing time effectively, monitoring and critically reflecting on progress, adapting the strategy to overcome difficulties.
- *Evaluating strategy and presenting results*: understanding audience and presenting outcomes appropriately, evaluating overall skills development and the effectiveness of the strategy for improvement, identifying strengths and weaknesses of the approach, and ways to move forward and further improve.

As with all learning, skills development rarely follows such a neat linear process and real students are likely to move backwards and forwards within this framework, revisiting some areas and adapting the approach to suit their own situation. However, the process seeks to encourage in the student a greater understanding of their own learning styles (that is, what does and does not work for them in tackling new learning situations), and to offer a 'skills language' they can use to identify and articulate their abilities and needs clearly to themselves and others.

This developmental framework for learning underpinning the national standards at the higher levels relevant to HE can be applied to extend and support SCONUL's Seven Pillars model of information skills. The Task Force suggests that 'the "pillars" show an iterative process whereby information users progress through competency to expertise by practising the skills'. The three-stage key skills framework offers an explicit interpretation of this 'iterative process' and paves the way for the proposal of a specification for information literacy skills that is compatible with national standards.

Information literacy: a new key skills standard?

The ongoing key skills work at the OU includes information literacy as a central component. An OU pack, U529 *Key Skills: making a difference* (Open University, 2001c), introduces the key skills approach to learning and uses the above three-stage framework to support the development of skills in both formal and informal learning environments. The pack covers all the six national standards, together with information literacy as a seventh key skill.

Since no national standard yet exists for information literacy, the OU work focused on identifying a set of skills that would define information literacy at an appropriate level for HE. In parallel with the work on SAFARI and MOSAIC, and informed by both the SCONUL Seven Pillars model and the existing structure of the QCA national standards, a specification for a key skills 'standard' in information literacy is proposed. The appendix gives the details of the specification. Key aspects include:

- establishing opportunities for using information literacy skills
- identifying a knowledge gap and the information needed to fill it
- planning and carrying out searches
- critically evaluating results, information and sources
- communicating and presenting findings accurately and appropriately
- reflecting on effectiveness of approach and adapting as necessary
- identifying own learning, successes and failures, and ways forward.

At the core of the OU's developmental approach lies an emphasis on increasing the awareness of the student of their own skills strengths and needs, and of their preferred learning styles. Specific information literacy skills are embedded in a framework that focuses on process as well as content, encouraging students to reflect on how they have learnt as well as on what they have learnt. In this framework the processes of planning, monitoring and critically reviewing progress, synthesizing and presenting results, and evaluating overall progress are understood as metaskills for taking learning forward into new situations.

Both SAFARI and MOSAIC support the specific skills with explicit teaching and examples, while the 'Making a Difference' pack draws out the generic process elements and provides a detailed commentary with examples for students tackling the information literacy requirements in the appendix.

Assessment across HE levels

SAFARI has no formal assessment but contains self-assessment activities for students to judge their own progress. Registered OU students can save their work on the system and build up their own profile of information skills as appropriate to their needs. Feedback linked to students' responses to the self-assessment activities, is generated automatically.

Both MOSAIC and the information literacy key skills offer more formal assessment linked to CATS credit points. Students studying MOSAIC are guided through a number of assessment activities as they work through the course. Each activity addresses specific course outcomes and requires the student to demonstrate and reflect on their learning of the relevant information skills. Proformas are provided for each task. Students can contact study advisors by telephone for guidance and advice on the course or the assessment. For the overall course assessment students must submit a 'portfolio' made up of their completed proformas and reflective accounts of their work. The portfolios are then assessed against the intended learning outcomes of the course, using a criterion-based system to record achievement. Criteria linked to the University's award guidelines are then applied to determine whether the standard of performance is sufficient for the award of ten CATS points at Level 1. All students receive a profile of their information skills assessed against the course outcomes irrespective of whether they gain CATS points for their work.

Key skills assessment is offered independently of both SAFARI and MOSAIC and references achievement to the national standards (Hodgkinson and Dillon, 2001). As described above, an information literacy key skill specification (see appendix) has been developed and is offered alongside the other six skill areas for assessment. Supported by the 'Making a Difference' pack, U074 *Information Literacy* is an assessment-only option which students can choose to take alongside their other studies (Open University, 2002b). Assessment is by means of a 'showcase' portfolio containing evidence and reflective accounts of the strategic planning, monitoring and evaluation processes used by the student in developing their information literacy skills.

Unlike MOSAIC this option is not a taught course but rather a means by which students can demonstrate awareness of how they have developed, applied and improved their information literacy skills in their own situations. Evidence may be drawn from the workplace or other activities, as well as from formal courses. The student's portfolio is assessed against criteria derived from the skills specification. Depending on their performance students can gain credit at Level One or Two. Those achieving the skills criteria equivalent to the national standards at QCA Level Four are awarded five CATS points at HE Level Two, while those achieving the standards at QCA Level Three are awarded five CATS points at HE Level One. As with MOSAIC all students submitting a portfolio for key skills assessment receive a skills profile.

Work is continuing at the OU to extend the key skills assessment framework, including information literacy, to cover all HE levels from entry to postgraduate and so provide a coherent structure for skills development and assessment across the curriculum.

Conclusion

At the Open University collaborative initiatives between specialist library staff in the Information Literacy Unit and academic staff involved in key skills and outcomes-based learning have resulted in the development and presentation of a generic information skills web-based resource (SAFARI), a standalone information literacy course (U120 MOSAIC), and key skills support and assessment materials (U529 *Key Skills: making a difference* and U071–7 *Key Skills Assessment Units*). The key skills work offers a specification for information literacy skills to complement existing QCA key skill national standards and the Seven Pillars model proposed by the SCONUL Task Force.

Information skills are increasingly understood as essential elements of the intellectual and learning skills of an educated adult, both within and beyond higher education. The development of the information-literate person is part of a wider view of skills enhancement at HE that should be seen as having equal value to the development of subject-specific knowledge and understanding.

References

Hodgkinson, L. (2000) Benchmarking Key Skills using National Standards: the Open University experience. In Jackson, N. and Lund, H. (eds), *Benchmarking for Higher Education*, Milton Keynes, Society for Research into Higher Education and Open University Press.

Hodgkinson, L. and Dillon, C. R. (2001) *Development and Assessment of Key Skills in the Open University Modular Environment*, 2nd Annual Skills Conference, University of Hertfordshire, 11–12 July, Hatfield. Available at www.herts.ac.uk/HILP/.

NCIHE (National Committee of Inquiry into Higher Education) (1997) *Higher Education in the Learning Society: report of the National Committee*, London, HMSO [Dearing Report].

Open University (2001a) *SAFARI (Skills in Accessing, Finding and Reviewing Information)*, Milton Keynes, Open University. Available at www.open.ac.uk/safari.

Open University (2001b) *U074 Key Skill Assessment Unit: information literacy*, Milton Keynes, Open University.

Open University (2001c) *U529 Key Skills: making a difference*, Milton Keynes, Open University.

Open University (2002) *U120 MOSAIC (Making Sense of Information in the Connected Age)*, Milton Keynes, Open University.

QCA (2000) *Key Skills Units (Levels 1–5)*, London, Qualifications and Curriculum Authority.

SCONUL (1999) *Information Skills in Higher Education: a SCONUL position paper*, London, SCONUL. Available at www.sconul.ac.uk/publications/publications. htm#2.

Appendix: Information literacy key skill specification

In developing a strategy, you need to know how to:

- establish opportunities for using information literacy skills over an extended period of time (e.g. in a programme of study, project or work to be carried out over three months or so)
- identify the outcomes you hope to achieve (e.g. by recognizing a knowledge gap and defining it in terms of the types of information needed to fill it, more effective searching, better use of information and critical abilities)
- identify relevant sources of information, including people and reference material (e.g. librarians, tutors, reference books, internet and databases) and research the information needed for planning purposes
- plan your use of information literacy skills (e.g. options, sequence of work, resources, level of expertise needed) taking into account factors that may affect your plans (e.g. access to IT, patterns of work, issues raised by the use of information such as intellectual property rights, copyright, data protection and plagiarism)
- make a reasoned selection of methods for achieving the quality of outcomes required (e.g. library catalogues, databases and internet search tools).

In monitoring progress, you need to know how to:

- explore different information sources, developing alternative lines of enquiry where appropriate (e.g. formulating questions appropriately, identifying types of information required, using different sources for different purposes)
- use a variety of search strategies and tools effectively (e.g. choosing search terms appropriately, using keywords and Boolean operators to narrow searches, using different search engines and user interfaces)
- record and critically evaluate the results of your search (e.g. establish, and apply systematically, criteria to assess the quality of results)
- monitor and critically reflect on your use of information literacy skills, including: obtaining feedback from others (e.g. colleagues, tutors, librarians, managers); noting choices made and judging their effectiveness (e.g. impact on the quality of work)
- adapt your strategy to overcome difficulties and produce the quality of outcome required.

In evaluating strategy and presenting outcomes, you need to know how to:

- interpret results and identify the main findings from your work, including evidence to support your conclusions (e.g. examine generalizations, assess coverage of your searches and authenticity and authority of sources)
- organize and clearly present information to suit your purpose and your audience, ensuring that the information is accurate (e.g. produce citations and a bibliography in a document using a consistent format)
- assess the effectiveness of your strategy, identifying factors that had an impact on the outcomes (e.g. availability and quality of resources, time, level of own expertise and confidence)
- identify ways of further developing your information literacy skills.

6

Does discipline matter?

Janet Peters, Helen Hathaway and Deborah Bragan-Turner

Introduction

One of the main questions raised at the 'Seven Pillars of Wisdom' conference (Corrall and Hathaway, 2000) was whether information skills can be taught effectively outside the academic subject curriculum or whether they should be embedded within it. In most UK universities, such teaching seems to be carried out by librarians working independently of the curriculum, even though the sessions are often timed to fit in with assignment deadlines or dissertation preparation. At the SCONUL (Society of College, National and University Libraries) conference, delegates concluded that it would be more sensible for information skills to be seen as an intrinsic element of the academic curriculum and integrated into the teaching of the subject disciplines. The key to success would be to work with academic staff as members of a team, with each contributing their expertise in the respective areas. Hepworth argued, both at the SCONUL conference and in a paper presented to IFLA (International Federation of Library Associations and Institutions) (Hepworth, 1999), that 'unless students learn this knowledge [information literacy and skills] in context and are shown how it can help them achieve better results then they are unlikely to absorb these relatively abstract ideas.'

At the same conference, the suggestion was also made that it would be useful to have a generic information skills programme, which could be followed by students in all subjects. The ECDL (European Computer Driving Licence) for IT (information technology) skills was an obvious parallel. But how could this be reconciled with the notion of embedding information skills into the subject curriculum? A sub-group of the Information Skills Task Force (the authors of this paper) undertook to find out what had been written in this area, and to carry out a survey of current practice in higher education. At the same time, the Open University began to develop a programme in information literacy, targeted at first-year undergraduates. Called MOSAIC (Making Sense of Information in the Connected Age), this was launched in May 2002, and the Task Force will take a keen interest in its evaluation (see also Chapter 5 in this book).

The literature

The literature search produced relatively little of direct relevance, although several interesting studies about information skills in general have been carried out, some of which include a subject focus. Most reports bemoan the difficulty experienced by librarians in becoming true partners in the educational process. For example, the first report of the JUBILEE (JISC User Behaviour in Information Seeking: Longitudinal Evaluation of EIS) project (Gannon-Leary, Banwell and Childs, 2001) paints a depressing picture of the lack of both ICT (information and communication technology) and information skills among undergraduates, and a low level of cohesion between those delivering such skills. Their recommendation is for a 'quadripartite relationship' between academics, library staff, IT technicians and administrative support, while recognizing how difficult it has been to achieve this.

Nonetheless, many librarians have attempted such a synergy over the years, some with a degree of success. In 1994 a series of case studies on integrating information skills into various subject curricula was published (Bluck, Hilton and Noon, 1994). Interestingly, Hilton concluded that, despite the apparent desirability of delivering subject-specific information skills sessions, the expansion in student numbers no longer made this form of delivery possible. A pragmatic solution was to develop an open learning programme, built upon a core of generic material, but with some subject-specific examples in the literature-searching section.

Although only focusing on the use of EIS (electronic information sources), the JUSTEIS (JISC Usage Surveys: Trends in Electronic Information) project (JISC, 2000) found that students tend to search in unsophisticated ways, often not really understanding what to look for, nor how to go about a search. Their survey also attempted to analyse differences between students in a range of subject disciplines, although it was noted that because of small sample sizes in some subjects, and differing responses to questionnaires and interviews, it was difficult to draw meaningful conclusions. Overall, however, the project has so far found that, with the exception of clinical medicine, search engines are used much more heavily than paid subscription services, particularly in the humanities and arts. The research also indicated the leading role played by lecturers (or other students), rather than librarians, in influencing students' use of information sources. A salutary point was that JISC (Joint Information Systems Committee)-funded subject gateways were hardly used at all. It is worth noting that students seem to be gravitating naturally towards the use of generic search tools rather than specific ones, which could indicate a general familiarity with web search engines, or a preference for open-ended searching, or, more worryingly, a lack of preparation for searching and consideration of the most appropriate tools.

Work was also being carried out by Webber and Johnston in Strathclyde, and later Sheffield, to find out whether students who were taught the concepts of information literacy in general (non-subject) terms could then relate this to using information effectively in their own subject area. Webber argued that information literacy is much more than a collection of skills, and that librarians who have to resort to extra-curricular, skills-based sessions may not be helping their students. 'The student may gain a few tactics which help him or her to negotiate some specific information sources. However, the student does not become information literate, capable of engaging in a fast-changing information society' (Webber and Johnston, 2000). Their research involved the provision of classes in 'information literacy' (rather than subject-specific skills) to undergraduate business school students. The authors found that, despite initial scepticism, the students gained a greater understanding of the role of information in their work, and were also able to apply their skills both to their subject and in other areas of their lives. However, Webber warns, 'from a pedagogic perspective, information literacy needs attention in its own right and should not always be subordinated to another discipline . . . the danger is that students learn in snatches and do not develop a coherent conception of what information literacy means to them' (see also Chapter 8 in this book).

Ongoing work in Australia and the USA is also promoting the topic of information literacy as a subject in its own right. Both the CAUL (Council of Australian University Librarians) and the ACRL (Association of College and Research Libraries) recognize that 'sheer abundance of information and technology will not in itself create more informed citizens without a complementary understanding and capacity to use information effectively' (CAUDIT (Council of Australian University Directors of Information Technology), 2001). Citizens need to be able to use 'critical discernment and reasoning' to engage with information, rather than focusing just on the skills. The Association of Research Libraries in the USA has also recognized the need for students to shift from achieving a specific knowledge base to mastering a set of learning outcomes. 'What students need to be able to do (critical thinking and creative ability), their ability to manage technology and implement an efficient information search, and their skills in communicating and collaborative reasoning are fundamental across many subject domains' (Smith, 2000).

Information literacy and its learning outcomes, as expressed in models such as the Seven Pillars, are intrinsically independent of the subject discipline. Information literacy implies an understanding of the information landscape, which can be considered at the conceptual level; at the practical – skills-based – level, it will clearly be more relevant to the student if examples relevant to their interests are employed. Information literacy should perhaps be seen as complementary to information skills rather than simply an accumulation of many skills at an expert level. This has an important bearing on the role played by the subject discipline in the acquisition of information literacy (as opposed to information skills).

Benchmark statements

The Task Force also analysed the QAA (Quality Assurance Agency) benchmark statements (QAA, 2000) to find out whether the information skills required in particular subjects varied. In most subjects, students were expected to become independent learners and critical thinkers, but the way in which this might be achieved was usually only expressed in very general terms. There were some notable exceptions that indicated how students might develop this capacity, which could be considered good practice, but there did not seem to be a pattern between related subjects (e.g. arts or sciences) (Peters, 2001).

The surveys

To find out whether there are intrinsic differences between the information skills expected of students in different disciplines, the Task Force sub-group decided to carry out a survey of both librarians and academic staff in a small number of subjects taught in UK higher education institutions. Three 'different' subjects were chosen for the pilot: Theology, Chemistry and Education. An e-mail survey of librarians involved in supporting these subject areas was carried out in 2000–1, and a web-based survey of academics was mounted on the appropriate LTSN (Learning and Teaching Support Network) websites at the end of 2001. The aims were to find out:

- how important information skills are perceived to be in each subject
- who delivers information skills in higher education institutions
- whether the teaching of information skills is embedded in the curriculum.

A total of 50 responses were received from the survey of librarians, and 93 from the survey of academics. It should be recognized that only those with an interest in information skills (and with some IT skills) are likely to have contributed to these surveys, and that the number of respondents is small (the overall pop-ulations of each group are not known). There is scope for a much larger survey in both these and other subject areas which may have differing views, such as law and health, for example, if the question of subject differences is felt to be worth pursuing.

Academic staff survey

In the survey of academic staff, between 90 and 95% of respondents indicated that information skills are considered to be very important or essential in each of the three subject areas, even though responses came from a differing selection of HEIs (Higher Education Institutions) across the subjects, as shown in Table 6.1:

Table 6.1 *Academic staff survey*

Subject	Pre-1992	Post-1992	HE College	Specialist College	Other
Chemistry %	70	23	7	0	0
Education %	51	33	9	2	5
Theology %	79	11	5	0	5

As portrayed in Figures 6.1–6.3, for both Education and Theology the Learning and Teaching Strategy was seen to be the key reason for the importance of information skills, whereas in Chemistry the QAA subject reviews and employer expectations were seen to be equally important. It is interesting that among Education lecturers, employer expectations were seen to be less impor-tant than for the other two subjects, which might indicate that schools are not

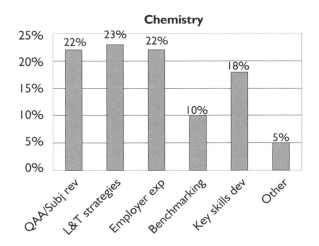

Fig. 6.1 *Why do you think IS are becoming more important?*

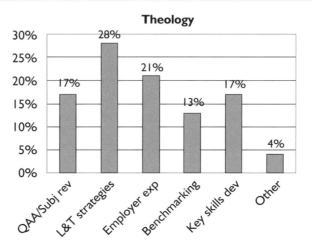

Fig. 6.2   *Why do you think IS are becoming important?*

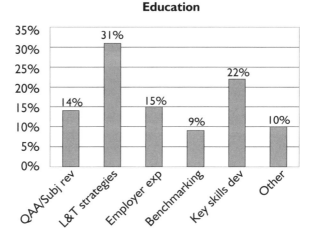

Fig. 6.3   *Why do you think IS are becoming important?*

yet persuaded of the need for teachers to have well developed information skills.

Why do you think IS are becoming more important?

In two of the subjects, respondents gave as a reason for the growing importance of information skills the changing nature of students at initial entry into higher education: 'Our students come in with low A [level] grades linked to poor learning and information skills' (Chemistry – HE College); 'Because current students coming with A level or other qualifications direct from school are of a far lower standard than 15/20 years ago. They need to be taught even the word "essay" for the most part!' (Education – post-1992 university).

The breadth of subjects taught in Education demands high levels of information-handling skills: 'Given that to be a primary teacher you are working in at least 10 separate subject domains, you cannot be expected to have all the relevant knowledge, hence the need to use information skills.' Information overload is another reason: 'Information is more widely available, but we are expected to be able to access it for ourselves (i.e. use the technology and be able to assess the quality and relevance when faced with what is often an enormous overload).' Theology respondents too highlight the need to cope with changes in society: 'The whole information-society ethos requires abilities/skills in information management.' However there were several comments along the lines of information skills having always been important, but not necessarily labelled as such.

How are these sessions offered?

Chemistry lecturers commented that they are more inclined to teach their students how to use information themselves, with the specialized nature of the tools (particularly at research level) given as a reason: 'Best taught by supervisor (i.e. professional user) rather than librarians or the like.' In the first year of the degree course, it is more likely that general skills modules will be provided, with more advanced skills delivered as required during a student's career. In Chemistry the demands made on undergraduate students may be quite high, since they need to use specialized tools to interrogate databases and to carry out formula searches.

Figures 6.4–6.6 indicate that, in Chemistry and Education, most information skills teaching seems to be within a subject module, although ad hoc sessions are also held by library staff. In Theology, most delivery also appears

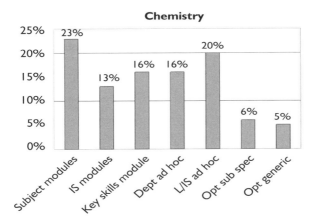

Fig. 6.4 *How are these sessions offered?*

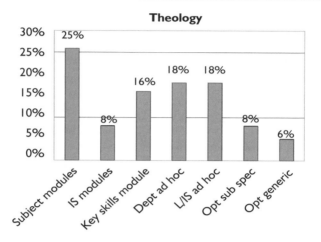

Fig. 6.5   *How are these sessions offered?*

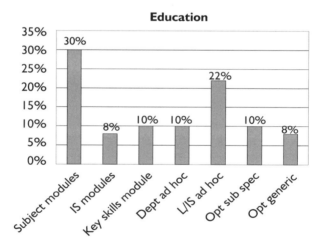

Fig. 6.6   *How are these sessions offered?*

within subject modules, but ad hoc departmental sessions are as common as library ad hoc sessions.

Librarians' survey

In the survey of librarians, most believed that they provided the information skills sessions in their universities, although there were some references to joint programmes run with academic staff. In the survey of academic staff, information skills were said to be delivered more or less equally by academic staff and by librarians. This raises the question of how well this is co-ordinated, whether there is some duplication, or whether it is an issue of terminology: 'Information handling is an integral part of our course, though it does not always have that label' (Education respondent). In all three subjects, the majority of the sessions run by librarians are not assessed as a formal part of the curriculum (although the highest proportion is in Chemistry) but there is considerable overlap in the learning outcomes expected. When mapped against the SCONUL Seven Pillars model (which indicates an ideal set of learning outcomes), it is clear that students are usually taught how to search for, locate and retrieve information, and to present their results in a properly formatted bibliography. In none of the subjects are the students taught how to recognize their information need, nor how to synthesize information to create new knowledge (although the latter is probably an issue of level – this skill would not often be expected of under-graduates, while it would be of doctoral students).

Conclusion

Our study showed a quite marked overall similarity of approach to the delivery of information skills training between the three subjects, both from the librarians' and the academics' perspectives. There were no major differences between subjects in delivery, assessment or drivers. From the comments received it appears that in Chemistry the skills tend to become more embedded into the teaching of the subject in later years of the course, or at postgraduate level. This finding is supported by the work of Gibbs (1994), who commented in relation to skills in general, that there is 'a gradual shading from, at one extreme, trans-ferable skills that are completely general and common to most endeavour, through specific forms of skills that are somewhat distinctive to the discipline, to the other extreme where the skills are almost entirely discipline specific'. Laurillard (2001) too sees similarities in the way in which students learn best, as part of a 'Reflective Practicum', where there can be generic learning activities for courses, especially when they are delivered online. Only the content varies between subjects, not the overall approach.

From the survey of academics, it can be seen that information skills are val-ued equally highly across all subjects, that delivery of these skills is perceived to be shared between librarians and academics, and that there are similar drivers for their importance. Comments were made in each case about the modern stu-dent often being ill equipped to deal with the information overload enabled by technology, and there is a broadly comparable amount of 'embeddedness' into a subject module.

For the librarians, discipline did not matter in terms of the learning out-comes even though, inevitably, the search tools used varied according to subject.

This small pilot study therefore suggests that there are no major differences in the way in which information skills are delivered in these different subjects, nor in the learning outcomes. The study has begun to provide some subject-based evidence and – it is hoped – taken forward the generic versus embedded information skills teaching debate.

Laurillard (2001) envisages the e-library supporting scholarship skills by offering generic information/research skills courses, which will 'support students in learning to carry out a rigorous systematic process of enquiry in whatever field they are engaged'. Reinforced by Webber's notion of the distinction between information skills and information literacy, where the overall concepts of information handling are independent of the subject, the Task Force therefore believes that it has a reasonably firm basis on which to proceed in the development of an information literacy programme aimed at first-year students. This work is already progressing in partnership with The Open University and its MOSAIC course. This will help to test the hypothesis that discipline does not matter, but the Task Force is fully aware that more work needs to be done in other subjects to investigate any differences, to contact people who do not respond to online questionnaires and to investigate further the learning outcomes set by academics. It would also be interesting to explore the literature regarding educational theory to assess whether students learn differently in different subject disciplines, and how this relates to their information-seeking activities, but this is beyond the scope of this chapter.

Finally, to return to the question, 'does discipline matter?' and to maintain the educational analogy – it seems that discipline may not matter, but literacy – information literacy – certainly does.

Acknowledgements

We would like to thank Dr Mike Gardner (University of Nottingham) for mounting the questionnaire on the web; the Learning and Teaching Support Network for publicizing the web questionnaire.

References

Bluck, R., Hilton, A. and Noon, P. (1994) *Information Skills in Academic Libraries: a teaching and learning role in higher education*, SEDA Paper 82, Birmingham, SEDA.

CAUDIT (2001) *CAUDIT Report*. Available at www.caudit.edu.au/caudit/information/projects/.

Corrall, S. and Hathaway, H. (eds) (2000) *Seven Pillars of Wisdom? Good practice in information skills. Proceedings of a conference held at Warwick*

University, 6–7 July, 2000, London, SCONUL.

Gannon-Leary, P., Banwell, L. and Childs, S. (2001) Enhancing ICT Skills: the how, who and when – illustrations from the JUBILEE project, *Vine*, **122**, 5–9.

Gibbs, G. (1994) *Developing Students' Transferable Skills*, Oxford, Oxford Centre for Staff Development.

Hepworth, M. (1999) A Study of Undergraduate Information Literacy and Skills: the inclusion of information literacy and skills in the undergraduate curriculum. In *Proceedings of the 65th IFLA Council and General Conference, Bangkok, August 20–28, 1999*, The Hague, IFLA, 1999. Available at www.ifla.org/IV/ ifla65/papers/107-124e.htm.

JISC (2000) *JISC Usage Surveys: Trends in Electronic Information Services (JUSTEIS) Cycle 1, report 6*. Available at www.dil.aber.ac.uk/dils/Research/ JUSTEIS/cyc1rep6.htm.

Laurillard, D. (2001) *Supporting the Development of Scholarship Skills through the Online Digital Library*, London, SCONUL. Available at www.sconul.ac.uk/ Conference/presegm01/Laurillard.ppt.

Peters, J. (2001) Information Skills and the QAA Benchmarking Statements, *SCONUL Newsletter*, **21**, 23–4.

Quality Assurance Agency for Higher Education (2000) *Benchmark Statements*. Available at www.qaa.ac.uk/crntwork/benchmark/index.htm.

Smith, K. R. (2000) *New Roles and Responsibilities for the University Library: advancing student learning through outcomes assessment*, Tucson, AR, Association of Research Libraries.

Webber, S. and Johnston, W. (2000) Conceptions of Information Literacy: new perspectives and implications, *Journal of Information Science*, **26** (6), 381–97.

7

Information literacy, but at what level?

Peter Godwin

Introduction

The need for everyone to be information literate has already been debated in Australia and the USA for several years. The sets of standards that have been developed have provided a firm foundation for these skills to become accepted and part of the learning process. In the UK the lead has taken longer to be followed, and is perhaps most visible in HE (higher education), particularly after the development of the SCONUL (Society of College, National and University Libraries) Seven Pillars of Wisdom framework. This is moving the agenda forward from the old idea of user education toward a defined set of skills taking into account the hybrid library. It is the contention of this chapter that these skills are cumulative and should be defined at various levels. The model suggested here is based on the needs of SBU (South Bank University), a new inner London university, and is a first attempt to provide benchmarks which can be used to define competencies at different student levels. The model helps understanding of the complexities of student need and provides a basis for gaining institutional understanding and commitment, as well as for assessing the effectiveness of any training given.

Student needs

User education has become information literacy because of the changing agenda in education, and the impact of the hybrid library. The era of mass higher education has led to the challenge of increasingly divergent student abilities, for example the Foundation student recently saturated with study skill training, the Masters student with a business background returning to education after a long break, and the ward nurse doing evidence-based practice assignments. Therefore the variety of skill levels and expectations has increased dramatically. The need to use a mix of print and electronic resources, and the explosion of material freely available on the web, has made the search for information seem easier to do and yet far more complex to manage successfully. The need is for a map through the maze, which is what information literacy can provide.

In the past, the guidance provided by librarians has fallen short of the ideal. There has been the cramming option where the librarian has an hour to imprison a group in the training room to tell them 'everything they should know about the library'. The result is overload. Then there is the all-embracing study skills unit in the first year which seeks to empower the student over the whole range of skills they will ever need, including exam technique. The result is lack of relevance. Finally, there is the librarian who pitches the teaching session to a Masters level, too high, not realizing that many students have little grasp of basic skills (e.g. locating a printed journal in a large library.) Such a mismatched session can lead to time-wasting confusion.

Information literacy is a cumulative process, and the speed at which these skills have to be developed will vary according to the level, nature and requirements of each course. Students within the same course arrive with assorted abilities. Any attempt to raise skill levels must take this into account. I have observed, and research has shown, that assessment-motivated students gain the skills best when they need them most – for example, just before an assignment.

Barriers to progress

There have been a number of barriers blocking the successful introduction of information skills into higher education. Foremost has been the lack of appreciation and ignorance shown by teaching staff. Their perception that all that is needed is to use a library catalogue, and perhaps the library databases, comes from their inability to find the time to grapple with the effects of the information explosion. Then there is the confusion that staff and students suffer from in mistaking information skills for IT (information technology) skills. Lack of institutional commitment to information skills combined with absence of time slots in the curriculum is still common. The final block is provided by students' belief that they already know how to get information and are apathetic about receiving any professional help.

The SBU model

To combat these trends, SBU has set up projects to benchmark information skills at five levels, along with IT, communication and career management skills, after the launch of its Core Skills policy in July 2000. We decided to base our benchmarks on the SCONUL Seven Pillars framework, and reference was made to a wide range of information literacy documents along with our SBU experience. A first draft of our model was prepared in March 2001, and revised in March 2002.

The model defines student competencies at five levels with Level 0 at Foundation, Level One at Undergraduate Year One, Level Two at Year Two, Level Three at Year Three and M level at Masters Level. The benchmarks define what a student should be able to do at the end of that level in their course. The model had to be able to accommodate courses of differing lengths with differing skill requirements to apply to a wide range of subject disciplines.

The model results in only very basic search skills at Level 0, whereas Level One develops understanding across Skills 1–6. Level Two builds upon these and encourages students to work more independently with less guidance. Level Three implies the building of skills to be able to undertake a project and ability to access a range of sources. Level M implies ability to research for a dissertation and use a wide variety of sources.

The availability of a model is useful as a planning document for formulating institutional learning and teaching policies, and at SBU for writing QAA (Quality Assurance Agency) Programme specifications for courses. The benchmarks can also be used as a framework to promote information literacy to academic staff. This is done by giving reference points for embedding the skills into courses at appropriate points.

The model has helped Library staff to understand the complexity of the information skills support offered. Some courses may require students to reach Level Three skills in one year, either because of the discipline or the course length. This explains the former difficulties of delivery and argues for acceptance by academic staff of more appropriate amounts of time to be available at the right stage. The transformation will come when these skills are seen as an essential part of the curriculum and not an optional extra. A model helps librarians and staff to be able to plan sessions at the appropriate level. Differing levels of student ability can be more easily appreciated and extra exercises built in to accommodate them. Diagnostic tests informed by the benchmarks could also be used to determine which students required extra help. The benchmarks encourage library staff to take a holistic view of information skills and avoid overconcentration on any particular skill. In the past this has often been searching a library catalogue or the vagaries of a particular database. This can be at the expense of seeing these in the context of the range of materials or search tools available. Evaluation of material found is probably the single most vital skill needed by students now, and may not have featured strongly enough in the past.

The future success of the model adopted at SBU will still depend on the ability of academic staff to have and use sufficient IT skills. The need of LIS to work with the SBU IT Training Centre to nurture this process will continue. Changing the attitudes of teaching staff is tackled through our Desktop Library sessions, where information advisers give individual hour-long sessions in staff offices, based on a standard list and delivered according to staff interest and requirements. Promotion of information literacy will continue to all staff with the benchmarks as a foundation. We are targeting all existing study skill and research skill units for inclusion of information skills. We will pilot diagnostic tests with a range of courses in all faculties to determine those groups that need assistance with basic web searching and then deliver training to them.

Conclusion

In the future, we can expect new generations to have different life skill requirements and expectations. Key skill initiatives in schools and information literacy in further education may mean that competencies set out in this model may move down so that many will arrive in higher education with Level One abilities already. However, this should not lead universities to conclude that these students will not need information skills training. The same error has been made with study skills in the past. All students have study and information skill needs. It is simply that they are at differing levels of development, which models such as the SBU one can help to define. The challenge of ever reaching agreement on a series of benchmarks at national level may not be insurmountable. The model presented here attempts to stimulate interest in the process in this area of information literacy, which can be of great benefit to us all.

Further reading

ACRL (2000) *Information Literacy Competency Standards for Higher Education: standards performance indicators and outcomes*, Chicago, ACRL. Available at www.ala.org/Content/NavigationMenu/ACRL/Standards_and_Guidelines/ Standards_and_Guidelines_by_Topic.htm.

ALA (1998) *Information Power: building partnerships for learning*, Chicago, American Library Association.

California Technology Assistance Project (n.d.) *Information Literacy Development*. Available at http://ctap.fcoe.k12.ca.us/ctap/Info.Lit/Benchmarks.html.

CAUL (2001) *Information Literacy Standards*, Canberra, Council of Australian University Librarians.

Central Queensland University (2000) *Information Literacy Marking Criteria*. Available at www.library.cqu.edu.au/informationliteracy/criteria.htm.

Florida International University Libraries (2002) *FIU Information Literacy Program*. Available at www.fiu.edu/~library/ili/.

SCONUL (1999) *Information Skills in Higher Education: a SCONUL position paper*, London, SCONUL. Available at www.sconul.ac.uk/publications/publications/htm#2.

Washington Library Media Association (2002) *WLMA/OSPI Essential Skills for Information Literacy: benchmarks for information literacy*. Available at www.wlma.org/Instruction/benchmarks.htm.

Appendix: South Bank University information skills benchmarks, 11 March 2002

Information Skill 1: Understanding the need to use information

Level 0	Understanding of need to use information to undertake everyday tasks
Level 1	Understanding of the dangers of information overload Ability to define specific information needs Ability to define concepts of a topic for a presentation or essay Ability to use general reference resources to increase familiarity with a topic Recognition that background information helps to focus topic
Level 2	
Level 3	Ability to redefine/modify information sought on basis of material found for project
Level M	Ability to redefine/modify information sought from research material found for major project

Information Skill 2: Packaging of information and choosing suitable sources for research

Level 0	Understanding of purposes and audience of resources: popular, scholarly Understanding of need to use both print and electronic resources
Level 1	Understanding of characteristics of information resources: primary, secondary, journal literature, print vs electronic Understanding of publication cycles, and issues of currency Understanding the research supply chain Understanding of print and electronic holdings of the home library Ability to select the most appropriate print and electronic sources for essay with some guidance Basic understanding of intellectual property

Level 2	Ability to select appropriate subject print and electronic resources for essay without guidance
Level 3	Ability to select range of appropriate subject resources for undertaking a project

Information Skill 3: Search tools and the need for a search strategy

Level 0	Understanding of everyday search tools Understanding the need to use appropriate search tools
Level 1	Understanding of library catalogue as a list of the holdings of the institution Understanding of the web as complex mix of free and chargeable material Understanding of limitations of web materials located by search engines Understanding of gateways and how they differ from search engines Understanding of LISA as the key gateway to premium information sources Understanding of the makeup of a database Ability to transfer a subject into a keyword search
Level 2	Ability to select most appropriate search tool, distinguishing between indexes, online databases, collections of online databases, and gateways Understanding of use of abstracts and indexes, and full-text electronic resources alongside print resources Understanding of other library catalogues as the way to discover holdings elsewhere
Level 3	Ability to choose range of electronic databases, printed abstracts to undertake project Ability to choose range of web search engines and search gateways to find material for project
Level M	Ability to choose full range of print and electronic search tools to undertake major project

Information Skill 4: Locating and accessing information

Level 0	Ability to use local library catalogue to search for specific books Ability to navigate around web using live links Ability to use web addresses to search the web
Level 1	Ability to use keywords to search for material on a topic Ability to use a library catalogue to find specific books, journal titles, books on a subject Ability to reserve and renew books Ability to use web gateways and search engines to locate material for an essay topic Ability to use databases and full-text services on LISA to locate material for an essay topic Understanding of electronic access anywhere in the University and off-campus Ability to use classification to locate all kinds of print materials in the library Ability to use help screens and help sheets to search for information
Level 2	Ability to use truncation and Boolean search techniques Awareness and use of different levels of searching on databases Ability to understand and use controlled vocabulary Ability to limit searches by fields Ability to display electronic results in various orders and understand all components of citations Ability to use variety of web search engines Understanding of interlibrary loan, access to other libraries, e.g. British Library and UK Libraries Plus
Level 3	Ability to construct complex searches and use across a range of databases, using different user interfaces, redefining terms and repeating searches as required. Ability to obtain interlibrary loans and access UK Libraries Plus libraries
Level M	Ability to search using comprehensive range of abstracts databases, using many different user interfaces Ability to use specialist collections or British Library Ability to set up e-mail alerting services Ability to save and re-use searches

Information Skill 5: Comparing and evaluating information

Level 0	Ability to read text, select material and summarize in own words for own use at basic level
Level 1	Awareness of issues of currency, bias and authority Understanding of issues of accuracy, relevance and comprehensiveness Understanding of presentation style used and messages this gives Understanding of nature of information freely available on the internet Ability to extract material by taking notes from print sources and from electronic by printing or saving to disk Ability to sift main ideas in information found for constructing a presentation or essay
Level 2	Ability to choose range of materials on topics, taking into account currency, bias, authority, accuracy, relevance and comprehensiveness Ability to sift information for application in essays
Level 3	Awareness of peer review process in journals Ability to read, analyse and evaluate wide range of materials on complex subjects identifying bias, and other factors, measuring against material already found Ability to sift information for project
Level M	Critical skills in assessing wide range of materials taking into account bias and other factors Ability to sift information for major project

Information Skill 6: Organizing, applying and communicating information sources to others

Level 0	Understanding of the need to keep records of searches and resources found
Level 1	Ability to keep basic records of searches made and resources found Ability to cite printed and electronic sources used for essay preparation as a book list Compliance with copyright and plagiarism rules

Level 2	Ability to create bibliography of variety of materials used to write essays
Level 3	Ability to keep systematic records of material found for major project Ability to compile a comprehensive bibliography of different types of sources: books, journals, websites, videos, and use either Harvard referencing or referencing as specified by the course, and to reference electronic materials. Understanding of copyright issues on the web
Level M	Ability to construct major bibliography and reference range of materials in major project

Information Skill 7: Keeping up to date and contributing to new information

Level 0	
Level 1	
Level 2	Understanding that existing information can be combined with original thought, experiment and analysis to produce new information
Level 3	Ability to create new knowledge in a project through synthesis and development of existing information Ability to reflect on problems encountered
Level M	Ability to create new knowledge in a major project through synthesis or development of existing information Use of mailing lists, discussion groups, newsgroups to obtain and exchange information

Part 3
Challenges to implementation

8

Assessment for information literacy: vision and reality

Sheila Webber and Bill Johnston

Introduction

The aim of this chapter is to identify the importance of assessment of information literacy, and describe factors and modes of assessment that form a framework for progress. We will start by setting this framework in the context of our vision of the information-literate university, peopled by information-literate students. We will also highlight what we perceive as problems in current practice in information literacy assessment.

Our definition of information literacy is an holistic one, compatible with models such as those of Bruce (1997) and SCONUL (Society of College, National and University Libraries). It can be summarized as: 'the adoption of appropriate information behaviour to obtain, through whatever channel or medium, information well fitted to information needs, together with critical awareness of the importance of wise and ethical use of information in society'.

As regards our definition of assessment, it is important to note that we are talking about assessment of student learning. Further definition will be given by explanation of factors and modes later in the chapter. The complexity of the subject areas implied by our definition of information literacy (and by other models such as those of Bruce and SCONUL) demands consideration of more than one type of assessment. In the context of formal education, assessment also confers credibility and marks the importance of the subject being assessed.

The information-literate student and the information-literate university

Before going on to address the issues of assessment, we will explain the context in which we see (or would like to see) assessment taking place.

The model of the information-literate student (see Figure 8.1) illustrates the ways in which an individual will experience changes that affect the type of information they need and the ways in which they access, evaluate, understand and use that information throughout their lives. Within the information society there are social and cultural changes which will impact both the nature of the curriculum and the student's own personal goals (for a discussion of these changes see Webber and Johnston, 2002). There are developments in the information economy which will, again, affect both the student's personal life and the way in which the curriculum is delivered, for example, legislation to do with freedom of information and copyright. Information literacy will be useful for lifelong learning, and it must be adaptable to changes through life.

This approach implies a body of knowledge concerning information literacy: certainly it implies more than a simple 'information skills' list. Additionally, it implies a context: the information-literate university.

This model of the information literate university (Figure 8.2) requires that all members of the university – administrators, academics and researchers, as well as students – become information literate. Management for information literacy implies strategic rethinking, which may affect planning, resource allocation and management systems. When academic staff become information lit-

Information-literate student: lifelong learning in the information society

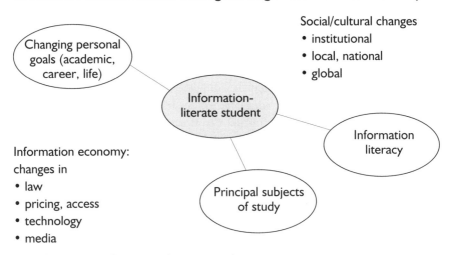

Fig. 8.1   *The information-literate student*

Our vision of an information-literate university

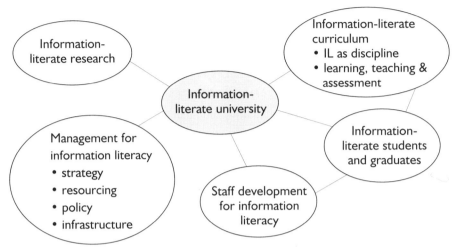

Fig. 8.2 *The information-literate university*

erate it can influence their pedagogic thinking and the way they conceive of their own discipline and its knowledge base. An information-literate university will be able to foresee opportunities for knowledge creation, extension and wisdom.

Barriers to this vision

We realize that there is some way to go to achieve this vision. Barriers include:

- lack of academic recognition of the value of information literacy, and the complexity of the subject
- librarians' lack of status within universities
- academic politics
- an obsession with ICT (Information and Communications Technology) training and e-learning, which can swamp agenda to do with other kinds of innovative teaching or with information management
- the fact that information literacy is not explicitly embedded into the curricula of many undergraduate and postgraduate programmes
- a library instruction/library skills focus. This results in other problems: it reinforces academics' conception of information literacy as a set of lower-order skills (which have little place in the curriculum), and it limits the vision of librarians.

These barriers can in turn lead to problems such as the one upon which we focus in the chapter: lack of appropriate assessment. This is a worry, because, 'It has long been recognised that probably the biggest influence on a student's approach to their studies is the assessment regime of the course' (Rust, 2001, 11).

Course design: assessment elements and modes

In order to achieve our vision we believe that teachers need to emphasize their role as course designers – specifically, designing courses to support student learning. Figure 8.3 places the teacher in a planning role and identifies four interacting elements of a course.

This shows a rational, problem-solving approach to pedagogical questions (such as assessment) regarding the nature, content and methods of curricula, courses and learning environments (Rowntree, 1982). The approach draws on concepts from general systems thinking, such as open and closed systems, feedback and the emphasis on setting goals and objectives. In summary, this approach allows a course of subject study to be conceptualized as a system. This system links:

- educational objectives
- course design for teaching, learning and assessment
- course evaluation, modification and improvement

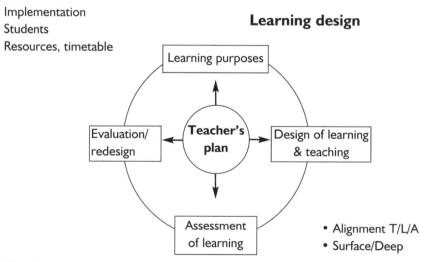

Fig. 8.3 *Learning design*

in a cyclical process of decision making, implementation, experimentation, data gathering modification and innovation. In practice the systems model is specifically linked to core educational concepts drawn from learning theories, communication theories and conceptual models of instruction (Richey, 1986).

This approach allows a comprehensive account of curriculum which foregrounds the dynamic and reflexive nature of a course. It lays the emphasis on designing courses as a key task for the teacher, and provides a disciplined but flexible method of proceeding with design tasks. The teacher's subject expertise and teaching experience is complemented by a body of knowledge which provides a means of conceptualizing a particular course and relating specific teaching and learning events to each other in a coherent manner. This supports decision making about resource inputs, infrastructure, aims, teaching strategy and methods, assessment of student performance and evaluation of overall educational quality and outcomes. Design is emphasized as a key element of the academic role in relation to curriculum, teaching, learning, assessment and evaluation. This is an important counterbalance to any tendency to focus attention largely on the nature and conduct of live or distance teacher–student interactions, and the associated questions of method and technique. The alignment referred to in Figure 8.3 is alignment of teaching, learning and assessment, as described by Biggs (1999). This means, for example, not assessing higher-order outcomes which require analysis and understanding through assessment such as multiple-choice tests, since the latter encourage a surface learning approach from students.

Assessment: unpacking the assessment box

Since much of our knowledge of assessment derives from experience in formal higher education, it is appropriate to draw on expertise developed in that area as a starting point to draft a framework for assessing information literacy. The essential principles and practices of educational assessment at the university level have been summarized by Wergin (1988) and elaborated by Miller, Imrie and Cox (1998). Catts (2000) discusses a number of problematic issues arising when such common features are related to the assessment of information literacy. A key theme of the literature is that assessment has come to be acknowledged as an integral part of the facilitation of learning and understanding, rather than as an end-of-course measurement activity (e.g. Ramsden, 1992; Marton, Hounsell and Entwistle, 1997). On the basis of this literature the following four factors and three modes can be advanced as essential elements of an assessment framework. We will describe these factors and modes, interposing reflections on problematic areas in practice as revealed by the literature of information literacy and bibliographic instruction.

Factor 1. Assessment should address a blend of purposes including:
- diagnosis (student entry-level behaviour and progression at key points)
- formative feedback (advice and guidance to improve performance)
- summative judgement (final adjudication of standards and levels attained)
- course evaluation and quality audit (student performance and progress data).

In the literature we observe an emphasis on diagnosis, course evaluation and to a lesser extent (where credit-bearing assessment is concerned) summative judgement. Diagnosis may take the form of pre-class and post-class tests (e.g. in Colborn and Cordell, 1998). Questionnaires are frequent (Roselle, 1997; Cribb and Woodall, 1997; Andretta, 2001; Hilliger and Roberts, 2001), often a blend of self-assessment of skills (e.g. marking on a scale the extent to which the student thought their internet searching had improved) and evaluation of the class (whether the student thought it relevant or well presented). It is notable that assessment of student learning and assessment of class delivery may be mixed together (and sometimes not distinguished in discussion). For example: the multiple-choice (credit-bearing) examination discussed by Niemayer (1999) includes optional questions at the end which ask the student to comment on the effectiveness of the computerized format. Formative assessment is not so much in evidence: it is dismissed altogether (and misunderstood) by Colborn and Cordell (1998), and on the whole would appear to be given on an ad hoc basis, e.g. what Higgins and Face (1998) call 'internal assessment': students dropping into the librarians' offices to discuss information problems. Importantly, even where summative and formative assessment of student learning is taking place, it is not necessarily being fed back to the student so that they can gain an insight into their level of attainment and identify ways to improve. Instead, the focus is on using the feedback to assess the performance of librarians and what they have taught.

Factor 2. An assessment regime should display certain conditions including:
- relevance (degree of congruence between factors assessed and learning objectives)
- consistency (extent of agreement between assessors using the same assessment)
- authenticity (degree of fit with real world performance contexts)
- practicality (congruence with availability of staff/student time and other resources)
- equity (commitment to inclusiveness and sensitivity to special needs).

Authors display anxiety about consistency and practicality. For example, Cribb and Woodall say that computer marking 'ensured consistent and standardised marking' (1997, 248) and was efficient: it 'saved us from having manually to mark 500 assignments'. Colborn and Cordell (1998) talk in the title of their article about 'moving from subjective to objective assessment'. This approach begs a lot of questions concerning what consistent and 'objective' marking means. Everyone will sympathize with the practicalities of marking work from large classes, but the need to align the assessment method with the desired learning outcomes is apparently being given a lot less priority. Williams (2000) provides a useful summary of some elements of assessment, and identifies more complex forms of assessment as appropriate to higher-level cognitive skills, but is concerned that marking 'may be subjective and is therefore susceptible to evaluator bias, which can affect fairness and validity' (333). This contrasts with the perspective of Ramsden (quoted by Biggs, 1999, 159): 'Be suspicious of the objectivity and accuracy of all measures of student ability and conscious that human judgment is the most important element in every indicator of human achievement.'

Factor 3. Recording of assessment should take a variety of forms in practice, for example:
* transcripts of test results
* portfolios of work
* learning diaries.

The information literacy literature shows a concentration on questionnaires, worksheets and online workbooks/tutorials, short tests (sometimes multiple choice) and bibliographies. While there are aspects of information literacy that can usefully be assessed by worksheets, tests and bibliographies, the first two only address lower-order skills, and neglect higher-order learning outcomes. While compilation of bibliographies can enable a student to develop a number of aspects of information literacy, without the student's reflective commentary on how the bibliography was compiled, the marker may be left to infer whether or not certain skills have been developed (e.g. search strategy, source evaluation).

Factor 4. Assessment should address the learner's concept of and approach to learning, for example:
* quantitative/qualitative concept
* surface/deep approach.

As will have been gathered from the commentary so far, it is our view that there has been too much emphasis on quantitative assessment and on methods that foster a surface rather than a deep learning approach. As an extreme example, in the Colborn and Cordell (1998) paper it is difficult to reconcile the ambitious learning outcomes with the multiple-choice format assessment. Buschman and Warner (2001) have noted the mismatch between the subjects that librarians are trying to teach – such as 'the highest cognitive level of critical evaluation' (62), and the sometimes inadequate methods – 'shallow and flawed' (63) – which they are adopting to assess student learning.

In addition to these factors, three main modes of assessment can be identified.

Mode 1: Expert assessment mode. Authority to make assessment decisions lies with a subject expert. Traditionally this mode has tended to be perceived as judgemental and objective, and has dominated practice in universities. Biggs, Ramsden and others consider such assessment a powerful factor in explaining surface approaches to learning by students (see e.g. Biggs, 1999). Case studies in the information literacy literature reveal a good deal of expert mode assessment (e.g. tests set and marked by librarians; bibliographies marked by librarians and/or academics).

Mode 2: Self assessment mode. Responsibility for assessment decision is taken on by the learner. Recording of assessment may take the form of actual information behaviour and related products rather than formal tests. There is evidence in the information literacy literature of self-assessment. However, the self-assessment is often without support or feedback which would help the student make a realistic assessment of their performance. For example, a student may be asked to say whether they feel that their skills have improved, that they are better at searching, evaluating and so forth. Such questions may encourage reflection, but, without guidance, students may overestimate their progress (see e.g. O'Hanlon, 2002).

Mode 3: Peer assessment mode. Assessment responsibility is shared by participants in group learning structures. Bhatt (2000), for example, characterizes experiential learning, informal peer reviews, and informal guidance as being conducive to effective learning and keeping up with changing patterns of knowledge in a learning organization. Although there is increasing interest in higher education, case studies in the information literacy literature do not reveal much use of this assessment mode.

In concluding this section, we would emphasize that we are concentrating on highlighting problem areas. There is evidence of some good assessment practice in the literature, but also clear evidence of these problematic areas which present challenges that need addressing.

Implications

We recognize that the barriers identified earlier in our paper are real. Meaningful teaching, learning and assessment is time consuming: time that librarians may find it hard to create, and that academics are reluctant to yield to them inside the curriculum. If the assessment is to be credit bearing, there needs to be recognition from the university (so that library-led courses are accredited) or from academics, who are willing to integrate information literacy into their programmes.

However, the implied information literacy curriculum is substantial. Most definitions of information literacy (for example, the SCONUL Seven Pillars model) include evaluation, comparison, synthesis and application of information. Assessment which aligns with appropriate learning outcomes for such a curriculum is likely to be complex, as has been noted also, for example, by Dunn (2002).

Ideally such assessment will include diagnostic elements (e.g. for straightforward tasks such as finding a known item on the catalogue, or using a specific piece of software), formative feedback to students which can help them to understand their strengths and weaknesses and identify ways to progress, and summative feedback which marks or grants progression. Course evaluation will be undertaken, but recognized as less important than assessment of student learning outcomes. Assessment will be varied, so that it is relevant to the particular area of information literacy being learnt, and also connects with real-world applications and problems where appropriate. Understanding may be tested through assignments such as identifying and applying evaluation frameworks in different contexts (e.g. evaluating an information resource from the standpoint of different types of user), synthesizing information to a specific brief, relating their own behaviour to models of information literacy, or presenting and critiquing search solutions. A blend of self, expert and peer assessment will encourage reflection and critical awareness, which is informed by 'expert' summative and formative feedback. Assessment will also reflect progression of learning through a course: so that a subject is not assessed once and then forgotten, but is revisited in different contexts and at a higher level, thus consolidating and deepening learning.

Conclusion

We have stressed the need to take assessment seriously, considering all factors and modes. Assessment is an essential part of the teaching, learning and assessment process, and is often the key focus for student motivation, but at the moment our contention is that it is the missing pivot that could swing information literacy into the foreground of students' attention. Progress involves work and collaboration. Assessment is an integral element of courses, so rapprochement between academics, librarians and students is essential. Librarians need to invest in self-development, in particular in learning more about pedagogy; academics need to recognize the complexity of information literacy and allow it time in the curriculum; and students also need to give more attention to information literacy (rather than just information technology) and show willingness to learn.

References

Andretta, S. (2001) Legal Information Literacy: a pilot study, *New Library World*, **102** (7/8), 255–64.

Bhatt, G. (2000) Information Dynamics, Learning and Knowledge Creation in Organizations, *Learning Organization*, **7** (2), 89–99.

Biggs, J. (1999) *Teaching for Quality Learning at University*, Buckingham, Open University Press.

Bruce, C. (1997) *The Seven Faces of Information Literacy*, Adelaide, Auslib Press.

Buschman, J. and Warner, D. A. (2001) Wider Access to Higher Education in the United States: an evaluative case study of the library. In *Centre for Research in Lifelong Learning. Researching Widening Access: international perspectives: conference proceedings*, Glasgow, Glasgow Caledonian University, 60–5.

Catts, R. (2000). Some Issues in Assessing Information Literacy. In Bruce, C. and Candy, P. (eds), *Information Literacy around the World: advances in programs and research*, Wagga Wagga, Charles Sturt University, 271–83.

Colborn, N. W. and Cordell, R. M. (1998) Moving from Subjective to Objective Assessments of Your Instruction Program, *Reference Services Review*, (Fall/Winter), 125–37.

Cribb, G. and Woodall, L. (1997) Webbook for Engineers: an interactive information skills programme, *New Review of Information Networking*, **3**, 245–53.

Dunn, K. (2002) Assessing Information Literacy Skills in the California State University: a progress report, *Journal of Academic Librarianship*, **28** (1), 26–35.

Higgins, C. and Face, M. J. C. (1998) Integrating Information Literacy Skills into the University Colloquium: innovation at Southern Oregon University, *Reference Services Review*, (Fall/Winter), 17–31.

Hilliger, K. and Roberts, S. (2001) Which Key Skills? Marketing graduates and information literacy, *International Journal of Management Education*, **2** (1), 31–41.

Marton, F., Hounsell, D. and Entwistle, N. (eds) (1997) *The Experience of Learning*, 2nd edn, Edinburgh, Scottish Academic Press.

Miller, A. H., Imrie, B. W. and Cox, K. (1998) *Student Assessment in Higher Education: a handbook for assessing performance*, London, Kogan Page.

Niemayer, C. (1999) A Computerized Final Exam for a Library Skills Course, *Reference Services Review*, **27** (1), 90–106.

O'Hanlon, N. (2002) Net Knowledge: performance of new college students on an internet skills proficiency test, *Internet and Higher Education*, **5**, 1–12.

Ramsden, P. (1992) *Learning to Teach in Higher Education,* London, Routledge.

Richey, R. (1986) *The Theoretical and Conceptual Basis of Instructional Theory*, London, Kogan Page.

Roselle, A. (1997) Using the ALA's Evaluating Library Instruction (1996), *Journal of Academic Librarianship*, **23** (5), 390–7.

Rowntree, D. (1982) *Educational Technology in Curriculum Development*, London, Harper and Row.

Rust, C. (2001) *A Briefing on Assessment of Large Groups*, York, Learning and Teaching Support Network.

SCONUL (1999) *Information Skills in Higher Education: a SCONUL position paper*, London, SCONUL. Available at www.sconul.ac.uk/pubs_stats/pubs/publications.html.

Webber, S. and Johnston, B. (2002) Information Literacy and Community: a UK perspective. In Booker, D. (ed.), *Proceedings of the 5th National Information Literacy Conference, University of South Australia, 30 November–1 December 2001*, Adelaide, Auslib Press, 68–80.

Wergin, J. F. (1988) Basic Issues and Principles in Classroom Assessment. In McMillan, J. H. (ed), *Assessing Students' Learning*, San Francisco, Jossey-Bass, 5–17.

Williams, J. L. (2000) Creativity in Assessment of Library Instruction, *Reference Services Review*, **28** (4), 323–34.

9

Measuring students' information literacy competency

Caroline Stern

Introduction

This chapter will identify the skills considered necessary to seek information from the internet, and the challenges these present to the instructional design process, before examining the results of a survey showing how students use information skills.

ILit (information literacy) has been a part of librarians' vocabulary for some time, but it is a relatively new phrase in the vocabulary of other educators. As a result of growing curricular interest in ILit, instructional designers are increasingly seeking to create tutorials that guide learners to a better understanding of how they can be information literate in the ways in which they access, evaluate and use relevant and reliable information from a variety of sources. ID (instructional design) 'refers to the systematic and reflective process of translating principles of learning and instruction into plans for instructional material, activities, information resources, and evaluation' (Smith and Ragan, 1999, 2). To be effective, this design process should be theory based and therefore organized on a cycle of activity that has clearly defined stages.

The instructional design process

More institutions of higher education are coming to understand what information literacy is and the value that it adds to the curriculum. However, theory-informed instructional design for information literacy instruction is still in the early stages of development at many colleges and universities. Schools that seek to add information literacy instruction to their curriculum could begin the instructional design cycle by:

- identifying and articulating the importance of ILit as a learning need, especially as it relates to lifelong learning
- describing the goals and standards for the ILit instruction and learning that would be applicable to their own student population
- referencing agencies such as the ACRL (Association of College and Research Libraries) and ALA (American Library Association) as a way of clarifying and promoting and understanding of ILit competencies (e.g. ACRL, 2000a; 2000b; ALA, n.d.)
- targeting learners and specifically defining their continuing need to learn ILit skills
- measuring students' incoming competencies in ILit skills and matching those against the desired exit-level competencies
- identifying and examining resources for instruction
- determining a design for the most effective delivery of instruction that meets the needs and builds on the strengths identified in the learning population
- delivering instruction and then assessing its effectiveness
- revisiting the instructional plan to improve on it.

The benefit of this type of systematic planning would be that information literacy instruction could be added to the curriculum in ways that are effective and efficient for learners, faculty and administration. Rather than randomly adding ILit instruction to the curriculum in a haphazard way, effective instructional design would work to infuse a variety of classes at different levels with systematic ILit instruction that cumulatively builds increasing competency in learners. This instruction could be accomplished in a variety of contexts. For example, freshman and sophomore composition classes, transition-to-college seminars, and interdisciplinary survey courses would all be suitable contexts for introducing ILit instruction to students.

A review of the literature on information literacy shows that many instructional designers are following these types of organizing cycles. Because most systematic ILit instruction is only just now being integrated into the existing curricula, the evidence of how this is being accomplished is more complete for the earliest stages of instructional design such as identifying the audience's needs or defining the exact skills that need to be taught.

The internet as a research tool

Skilful use of the internet as a research and learning tool is one such clear need for students who wish to be successful in industry, commerce and academia. Because digital information is often unregulated by editors, publishers or peer review, learners need to be information literate. Readers in digital media such as the internet must be critically alert and evaluate each internet source they use for reliability and validity.

Because this level of critical thinking is not intuitive, learners from elementary to higher education need to be guided in their information literacy in the same way in which we educate them in the traditional literacies of reading paper texts. These ILit skills represent an expansion, revision or addition to the traditional information management practices of a paper-based information society. All readers, researchers and information users can benefit from instruction that advances their ILit skills and prepares them to be lifelong learners capable of navigating the full spectrum of information sources. As lifelong learners who are information literate, they should be able to effectively find, analyse and apply relevant and reliable data from a variety of regulated and unregulated sources such as are found on the internet.

With traditional information filters and supports appropriate to paper texts absent, those who use the web for information gathering must become researchers and information managers with the ability to individually:

- use critical thinking to evaluate the enormous variance in the quality of information published on the web
- sort through the large quantity of information available from a wide variety of sources
- separate subject content, media presentation and information delivery as modes of shaping information quality
- use appropriate technologies to access, manage, process, and store information
- understand that digital information is often dynamic and not 'locked' into print the way paper texts are
- employ search skills that consider the various and distinct capabilities of search engines, meta-crawlers, intranets and browsers
- design keyword and Boolean search strategies that target the best possible pool of research resources
- apply copyright law and ethics to use information in fair and legal ways
- synthesize information from a wide variety of media
- create communication and information storage that effectively use the appropriate media
- understand the public nature of information that is published without password protection in full access media such as the internet
- stay current with emerging technologies that shape information management.

Instructional designers are experimenting with ways to accomplish this goal. There is a long history of reading literacy instruction being most effective when it is systematic, cumulative and guided by learning theory. It follows that information literacy, like so many other core learning skills such as reading literacy, critical thinking and communication, should also be systematic, cumulative and guided by learning theory. Learners can be guided to higher levels of information literacy in ways that are specific to their own needs, skills and resources. To do this, educators must first begin with a clear definition of what information literacy constitutes and then decide how ILit instruction fits into the overall curriculum.

Instructional practices

The challenge to instructional designers is that because information literacy is a relatively new field, there are not many tested models of effective instruction specific to this field. Educational institutions, therefore, must begin the ID cycle for information literacy by studying other forms of library, bibliographic or research methodology instruction to determine best practices that transfer to ILit. For example, in the case of online tutorials for information literacy, educators must carefully consider how digital contexts impact on learning. Early research suggests that instructional designers can optimize digital learning in many ways such as by:

- teaching through practice that page design should not be confused with content value
- limiting the colour range to five colours a screen and seven within the domain's palette
- recognizing that it is harder to read text on a screen, and so not crowding a digital page with dense text or distracting graphics or animations
- using clear hierarchies of meaning to chunk information so that learners will visually see and understand the relationship between ideas and concepts
- using lists that learners can skim to glean the main ideas rather than having to search them out in prose paragraphs
- employing site maps to help learners easily locate and understand relationships between ideas
- limiting the links that take readers away from the original document
- providing navigational aids to make clear to users the difference between hypertext within a site and linking away from the site
- clearly establishing the authorship and currency of information, because they influence the interpretation of content.

A survey of information literacy skills

Even using these design principles, the picture of the instructional need is not met unless one considers the students' ILit competency. In a research survey conducted in the summer of 2001, this writer surveyed 1184 of the 2345 incoming college freshmen who passed through summer orientation at Ferris State University in Big Rapids, Michigan (www.ferris.edu). Most of the almost 10,000 students at this residential state institution are from Michigan. Most are traditional-age college students and come from every county in the state with about a four-to-three male to female ratio in the student population. According to Ferris's institutional research, this four-year, comprehensive, undergraduate institution enrols a student population that has an average high school GPA (Grade Point Average) of 2.9 on a 4.0 scale and an average ACT (American College Testing) composite score of 20 on a scale of 36.

In an effort to better understand the information literacy competencies of incoming students, this writer designed a 20-question, multiple-choice, voluntary survey to gather information on how students from the target population of incoming freshmen used the internet for general and academic research. A survey of the student population was completed during the summer orientation/registration sessions in 2001. A portion of the results is reported below.

Some 9.8% (116 students) in the population of 1184 respondents reported never having used the internet. Another 36% (426 students) reported using the internet for one to two hours a week and 35.7 % (422 students) reported using it three to seven hours a week. The remainder, 18.5% (218 students), reported using the internet for more than eight hours a week. Of that same group, 4.7% (56 students) never used the internet for a school project, while 10.4% (123 students) used it one or two times. The majority of students self-reported that they used the internet for school research with 25% (296 students) using it three to five times, 20.7% (243 students) using it six to ten times and 39.2% (463 students) using it more than ten times.

A combined total of 27.5% of those same students (413) never or seldom made judgements about the quality and reliability of the information they found on the internet, while 36.2% (428 students) usually made judgements, 15.7% (187 students) often made judgements, and 13.2% (156 students) always made judgements. An operational rule of sophisticated users of the internet has always been that one cannot trust what is out on the web. Digital researchers and paper-print readers should always judge the reliability of a source before using it as a reference. So, this response is a troubling one that should be addressed by some kind of instruction.

It could be that students need more education in how they gather research. One clue to the nature of this problem could be the pattern of library usage that the survey population reported concerning the times they used a library in high school. The students in this survey reported that 15.7% (186) never used the library, 25.4% (301 students) used the library only one to two times in the last school year, 28.4% (336 students) used the library three to five times, 15.3% (2181 students) used it six to ten times and 15.2 (180 students) used it more than ten times. Yet, in a separate question, 81.9% (970 students) reported that when they do research they use a combination of the internet, books, magazines and other sources with only 8.5% (101 students) saying that they use only the internet. The question remains as to what the formula is for that combination of information sources. Is it one book and 20 internet sources? Or are high school teachers perhaps – as some college professors still do – still restricting the amount of sources a student can pull from the internet? This type of restriction may be well intentioned, but it is not realistic in terms of preparing to be lifelong learners/students who will be using the internet for research in their professions and personal lives.

Surprisingly, in this age when internet expertise has become almost an academic presumption, a group of 13.8% (163 students) ranked themselves as having no or little expertise on the internet. Some 46.9% (555 students) considered themselves to have intermediate abilities to use the internet for school projects. The remainder, 39.3% (464 students), saw themselves as having advanced or expert knowledge in the intricacies of using the internet as a research tool and resource. What is even more interesting is that 50.2% (593 students) reported that they learned to use the internet on their own while 22.8% said that they learned together with friends. Only 18.6% (220 students) reported that they had learned through classroom instruction. One might consider how this compares with the instruction the educational system offers in using traditional print resources and the information repository of the library. When asked how much more training they need to use the internet for college projects, 11.8% (139 students) said they need a beginner's class, 35.1% (415 students) needed to 'brush up' on their skills and 37.6% (445 students) said they already 'knew enough' to use the internet for school projects. A group of 12.4% (147 students) wanted to advance their internet skill to the 'highest level'.

The last five questions on the survey used multiple-choice responses to determine the students' ability to craft a keyword search and analyse a URL (Uniform Resource Locator) to begin the process of determining the reliability of a website as a research information source. The results from these questions show that a large number of students, despite their confidence in their own information literacy for using the internet for research, could benefit from systematic and cumulative formal instruction on internet usage. This survey is a beginning step in proving that a need exists for systematic and cumulative information literacy instruction to take place – especially in the area of internet use where so much academic research information is now hosted.

Conclusion

Perhaps the most significant finding from this survey is that such a large percentage of students do not evaluate the reliability and quality of web sources. This is a danger given that they self-report using the internet as their main source of information for school projects. Not judging the quality of information sources is not a new phenomenon in student research. A glance at freshman composition handbooks quickly reveals that they universally teach how to decipher a reliable from an unreliable source. Most college composition research has been traditionally conducted in library databases that are screened and supported by the academic infrastructure of the library, publishing house and subscription-based academic journals. In other words, there was a professionally developed and maintained information infrastructure to keep the student researcher from straying too far from reliable sources. These library supports are very important, especially for novice researchers, because they fill the gaps between what a researcher knows and what they need to know in order to find, evaluate, use and communicate information. Many times these supports buttress the users' own critical thinking skills or initiate the novice researcher into the role that critical thinking plays in successful research. For many who are new to the research process, the library – even with its 'high-support' environment of reference desks, instructional librarians and self-guided tutorials – presents a high-challenge learning environment. But even then, libraries are supportive to research in ways the internet cannot be.

Higher education must better understand how student researchers are gathering information and then create curricula that address the digital ways in which information is and will be managed. Designing instruction that serves this purpose must be informed by research that determines what students know, what they think they know and what they need to know. We must not operate on intuitions when careful research can better inform instructional design for information literacy.

References

ACRL (2000a) *Information Literacy Competency Standards for Higher Education: standards, performance indicators and outcomes*, Chicago, American Library Association. Available at www.ala.org/acrl/ilstandardlo.html.

ACRL (2000b) *Standards for University Libraries: evaluation of performance*. Available at www.ala.org.acrl/guides/univer.html.

ALA (n.d.) *Presidential Committee on Information Literacy.* Available at
    www.ala.org.acrl.nili/ilit1st.html.
Smith, P. L. and Ragan, T. J. (1999) *Instructional Design*, 2nd edn, New York, Wiley.

10

IT skills are not enough

Peter Reffell

Introduction

Chapter 8 of the 1997 Dearing Report outlines the UK Government's vision of the university in the 'information age'. In Dearing's vision HE (higher education) colleges and universities will increasingly look to information technologies to provide 'a central role in maintaining the quality of higher education', as well as becoming the focus for the delivery of teaching materials, overcoming 'barriers to higher education', and making 'higher educational services . . . become an internationally tradable commodity within an increasingly competitive global market' (NCIHE, 1997, Chapter 8). Dearing is not the first to place so much stock in the power of IT (information technology) to resolve the problems of an under-funded education system. Indeed the appeal of a 'technical fix' has long held considerable currency despite solid arguments that challenge the veracity of any kind of technical fix to what are essentially social and economic problems (Robins and Webster, 1989). Whether we like, or subscribe to Dearing's future vision, we can hardly deny that the introduction of information technologies has changed the way in which higher education operates. Most universities have accepted that information technology is now a crucial part of the university at all levels, and it seems that now the question is not should we charge into the wired future, but how do we do it as quickly and profitably as possible.

But how do we enable our students to exploit this future? In this chapter issues surrounding delivery and certification models, and the value of a diverse approach, are considered.

Searching for a solution

Dearing (NCIHE, 1997) sees a great many of the proposals he puts forward as being in place by the end of this decade, and this is especially the case with his vision for the role of IT within the university:

> Within the UK, by the end of the first decade of the next century, a 'knowledge economy' will have developed in which institutions collaborate in the production and transmission of educational programmes and learning materials on a 'make or buy' basis. We must expect and encourage the development and delivery of core programmes and components of programmes, and sharing and exchange of specialist provision, to become commonplace.

HE institutions in the UK have approached this problem from a variety of different angles, with different mixtures of home-grown induction sessions, library-supported training days, departmental-accredited modules and, increasingly, off-the-shelf training initiatives such as the ECDL (European Computer Driving Licence).[1] The focus of IT training and education has shown a tendency to centre around the acquisition of technical skills (using a word-processor, spreadsheet, etc.), while paying scant attention to the more discursive and less technical areas of the role of IT and information in society. Neil Selwyn (1997a) has noted that the bias towards technical competency also pervades educational computing research: 'In particular three main constraints to past and present research are conspicuous: . . . the overtly optimistic tone that permeates the vast majority of the literature; the avoidance of qualitative methodologies and the distrust of a more theoretical analysis of the role of the computer in education and therefore society' (305).

Selwyn describes the optimism that surrounds what information technologies may bring us in the future as the 'techno-romantic' view that sees computers as 'unequivocally a "good thing" for education', or, as Joseph Weizenbaum is cited as saying about computers in general in Roszak (1994), computers are 'a solution in search of problems' (51). Michael Gell and Peter Cochrane (1996) typify the more enthusiastic of the 'techno-romantics' when they talk about 'learning and education in an information society':

> An important characteristic of the ICT (Information and Communication Technology) based experience society will be the emergence of 'creativity enterprises', such as international virtualised education and training operations . . . development of round-the-clock creativity enterprises . . . being delivered by the services of an experience industry which is implicitly dependent on ICT for its opening up

of international markets and wide ranging possibilities for co-operative wealth creation. (262)

Given the tenor of the Dearing Report it is little wonder that such views should persist, for Dearing, like Gell and Cochrane, clearly sees IT as unequivocally good for higher education: good for the students, and good for reaching the UK government's target of increasing participation in HE to 50% of the under-30 population by 2010 (Great Britain. DfES, n.d.). However, while it is made clear that information technologies and the requisite skills to use them are the solution to many of our educational 'problems', it is less clear what skills are required or useful to students in higher education. Clearly any such skills should both augment the students' studies in an increasingly online learning environment, as well as providing a solid foundation for participation in the 'information society' and 'knowledge economies' of the future. The problem that faces teachers in HE is how to identify and deliver these key IT skills to a wide range of different students, many of whom have different abilities, needs and perceptions of information technology.

The somewhat pressing 2010 deadline for achieving the twin targets of increased participation in HE and IT skills provision for all undergraduates may be partly responsible for universities and colleges opting for a 'one size fits all' solution for IT training provision. Cost and convenience will also figure in any decision-making process, especially if there is no coherent college-wide IT skills programme already in place. International initiatives such as the ECDL provide just such a 'one size fits all' solution: an internationally recognized qualification; online delivery of the teaching materials and assessment; flexible modular course structure; in the UK, accreditation from the British Computing Society, and a part of the cost is covered by the student in addition to their normal tuition fees. Moreover, the ECDL does not just sell itself as one among many IT training programmes, the promotional literature informs us that the ECDL provides a standard 'for everyone who uses a computer in either a professional or a personal capacity', and a 'yardstick by which to measure [one's] computing abilities' (British Computing Society, 1999). As educators who wish to retain our more critical faculties, even within the brave new discourse of IT, we have to ask what standards are being set, and how is this shaping the way in which we understand and teach information technology? Are the IT skills provided by the ECDL and similar programmes always appropriate and sufficient to be considered as such a universal 'yardstick', and what 'computing abilities' are being fostered?

Setting 'standards' in IT education

Most students in higher education require a wide and diverse range of computing skills, many of which straddle the divide between 'IT skills' and more formal 'computing', while others emphasize the research-based nature of HE work. Of course HE students, as with all learners of information technology, still require a basic understanding of the principles of IT, but within a learning environment such as a university should providers of IT skills stop at teaching such basic principles? For many students the most important skills they require are not centred around the leading Microsoft packages, but in the use of applications and technologies relevant to their discipline. Moreover, where students do use the more standard office-type applications, it is likely that they may have to think outside of the clerical and administrative practices that form the basis for so much IT training.

At the University of Leeds a small panel was asked to consider these and other questions with a view to offering undergraduates ECDL accreditation. Representatives from a number of interested parties viewed the various coursewares and discussed the merits and the possible pitfalls. Being part of a team that is responsible for providing undergraduates with a range of IT skills, my colleagues and I assessed whether we could change our syllabus to allow for ECDL accreditation. Our main concern was whether the range of skills covered by the ECDL would be sufficient and appropriate for undergraduate students at the University of Leeds. Our own syllabus covers a wide range of different IT and introductory computing skills that students can choose from to construct their own ten credit modules. At Leeds, as is probably the case at all universities and colleges, the IT skills that are of most use to undergraduates are often quite diverse: being able to successfully navigate and use the internet for research, generating statistics for social and biological sciences, introduction to programming concepts, broader social and legal implications of IT, using computers as translation tools, understanding the use and generation of electronic texts, web design, using non-Western texts on the PC, using long document techniques and analysing data. Moreover, not all students will spend their undergraduate time sitting in front of a Windows PC; many departments run a considerable number of applications on Unix systems and Apple Macs. (A more comprehensive overview of the IT Skills Programme at Leeds can be found at www.leeds.ac.uk/acom/.)

Being able to maintain our 'home-grown' brand of IT education was extremely important to us, having developed our courses over a number of years and in collaboration with many different departments. Although providing the necessary support for ECDL accreditation would require a considerable amount of restructuring and adjustment to our current programme, the problems were not insurmountable and it was felt that the ECDL could work along-side our own syllabus. Indeed, many of the areas that we covered in our introductory courses appeared to sit quite well with the ECDL syllabus. However, although many of the same subject areas were addressed, there were considerable differences in emphasis and goals. Because we offer IT electives for a wide range of students from nearly all faculties, we have had to create a programme that provides both the skills they can use while at university, and a broader set of skills that may be of use beyond their formal education. It was the latter concern that initially aroused our interest in the ECDL. Could the ECDL provide undergraduate students from across the university with a standard set of skills that would be of use to them when they leave, and engage their interest sufficiently for the skills to be useful? After much consideration we identified a number of issues and concerns that not only led to us rejecting the ECDL for undergraduates at Leeds, but also forced us to consider whether a standard model for IT education could ever be appropriate, and if it could, would IT skills, in the form of those offered by the ECDL syllabus, be enough?

One size does not fit all

Our concerns centred around two main areas; flexibility and range of skills, and appropriateness of the skills offered. Although the promotional material for the ECDL made much of the flexible nature of the programme, and appeared to go beyond word-processing and spreadsheets, we found the syllabus to be very much biased towards the MS (Microsoft) Windows platform running MS Office. While it is understood that the majority of personal computers will be Windows machines, to provide no alternative to this both limits the students' understanding of what constitutes IT and computing, as well as tying the skills to a very specific set of applications. The very limited range of subject areas and the focus of the learning objectives further compounded these limitations. It appeared that most of the skills were appropriate for administrative and clerical work, or home use, but not for developmental and problem solving tasks. Where there was scope to explore these areas, as with MS Access database development and the world wide web, the students were channelled into the role of 'user' rather than 'developer'. In the case of MS Access, the module that dealt with this signally failed to provide even the most cursory introduction to relational database theory and design. Without such important foundational principles, one's use of the application is severely restricted. It is acknowledged that any introductory IT course cannot cover the more involved areas of computing and IT; however, this should not mean that the teaching materials are 'incomplete'. Furthermore, it is important that students are encouraged to develop their problem-solving skills; thus use of a specific application (MS

Word, Excel) is often secondary to the skills that enable one to understand what that application can do (word-processing, data handling). The ECDL puts far too much focus on technique and not enough on understanding the relationship between the problem and the means of solving it using IT. This underemphasis on developing problem-solving skills was made even more apparent when we looked at the assessment of the modules. Many of the questions were multiple choice or involved completing very specific tasks. There was little scope for choosing alternative routes to achieve the same goal, and the absence of any project-based work seemed to run counter to how IT is used in the workplace.

For students in higher education we also felt that the uncritical approach to IT presented by the ECDL was inappropriate in terms of developing a broader understanding of IT and information issues. Where such implications were considered it was usually in a way that was too prescriptive and simplistic for HE students. When one considers the range of different people the ECDL is designed for and the method by which it is assessed, it comes as little surprise that the more discursive elements of information technology skills may not be adequately represented. One could perhaps excuse this as an inevitable, but necessary, sacrifice in exchange for making IT skills provision more inclusive. However, the skills that are not developed are those that may actually allow people to participate in the 'information society' and make it their society where their views are represented. Tom Conlon (2000) illustrates this point in his paper on the unlikely combination of IT education and postmodernism. Conlon (2000, 109–10) argues that, 'The questions that dominate the discourse of IT in education are mostly at the technicians level', whereas 'visionary questions relating to technology and education [are to] be avoided or their answers taken for granted.'

Initiatives like the ECDL reinforce the idea that the technology, and the techniques required to work the technology, are the central concern of the learning process, rather than developing both the information skills required to work within an information environment, and the technical understanding required to use the appropriate tools. Other authors have made similar points (e.g. Rowley, 1997; Selwyn 1998, Selwyn 2000, Bruce, 1997), suggesting that a standardized approach to IT education ignores the important, and highly variable, role of information skills. In the ECDL promotional literature, prospective students are informed that the ECDL can prepare one for 'full participation in the Information Society' (British Computing Society, 1999), yet it is unclear how simple technical competency, coupled with a simplistic and unquestioning acceptance of the idea of the 'Information Society' promotes an understanding of the issues surrounding the use of information (Webster, 1995). In order to participate in any kind of social sphere, one must be able to make informed choices about the society within which one exists or with which one wishes to engage. In the case of the so-called information society and our need, perceived or otherwise, to participate in it, we need to know how to use IT in an appropriate way. The alternative, a blind acceptance of the power of IT, is unlikely to engender the critical skills that are essential to problem solving and understanding, and that are so much in demand both in education and employment.

Promoting educational and technological diversity

Of crucial importance to problem solving and understanding the appropriate use of a technology to resolve problems, is context. A standardized approach to IT education obfuscates the important issue that because of the complex nature of the technologies and how they are situated and used, there is considerable difference between one user or group's understanding of information technology and another's. Commentators have consistently underlined the importance of age, gender, class and nationality in understanding how different technologies are used and appropriated by different people and special interest groups (e.g. Schwartz Cowan, 1976; Pacey, 1983). There is no reason why information technologies should not be subject to the same considerations (e.g. Barker and Downing, 1980; Gooday, 1998), and these ideas brought into the learning and teaching environment. It is the localized nature of both the learning experience and the context within which the technology is applied that allows people to understand and use a technology on their terms. In other words learners need to understand both how and why they should be making use of a new technology.

In two studies of students' attitudes toward educational computing in further education, Neil Selwyn (1997b, 1998) illustrates this point very clearly, as well as demonstrating how important the students' local environment and social sphere is to the learning experience.

> Richard: 'Yeah, every time you've got an idea you can't just go over to the computer and turn it on and off you've got to sit down in front of it and churn it out. Usually you come up with an idea, you have to write it down on a piece of paper and when you go back to the computer later it's just more typing and more time'.
> (Selwyn, 1998, 203)

> Helen: 'Because we talk more . . . we'd rather talk with our friends rather than sit down and use a computer, we socialise more. Boys sort of socialise when using a computer and then they'll talk about that. If you go into the IT workshop at lunchtime they're all in there using the Internet.' (Selwyn, 1998, 206)

At Leeds we can sometimes face a similar response to our own courses, as this response from an anonymous course evaluation questionnaire illustrates: 'I didn't think the bibliography exercise was very useful. It seemed a lot of effort just to make a ten line long list of references for the end of an essay.' While it will not be possible to please all the people all of the time, Selwyn (1998, 210) argues that, 'The emphasis should . . . lie in changing the nature of educational computing to fit the needs of the students, not the other way around.'

This is not to say that teachers should stop teaching a particular area because a student finds it boring, rather it is that as teachers we should try to ensure that students are able to see how information technologies can be used where appropriate. It is unlikely that a student who does not use a wide range of published material in their main degree will be able to see the benefit of generating bibliographies and citations from a database. It is, however, quite the opposite story if a great deal of one's time is spent formatting bibliographies. 'The idea of gaining extra marks for using EndNote with Word pushed me to try this out, instead of simply using the most basic, and now I can use this with my other degree work – very useful. Thanks for the incentive' (from an anonymous IT Skills course evaluation questionnaire, 2001, School of Computing, University of Leeds).

Information technologies enable people to better use and manage other information resources. But while it may be the case that people will be using the same core technologies, specifically computers, it is not necessarily the case that people's information needs, and thus skills, are going to be the same. Librarians, researchers, students, office workers, and so forth, all have a very different set of information requirements and require a different set of skills to manage them. Both the skill set and the method of teaching should be sensitive to the needs and requirements of the learners if the teaching and learning of IT is to progress towards a greater understanding of the use and role of IT in society. Learners must be able to see why information technologies and information is relevant to them beyond the rhetoric of the great IT salvo. To not foster a deeper understanding of the issues surrounding information technologies is to risk increasing the divide between the 'information rich' and the 'information poor' (Schiller, 1996; Webster, 1995).

It is not only the learners' capacity to understand the potential and limitations of a technology that it is not being addressed with programmes like the ECDL; there is also an assumption that businesses and organizations that use IT have the same basic information requirements from locale to locale. This is not necessarily the case as was noted in the ICT skills gap workshop at the European E-Learning Summit (Selinger, 2001, 9), where it was recommended that, 'Education needs to work with industry and government to . . . tailor make [ICT] education for the unemployed in shortage areas, for SMEs, for women, and members of ethnic minority groups.' Whether we do live in an information age or not, it is undeniable that the processing and management of information at all levels plays an increasingly significant role in many aspects of our lives. If, as educators, we are to provide learners with a set of skills that will genuinely enable them to participate in the information society, we need to consider how such skills can be relevant to people's information requirements, as well as ensuring that participation is full and equal.

Universities and HE colleges are well placed to be able to implement key strategies that would be instrumental in changing the way in which IT education is undertaken as:

- IT education should take advantage of the skills a student is learning in their main subject and seek to dovetail the delivery of IT education with these skills.
- IT skills that are used in a working and learning environment will demand more general problem-solving skills as the learner demands more from the technology than they otherwise would if the skills were learned in isolation.
- These skills can then be fed back into the local community through university initiatives within the region. The broad set of skills gained through such an exchange is invaluable in terms of the students' education and the relationship between the university and its region, as well as taking real steps towards widening participation in HE.

IT educators should also be mindful of the research that currently does and could inform both teaching and policy. If information technologies are as important to our educational and societal future as Dearing suggests, they should be subject to the same degree of critical analysis as other significant technologies and the disciplines that use them. What we learn from such an approach should be reflected both in what we teach, and in the way we teach. Initiatives like the ECDL are based upon the assumption that information and information technologies are morally and politically neutral, and thus in the new age of information we are all able to start as equals. This is simply not true, as historians of science and sociologists are apt to tell us (e.g. Gooday, 1998; Webster, 1995). We need to acknowledge and understand the differences between people's information needs and provide them with the appropriate tools. It may be that many of the 'tools' that people require do not involve a great deal of 'button pushing', but make use of critical thinking, organizational and communication skills. Knowing how to use a web browser may allow one access to over two million pages that mention William Shakespeare, but knowing how to source web pages for scholarly integrity will actually enable the user to get to the relevant information.

Conclusion

The techno-romantic view of the computer, coupled with a sense of urgency to increase the use of IT within HE, can make us less critical of the technologies we are using and teaching, leading to inappropriate use at many different levels. Over-emphasis on quantifiable results can sometimes obscure the subtleties of the learning process, especially where it may not be immediately evident how IT may aid what one is already doing to a good standard. If we are to develop and teach a broad understanding of IT skills, then it is important that we start to think about information technologies with the same conceptual tools as we apply to other technologies. We can learn a great deal from the histories of other technologies, how they are used in different contexts, how people are able to use them in different and diverse ways, and the consequences when local issues and concerns are ignored.

As universities and colleges are under increased pressure to ensure that all undergraduate students are provided with IT skills, so it seems likely that off-the-shelf solutions will be deployed to satisfy this demand. But as information skills play an increasingly important role in many people's lives, and new technologies extend the range of available tools, so we have to consider whether IT skills in the narrow, technical sense are enough. I have argued in this chapter that we need a broader, more theoretical, knowledge base from which we are able to explore and participate in this 'information age'. We also need to ensure that any use of IT augments and complements our use of information resources, reflecting cultural, national and personal concerns. Genuine participation requires open dialogue between the interested parties; it is hard to see how the ECDL is anything other than a monologue that reiterates the convenient rhetoric of the technical fix as a solution to educational and social problems and concerns. Throughout this chapter I have argued that IT skills training packages like the ECDL are not appropriate for students in HE. This does not imply that the ECDL has no educational use, or that it will not serve some groups of people well, only that we are unlikely to find a 'one size fits all' solution to people's information needs. The challenge we face in higher education is to ensure that we are able to meet the needs of a diverse student body working with a diverse set of technologies. We should be exploiting such diversity, not trying to fit it into a single standard.

Endnote

1   The range of different approaches to the 'problem' of providing HE students with IT skills was brought into sharp relief at the First IT&ILit Conference in Glasgow 2002, and is reflected in the chapters in this book. An overview of the papers delivered at the conference can be found at www.iteu.gla.ac.uk/

elit/itilit2002/papers.html. The IT&ILit event has been succeeded by the eLit series of conferences; see http://elit2003.com/.

References

Barker, J. and Downing, H. (1980). Word Processing and the Transformation of Patriarchal Relations of Control in the Office. Reprinted in MacKenzie, D. and. Wajcman, J. (eds) (1985) *The Social Shaping of Technology*, Buckingham, Open University Press, 147–64.

British Computing Society (1999) European Computer Driving Licence promotional literature, BCS.

Bruce, C. (1997) *The Seven Faces of Information Literacy*, Adelaide, Auslib Press.

Conlon, T. (2000) Visions of Change: information technology, education and post-modernism, *British Journal of Educational Technology*, 31 (2), 109–16.

Gell, M. and Cochrane, P. (1996) Learning and Education in an Information Society. In Dutton, W. H. (ed.), *Information and Communication Technologies: visions and realities*, New York, Oxford University Press, 249–63.

Gooday, G. (1998) Taking Apart the 'Roads Ahead': user power versus the futurology of IT, *Convergence*: *The Journal of Research into New Media Technologies*, 4 (3), 8–16.

Great Britain. Department for Education and Skills (n.d.) *The Excellence Challenge: what is the excellence challenge?* Available at www.dfes.gov.uk/excellencechallenge/whatis/.

NCIHE (National Committee of Inquiry into Higher Education) (1997) *Higher Education in the Learning Society: report of the National Committee*, London, HMSO [Dearing Report].

Pacey, A. (1983) *The Culture of Technology*, Boston, MA, MIT Press.

Robins, K. and Webster, F. (1989) *The Technical Fix: education, computers and industry*, London, Macmillan Education.

Roszak, T. (1994) *The Cult of Information: a neo-Luddite treatise on high tech, artificial intelligence, and the true art of thinking*, 2nd edn, Berkeley, CA, University of California Press.

Rowley, J. (1997) Open Learning and IT Skills Acquisition in Higher Education, *British Journal of Educational Technology*, 28 (1), 64–5.

Schiller, H. (1996) *Information Inequality, the deepening crisis in America*, New York, Routledge.

Schwartz Cowan, R. (1976) The Industrial Revolution in the Home. Reprinted in MacKenzie, D. and Wajcman, J. (eds) (1985), *The Social Shaping of Technology*, Buckingham, Open University Press, 181–201.

Selinger, M. (2001) *The ICT Skills GapWorkshop. Discussion paper presented at the European elearning summit, Brussels, 10–11 May 2001*, IBM Web Lecture Services website. Available at www.ibmweblectureservices. ihost.com/eu/elearningsummit/ppps/downloads/sgprint15.pdf.

Selwyn, N. (1997a) The Continuing Weakness of Educational Computing Research, *British Journal of Educational Technology*, **28** (4), 305–7.

Selwyn, N. (1997b) Students' Attitudes toward Computers: validation of a computer attitude scale for 16–19 education, *Computers and Education*, **28** (1), 35–41.

Selwyn, N. (1998) What's in the Box? Exploring learners' rejection of educational computing, *Educational Research and Evaluation*, **4** (3), 193–212.

Selwyn, N. (2000) Researching Computers and Education – glimpses of the wider picture, *Computers and Education*, **34**, 93–101.

Webster, F. (1995) *Theories of the Information Society*, London, Routledge.

11

ICT training: models of delivery

Catherine McKeown and Caitriona Curran

Introduction

ICT (information and communication technology) is becoming increasingly crucial as an underpinning tool to support learning and teaching, research and administration at Queen's University. This change is the result of a number of factors: the Dearing Report, national agendas such as Key Skills, the introduction of the university's VLE (virtual learning environment) and Queen's Online, and changing expectations from both staff and students. Within this context, it is critical that both students and staff have sufficient ICT knowledge and skills to allow them to make effective and efficient use of technology in their working and learning environments.

Queen's University has for many years offered a range of services to support the development of staff and student ICT skills. For students, these have included ICT orientation for all new students, access to ICT training resources and self-study materials, and an assessment centre for ECDL (the European Computer Driving Licence). While this provision is supplemented by School-based ICT-related training on some courses, many students receive no training beyond the ICT orientation. Current uptake of central ICT services and resources is sporadic across the University.

For staff, services have included ICT training courses, access to ICT training resources and self-study materials, an assessment centre for ECDL, and support for teaching staff wishing to embed ICT into the curriculum.

However, with the overall growth in the use of ICT, the University recognized the need to develop a coherent strategy to institution-wide ICT training. Queen's University Belfast, in 2000, established a three-year TAP (Training and Accreditation Programme), within the Educational Technology Unit,

Information Services. This programme is funded by the Northern Ireland Department for Employment and Learning. TAP has developed and implemented a number of initiatives for its three target groups – students, academic staff and administrative/clerical staff. The findings of the combined key activities have acted as a catalyst for the development of a University-wide ICT training strategy, currently being planned for implementation over the next three years. This chapter discusses the outcomes of the TAP initiatives and describes the resulting proposal for an institution-wide ICT training strategy.

Changing needs: post-primary sector (Northern Ireland)

Within Northern Ireland, at Key (Skill) Stages 3 and 4, ICT is a compulsory element within the curriculum but significantly, is not an independent main subject, such as English, Mathematics or Science, Technology and Design. It is cited under the umbrella of 'Six Educational Themes', which are 'not separate subjects but are woven through the main subjects of the curriculum' (Northern Ireland CCEA (Council for Curriculum, Examinations and Assessment, 1996)). An Inspectorate Report published by the Department of Education in 2000 does indicate that at best, in a minority of schools, ICT provision is above the required national standard and is effectively embedded throughout the curriculum. At worst, ICT provision is either non-existent or confined to 'discrete typing and basic information handling activities' (Education and Training Inspectorate, 2000).

There are a number of initiatives currently in place to enhance ICT provision within the post-primary sector, based on recommendations put forward in the Department of Education's document, *A Strategy for Education Technology in Northern Ireland* (Department of Education Northern Ireland, 1997). For example, an official but optional Key Stage 3 ICT Assessment was introduced by CCEA in September 1997 and there has been a significant and steady increase in its uptake. These initiatives will have an impact on raising the ICT skills of new undergraduates, but this will be a gradual development over the coming years.

IT skills survey of new Queen's undergraduates

Annual surveys of new undergraduates at Queen's demonstrate that between 1998 and 2001, there has been a gradual increase in the number of students who feel confident with their level of ICT skills in a range of different areas, on entry into the University. This confidence, however, is significantly higher when dealing with more basic ICT skills such as creating a Word document or finding a web page, rather than tasks such as inserting Clipart, creating a table and bookmarking web pages. However, also significant is that approximately 50% of the students surveyed stated that they felt they needed more computer training and would be interested in attending training courses. Therefore, the ICT skills that Queen's can expect new undergraduates to have are still difficult to measure. The primary implication of these findings is that Queen's cannot assume that the majority of new students will have a certain common level or set of ICT skills. Furthermore, the types of basic skills that students will need to have will also evolve over the next few years, as developments in e-learning within Queen's will require students to be much more web literate.

ICT training and accreditation programme strategy

The analysis stage of TAP identified three levels of training as important for both staff (academic and administrative/clerical) and students:

1 *Awareness Raising*: An introductory level, focusing on developing an appreciation of what technologies are available and how they can support/improve the working/learning practices of staff and students.
2 *Skill*: Focuses on generic skills, i.e. the basic skills required to manage a personal computer and its associated core applications in a networked environment and specialist skills, e.g. using QUB (Queen's University of Belfast) administration systems or a statistical package.
3 *Application*: Focuses on understanding how ICT can be used to support staff in their work and students in their learning, how to identify areas where improvements could be made and the factors that need to be considered.

The programme adopted a multifaceted approach, which can be characterized as:

- *Proactive*: Targeted at specific groups, i.e. clerical staff, administrators, office managers, lecturers and students.
- *Tailored*: Responsive to staff, student and organizational needs.
- *Flexible*: Where appropriate, trainees can choose methods (tutor-led, CBT, etc.), materials, timing, participation and pace.
- *Partnership*: Working with representatives of staff, units and relevant groups to ensure that the training is meeting user and organizational needs.
- *Accredited*: Where possible accreditation, e.g. ECDL, is provided.
- *Embedded*: The intention of the programme is to embed ICT into the working life of staff and students. It is critical that all activities are designed and developed to exist beyond the life of TAP.

TAP implemented a number of key activities including the following:

- ICT-related briefing series were delivered to specific groups with the support of the relevant senior management: 'Learning and Teaching in the Information Age' for Heads of Teaching; 'Office Management in the Information Age' for senior clerical staff; and 'Administration in the Information Age' for middle management administrative staff.
- There is a centralized, flexible ICT training pilot, linked to the ECDL. The model of training adopted was self-study utilizing CBT (computer-based training) materials. Senior clerical staff nominated a member of staff from each office across the University. Almost 100 nominees obtained full ECDL certification within the first year. The number of self-selecting students enrolling for ECDL training and accreditation was 194.
- Work with academic staff focused on three key activities:

  — Offering consultancy to Schools to advise and support lecturers who wish to use computers to support their students' learning. Some of the work was with individual staff but more of it involved small groups of staff within Schools.
  — Offering a programme of workshops on the use of technology to support learning and teaching. Fifteen workshops were offered focusing on topics such as using PowerPoint in lectures and presentations, planning for publishing lecture notes on the web, and using computer-assisted assessment tools. The workshops were attended by over 200 staff and evaluated positively.
  — Offering a programme of workshops on the use of the Queen's VLE. Training and support was offered to staff both individually and on a School basis. The TAP team have also conducted an evaluation of the use of the VLE to inform further support and training required.

ECDL: comparisons and findings

It is not possible in this paper to consider all the results and implications of the activities carried out under TAP. However, analysis of the two parallel ECDL pilots showed interesting contrasts and has influenced the new institution-wide ICT strategy. The data from the ECDL pilots showed that staff and students had reacted very differently to the flexible self-study model of training/accreditation.

Clerical staff

Clerical staff responded well to the self-study model of training and accreditation. In the first seven-month phase, 86 people from 66 offices passed 466 tests in 30 test sessions. Over 50 attendees completed the full seven modules, with the majority of the remainder continuing to complete ECDL in the second phase which was set up to cater for those on the waiting list. There were three strands to the service offered and these were induction, self-study CBT, and weekly testing. The flexible intensive testing timetable proved popular with staff. The sessions usually lasted two or three hours during various times in the day/evening and Saturdays. The popularity of lunchtime and evening sessions indicated that for many being absent from their desk during core hours was a problem. This was particularly the case for those in small offices with no cover, e.g. for telephones.

A questionnaire was issued to all Phase 1 attendees with over a 50% response rate (45 responses). All of the staff indicated that they had used the CBT with 90% doing so from their office. However, over 40% also used the CBT at home. Over 85% indicated they planned to continue to use the CBT. Over 90% would recommend that other staff use the CBT and over 95% would recommend to other staff that they should complete the ECDL.

When attendees were asked about the effects of participating in the ECDL pilot, the results show that this will have a lasting impact on training and skill development. (See Table 11.1.)

Table 11.1   *Effects of ECDL pilot*

The staff were asked how likely they would now be to:

	No difference	More likely	Less likely
1. Help others in the office	19%	81%	–
2. Find solutions to IT problems	5%	93%	2%
3. Attend IT training courses	32.5%	55%	12.5%
4. Encourage others to attain IT qualification	4%	96%	–
5. Pursue further IT qualifications	28%	67%	5%

Staff were asked to rate their IT competence having completed/started ECDL. Over 75% felt that there had been an improvement in their IT competence. Of this percentage, 40.9% stated that they would be more confident in their own use while an additional 36.4% now felt that they were sufficiently proficient to be able to help others. Staff also provided specific examples of how this increased knowledge was being used to improve the working practices of both staff and, by extension, their offices.

The success of the staff pilot can be attributed to five factors. They are:

- the flexible and tailored training approach
- a perception that ECDL could be beneficial to staff careers
- a perception that ECDL could benefit staff current working practices
- a non-threatening exam environment suiting people who have not sat exams in some time
- the fact that attendees had been nominated by senior staff and were representing their unit. No further places were given to their unit until they had completed the full ECDL.

In conclusion, the ECDL staff pilot successfully increased training, accreditation and skills among clerical staff. The methods used during the pilot have now become embedded within the University with currently over 120 registered for ECDL.

Students

Over 295 students attended initial ECDL briefings with 194 registering for ECDL. The students were required to make a nominal contribution of £30 with the remaining costs subsidized by TAP. The students were offered regular testing sessions and access to CBT materials. In addition, clinics were offered on a regular basis. However, the clinics were very poorly attended except in cases where lecturers had advised students to attend a particular session on a specific skill. Despite contributing financially, only 37 (19.1%) completed the full ECDL during the academic year of the pilot. Exactly half (97) completed three or fewer modules. In addition, only 54 took up the offer to complete ECDL for free in the subsequent year. (See Table 11.2.)

Table 11.2 *Student ECDL figures October 2000–June 2001*

Students attending initial ECDL briefing	295
Students enrolled for ECDL	194
Students having gained full accreditation	37
Students with 3 or fewer modules completed	97
Students with 4 or more modules completed	60

These figures, combined with discussions with students, indicate that the model adopted was only appropriate for approximately 20% of students. Based on analysis, it has become apparent that, while many students were interested in developing ICT skills, large-scale voluntary training programmes will not be effective for this constituency. A more realistic and appropriate approach to student ICT skill development requires lecturer involvement and embedding within existing modules and programmes of study. This has significant implications for both student and academic staff training. In this context, it will be essential to devise and implement strategies that also develop academic staff ICT skills and awareness, in order to enable them to map and embed ICT skills into course curricula and provide effective delivery of these skills to students.

Proposed Queen's ICT training framework

The outcomes of the TAP experience have informed the University's proposal to embark on an institution-wide ICT training framework for students. While recognizing the need for a similar framework for staff ICT skills development, this process is still in its early stages; therefore the focus of this discussion is the training framework for students.

TAP demonstrated that students' level of interest is a key issue contributing to the success of voluntary development of ICT skills. However, interest alone is not sufficient. It needs to be supported by making ICT skill development a course objective, either through generic training and/or embedding and contextualization. In addition, a model of training that has student motivation as a core attribute must build in 'added value' that is clearly visible to the student. It is imperative that any model of ICT training addresses these issues.

In the ICT framework being planned by Queen's, it is envisaged that ICT skill development will be a course objective and added value will primarily be incorporated into the training model in three ways. They are the introduction of assessment for ICT elements, embedding ICT in course curricula elements, and contextualizing ICT for students within their own subject areas so that they understand the relevance of the skills.

The overall aim of the proposed ICT training framework is to ensure that students develop appropriate ICT skills to support their learning and work. The objectives need to ensure that:

- students have the necessary ICT life skills required to support their learning
- subject areas offer students the opportunity to practise and apply their developing ICT skills
- staff in subject areas contextualize the use of ICT to support the subject area
- students have an appropriate level of ICT skills and knowledge to prepare them for the workplace.

Three different student types, within the context of current ICT skill levels, have been identified, which have direct impact on the training delivery model adopted. They are:

- *Beginner*: Will have minimal experience of using a computer, with skills limited to turning a computer on and basic mouse operations.
- *Post-Beginner*: Will have basic experience of using a computer, with skills limited to, for example, basic browsing of the internet or creating a basic Word document. Skills will not extend to familiarity with any of the other Microsoft Office applications.
- *Intermediate*: Will have a range of basic or above basic ICT skills, for example, familiarity with word-processing, presentations, file management, internet and e-mail.

Table 11.3 characterizes the different types of ICT skill requirements identified for Queen's students:

Table 11.3   *ICT skill types*

Skill Type	Description
Orientation Skills	An overview of Queen's ICT facilities and skills required to use the system, e.g. logging on, accessing CBT material.
Life Skills for Learning	A baseline of basic skills in the following areas: word-processing, file management, internet and e-mail.
Advanced Skills for Learning	Skill set drawn from a generic list of further ICT courses, e.g. advanced word-processing, presentations, spreadsheets.
Subject-Specific Skills	Skill set varies between subject domains. Examples of these skills include SPSS (statistical analysis) for Psychology students, Spreadsheets (calculations and projections) for Science ones.
Work-Related ICT Skills	This will comprise a generic set of ICT skills and subject-specific ICT skills, many of which will have already been covered in the previous skills categories.

To meet the aims of the ICT framework, three major actions have been proposed: the introduction of an ICT Life Skills for Learning certificate, the facilitation of ICT embedding in pathways, and the preparation of students for the workplace. It is also recognized that central to achieving the framework's aims is establishing a collaborative partnership, which includes input from the central support agencies, teaching policy makers and the academic schools and departments. The following sections consider each of the proposed actions in turn.

Introduction of an ICT Life Skills for Learning certificate

As outlined previously, students entering Queen's have differing levels of ICT skill. The proposed scheme allows the University to assume that all students have core ICT life skills for learning. Key elements will include:

- Encouraging every new student to attend the current ICT orientation session. The current session would continue to be offered but would be increased to two hours, culminating in the opportunity for each student to carry out a self-audit of their ICT skills. It is recommended that this course should become mandatory. It is proposed that this is negotiated on a faculty-by-faculty basis.
- Streaming students through an online self-audit process at the end of the orientation session to establish their skill category and training needs.
- Depending on the self-audit 'score' the student has attained, categorizing each into one of three groups: intermediate, post-beginner or beginner.

On successful completion of the automated assessment the student will receive the ICT Life Skills for Learning certificate. Working in conjunction with each associated faculty, Information Services will offer training sessions during Week One of Semester One. It is recommended that this exercise be piloted with one faculty in the first instance.

Figure 11.1 shows the procedure necessary to obtain the certificate.

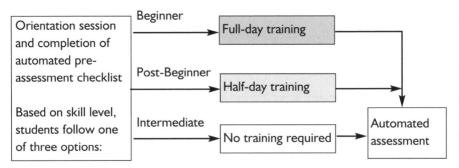

Fig. 11.1   *Procedure in order to receive the ICT Life Skills for Learning certificate*

Facilitation of ICT embedding in pathways

Students' achievement of the Skills certificate is to be viewed as the springboard to:

- Enabling students to move on to develop their understanding and application of ICT to their learning and, in time, to their work. This development will be fostered through the appropriate and sustained use of ICT in taught courses at the University.
- Ensuring that lecturers can assume a certain level of ICT skill, which would establish a foundation for developing ICT programmes within subject areas.
- Easing some of the pressures on students who are currently being expected to use basic ICT skills in their studies.

In order for students to develop sustainable ICT life skills, both for learning and work purposes, it is vital to the strategy that these are embedded into the curriculum of subject areas, otherwise skills that are learned are forgotten through both lack of practice and actual need. The strategy distinguishes between two types of ICT embedding which are:

- tasks that are within the requirements of a curriculum but are not essential to the completion of a subject specific task, e.g. a Humanities module making word-processing of essays and a presentation compulsory.
- subject-specific tasks, which require the use of ICT for successful completion, e.g. the use of spreadsheets to process data and perform calculations of a laboratory experiment.

The model to support embedding will comprise the following. An Information Services ICT skills consultant will be allocated to work with each faculty, establish partnerships with relevant pathways, ensure all students have the Skills certificate, enable pathway co-ordinators, in consultation with central support agencies, to analyse the learning outcomes of each pathway and identify opportunities for ICT embedding, and introduce learning activities that use ICT. Essential to the success of embedded ICT skills delivery and subsequent use are academic staff who have sufficient ICT knowledge to support each faculty's strategy. Therefore academic staff training will become a major consideration in the ICT embedding strategy for each faculty.

Preparing students for the workplace

It is the premise of Queen's that all graduates should have the appropriate ICT skills required to function in a modern business environment. These will comprise a generic set of ICT skills and subject-specific ICT skills. Arguably the initiatives discussed earlier in this paper will lead to graduates with the ICT skills required for the workplace. This would leave a short-term problem of current students who would not benefit from the scheme outlined. Factors currently being considered to bridge this skills gap include the role of ECDL, widening access to the Skills certificate, and encouraging embedding of work skills into the curriculum.

ICT skills for staff

A new staff training strategy is being developed based on a recognition of the proven benefits, within Queen's, of a flexible and tailored training approach. It is the aim of this strategy to introduce new areas of training, tailored to specific audiences, delivered at flexible times and utilizing CBT and online resources. Analysis of TAP activities with academic, administrative and clerical staff showed that flexibility in both time scheduling and training materials make a significant difference to motivation and the achievement of both personal learning objectives and organizational objectives. This strategy will focus on developing the existing, traditional approach to staff training, which delivers a generic central programme of training sessions. New initiatives will provide tailored, contextualized training to all types of staff. This new approach is currently being offered to academic staff via the Educational Technology Unit's programme of workshops, which focus on delivering tailored training on a range of ICT-related learning and teaching themes. Tailored training is also being offered to various academic audiences, focusing on the different uses of the Queen's VLE by different academic disciplines.

Conclusion

The models of ICT training delivery outlined in this paper point to the importance of developing strategies that address both staff and student ICT skill levels. In the past, ICT skills delivery has largely been a voluntary undertaking. However, as ICT becomes more widely adopted within universities, it is imperative that all staff have the skills to function within the workplace, both for personal development and contribution to business objectives. From the student perspective, it is imperative that all students develop ICT learning and life skills that are embedded and practised in programmes of study. By implementing the institution-wide flexible and tailored training approach described in this paper, Queen's hopes to enable its staff and students to meet the demands of an ICT-rich business and learning environment.

Acknowledgements

We would like to acknowledge the help of Randall Thompson and Maria Lee in preparing this paper and in particular for allowing us to use extracts from the internal report *ICT Skills for Students* (Information Services, Queen's University Belfast, November 2001).

References

Department of Education Northern Ireland (1997) *A Strategy for Education Technology in Northern Ireland*, Belfast, DENI. Available at www.deni.gov.uk/about/ strategies/d_ets.htm. [Accessed 17 June 2003]

Education and Training Inspectorate (ETI) (2000) *Information and Communications Technology in Post-Primary Schools 1999–2000*, Department of Education Northern Ireland (DENI). Available at www.deni.gov.uk/inspection_services/ publications/surveys/ICT. [Accessed 17 June 2003]

Northern Ireland Council for Curriculum, Examinations and Assessment (1996) *Northern Ireland Curriculum (Education Order)*, Belfast, Department of Education Northern Ireland. Available at www.ccea.org.uk/nicurriculum.htm. [Accessed 17 June 2003]

12

Integrating information literacy into higher education

Lindsey Martin and Sylvia Williamson

Introduction

Much has been written about how information and communications technology has created an 'Information Revolution' as the quantity of information has expanded and the formats in which it is held have developed and changed. Libraries are no longer just bricks, mortar and collections of books; they are gateways to an almost infinite world of electronic information delivered over the internet. However, the information revolution has brought with it the curse of information overload. Information technology has made information superficially much easier to access but it leaves the user with the responsibility for deciding what is quality information and what is not. Students need to become critical consumers of information in order to avoid overload, and to develop new intellectual skills in order to manage information effectively and transform it into usable knowledge.

This collection of new intellectual skills has come to be known as 'information literacy'. According to Bruce (1999), this involves critical thinking, an awareness of personal and professional ethics, information evaluation, conceptualizing information needs, organizing information, interacting with information professionals and making effective use in problem solving, decision making and research. Information literacy is increasingly regarded as an essential workplace skill appropriate to today's workplace which has been described as, 'Knowledge driven and technology impacted; and where learning is lifelong, and change is the only constant' (Goad, 2002).

Higher education institutions are under increasing pressure to 'add value' to the student experience by the provision of opportunities to develop these skills as part of their education. The merging of teaching and learning with technology in higher education began because most institutions believed they had no choice (Ehrmann, 1996). Most of them believe that technology will give them the edge in competition for students and funding (Gilbert, 2000). The available evidence suggests, however, that students make a low level of use of the wide range of subscription and HE (higher education)-funded EIS (electronic information sources) available to the academic community. Student use is focused upon the web, e-mail and library catalogues and they use search engines and sites they are familiar with as the starting point for most academic queries as well as for their personal queries. However, they have not developed information literacy skills and do not appear to understand the nature of the EIS that they use (Rowley, 2000).

In this chapter we outline and evaluate the approach taken to integrating information literacy into discipline-based courses at Edge Hill College of Higher Education.

The local context

Edge Hill College is a medium-sized higher education institution in the northwest of England. It is an established education provider that has delivered higher education courses for over 100 years. Over recent years, the college has diversified the range of courses on offer to include programmes for undergraduate and postgraduate students, full time, part time and distance learning. The institution is well known for its teacher education provision and varied health portfolio as well as a diverse modular programme. There are currently 8000 students on undergraduate and diploma courses and a further 6000 undertaking continuing professional development and postgraduate courses. There is a large body of non-traditional students as a result of the college's widening participation initiatives. In 2000, the college successfully bid for an award from the HEFCE (Higher Education Funding Council for England) Good Management Practice fund. Its purpose was to explore the possibilities of partnerships, both internally and externally, in using ICT (information and communications technology) as a change agent within learning and teaching. There is a top-down commitment to embedding ICT at all levels within the institution.

IMS (Information and Media Services) at Edge Hill is a converged service comprising library, IT (information technology) and media facilities, resources training and support. The service also works closely with academic areas on the resource requirements of new courses and the embedding of information literacy skills within the curriculum. The service is actively represented on the academic committees that develop institutional strategies. The service aims to be proactive in marketing and promoting IMS and its resources. This is considered to be an essential aspect of the role of the liaison team along with building effective relationships with other central support services (such as Teaching and Learning Development, and Partnerships), academic teaching staff and external partners (such as further education colleges). IMS recognize that the way students learn and how learning opportunities are presented to them have changed. The service sees itself as a hybrid library and as a matter of policy now considers it essential that all new purchases of electronic information resources should be accessible from off-campus wherever possible.

Increasingly, staff within IMS have come to regard themselves as teachers or facilitators of learning and members of the new, multi-disciplinary academic teams that are developing within college. This is largely as a result of work done on disseminating the importance of information literacy skills, and participation as learners on internal courses usually available only to academic staff (such as the Postgraduate Certificate in Teaching and Learning in Higher Education, an eight-week WebCT module 'Developing and Delivering Teaching and Learning Online', and a module on the Postgraduate Certificate for Research Supervisors).

Delivering information skills

The delivery of information literacy to students has developed in an ad hoc and patchy way but has increased year on year. If you were to view the bulleted list below as a time-line, it would show the development of delivery as follows:

- Generic, voluntary workshops on using resources. This favoured a mechanistic or 'point and click' approach to skills development.
- As the marketing of learner support began to take effect, teaching staff would ask IMS learning support advisers to deliver short, single workshops within core modules. Attendance was still voluntary.
- The evaluation of workshop delivery and user feedback enabled learning support advisers to negotiate longer workshops within core modules with attendance compulsory and material linked to a piece of assessment. The aim was now to encourage students to develop the conceptual skills needed to search, sift, retrieve and evaluate information.
- With revalidation of new courses, some modules are currently integrating information literacy programmes. Attendance is compulsory and coursework is set and assessed by IMS staff who are full members of the academic course team.

In practice, this development has not been so linear. Examples of all the above workshop models and programmes continue to be delivered side by side.

Case Study 1: An introduction to critical analysis

This module is being held up within Edge Hill as an example of good practice in terms of encouraging Level 1 students to think critically. The module 'Critical Analysis: an Introduction' is a Level 1 module delivered within the joint and minor honours programme for Critical Criminology. The head of subject provided the impetus for IMS involvement with the module and the IMS role was embedded within the course planning documentation. The IMS contribution to the module has been tailored specifically for this module and IMS staff are considered to be part of the teaching team. Students are required to submit a portfolio that demonstrates their acquisition of information literacy skills and is assessed by the IMS staff delivering on the module. One particularly challenging aspect is that the module is also taught by teaching staff at one of Edge Hill's FE partner sites. Under the partnership agreement, the FE teaching staff must deliver the IMS contribution to the module also. We have developed a complete teaching pack for use by our FE partners.

IMS learner support staff deliver four workshops within the module. The skills that they aim to develop are based upon established models of information literacy and follow the SCONUL (Society of College, National and University Libraries) model closely. The focus is on developing transferable skills. Teaching methods favour a student-centred delivery that aims to encourage a deep approach to learning. The emphasis is on the processes involved in finding and evaluating information, not just the final product. Students complete self-audit questionnaires of their information literacy and IT skills at entry and exit to the programme. We use the entry forms to allocate the students into groups based on their perceived skills levels. The exit-point questionnaires indicated that all the students considered their skills levels to have improved through attending the workshops. To this end the IMS programme sought to spend time explaining the context or why information skills are important. The students are encouraged to construct their own knowledge through experiential learning. A variety of teaching methods have been used in order to facilitate student learning. In addition to the usual 'hands on' approach to workshops the team use group work, discussion and reflection. The IMS programme within the module is subject to a cycle of evaluation and review. IMS staff are encouraged to reflect both as individuals and as part of the team. Further feedback is obtained by student feedback forms, entry and exit self-audit questionnaires and most importantly, by the portfolios submitted.

This year we developed a WebCT unit to accompany the module. This did not deliver any teaching but provided access to course materials, resources and communication tools. Student feedback and WebCT usage statistics suggest that students would welcome further opportunities to engage with WebCT on this module.

This is the second year that this module has been delivered and the IMS team are growing in confidence. For the next academic year, it is planned to use the WebCT platform to deliver teaching and learning opportunities to the students. Student portfolios will include the keeping of a reflective journal to record their growing understanding of the conceptual skills that they are developing. There will also be explicit linking to a UK information literacy model that offers the potential for accreditation – perhaps the SCONUL model.

Case Study 2: PGCE Secondary English

This is an ICT module delivered exclusively by IMS learner support staff since 1999. The English subject team approached IMS with a request that they deliver ICT to postgraduate students. The emphasis would be on enhancing teaching and learning processes in English through use of ICT. The purpose was to ensure that prospective teachers were equipped with expertise in areas of the curriculum that reflect current professional needs and practice. The PGCE (Postgraduate Certificate in Education) is a requirement for graduates entering the school teaching profession. 'Secondary English' refers to the teaching of English in secondary schools.

A new module methodology was introduced for the 2000–1 academic year. As an integral part of the course, and in order to foster effective and efficient communication among trainees and with tutors, it was decided to use WebCT. The use of WebCT as the module platform was considered to be appropriate as 24 of the 36 weeks of the course are spent in partnership schools and colleges practising and developing teaching skills. It meant that students could always gain access to an up-to-date flexible learning environment, obtain course information and contact members of the group and tutors regardless of time and place.

The module contains seven face-to-face workshops delivered by IMS learner support staff:

- creation of a student home page in WebCT – students are encouraged to add information and links to useful resources on their home pages to encourage peer learning and support
- ICT and communication
- classroom resources – finding and evaluating resources and information that can be used in the classroom
- continuing professional development resources – finding and evaluating resources that will enable further development of teaching skills

- developing pupil literacy using technology
- lesson planning
- lesson delivery.

Complementary sessions were also laid on for students. These included online support sessions and videoconferencing with examiners.

The IMS course team aim to provide a responsive approach to student needs. To this end course developments have taken into account student feedback. Extra sessions have been laid on at the specific request of students. These included a speaker from Channel 4; sessions using media and AVA (audio visual aids) classroom equipment; and QTS (qualified teacher skills) skills test workshops.

Common factors of both case studies

The two case studies appear very different at first glance. However, it is possible to identify a range of common success factors. These are:

- *Top down support*: In each case the IMS teams were approached by subject leaders who could clearly perceive the benefits to the student experience of having information literacy embedded within the curriculum.
- *Effective collaborations and partnerships*: In both of the case studies, IMS are not offering bolt-on workshops. They have developed customized programmes developed in collaboration with teaching staff and other central support services staff.
- *Part of the academic course team*: The IMS teams delivering on these two modules are considered to be academic team members and are viewed as such by teaching staff and students alike.
- *Skills embedded into the curriculum*: Information literacy skills and electronic information sources have been embedded into the curriculum. All tasks and examples relate to specific course material.
- *Transferable skills*: In both cases the emphasis is on the development of conceptual skills that can be transferred to other resources and situations.
- *Commitment to evaluation and review*: The teams are willing to learn from the module participants and their own reflections in order to ensure that module delivery remains effective and up to date.

Conclusion

Information literacy models have provided us with an information literacy curriculum. At Edge Hill we have discovered that to be fully effective, this curriculum is most effectively assimilated when it is embedded within the subject curriculum. The generic training approach would appear to add little to the student experience and does not encourage experimentation with or increased use of electronic information sources. Student feedback suggests that they benefit from being taught by IMS learner support staff within modules. Teaching staff enjoy a privileged relationship with their students that develops over a period of time. When viewed as members of the academic team, learner support staff are able to develop student information literacy skills and encourage effective use of the growing portfolio of electronic information sources.

However, there are issues to consider if we are to avoid becoming victims of our own success. Most notably, how do we deal with the prospect of increased demand for our skills within the existing IMS staffing budget? Within learner support we are presently examining ways of dealing creatively with this issue. Some options we wish to test are: using a team approach to all delivery, where subject specialists within IMS will work with teaching staff to develop module materials that can then be delivered by the wider team; continuing to work on changing IMS staff perceptions that they are not teachers or facilitators of learning (this has in the past been a barrier to our further development in the area of information literacy delivery); and using VLEs (virtual learning environments) to facilitate learning and to offer support.

References

Bruce, C. S. (1999) Workplace Experiences of Information Literacy, *International Journal of Information Management*, **19** (1), 33–47.

Ehrmann, S. C. (1996) *Ivory Tower, Silicon Basement: transforming the College*, The TLT Group. Available at www.tltgroup.org/resources/Visions/ITSB.htm.

Gilbert, S. W. (2000) *A New Vision Worth Working Toward: connected vision and collaborative change*, The TLT Group. Available at www.tltgroup.org/resources/vwwt.html.

Goad, T. W. (2002) *Information Literacy and Workplace Performance*, Westport, CT, Quorum.

Rowley, J. (2000) JISC *User Behaviour and Monitoring Framework*. Available at www.jisc.ac.uk/pub00/m&e_repl.html.

13

The Information Commons: strategies for integration

Susan Beatty

Introduction

The Information Commons at the University of Calgary Library is an integrated service facility, which provides an environment for teaching, learning and practising both information technology and information literacy skills. A dynamic vision of service to students prompted two units from the University of Calgary, IR (Information Resources), of which the library is a part, and IT (Information Technologies) to combine energies to create a unique service unit focusing on what students need to succeed in the information age; new skills, access to information, a flexible facility, and help when they need it. Integration and convergence of services focused on the user underlie the models of planning, service development and service delivery for the Information Commons. This chapter discusses the background of the Information Commons project, the planning process, the key elements of the service design and delivery, and the results. It describes a strategy of integration and convergence and its influence on the user's learning.

Background

The Information Commons plan did not spring fully formed into the mind of an administrator or of any one person. Previous to the development of the plan, the focus of the University community was on strategic transformation. As a part of the examination, IR and IT produced four significant documents which underlie the development of the Information Commons plan. The *Technology Integration Plan* (1997) discussed learner benefits that could result from the integration of IR and IT. The Library Task Force (1997) and the Library of the

Future Task Force (1998) focused on the impact of the changing information environment on the library and on the user. Coincidentally, and finally, during the planning and creation of the Information Commons, the Learning Support Needs report (Kearns and Scharnau, 1999), a collaborative research initiative between the library and Student and Academic Services, reported on the support students need in order to learn. Overall this report notes that, 'Learners will not be successful if they: do not possess adequate technological and information literacy skills; do not have adequate access to technology'. The Library of the Future Task Force Report as well as the other reports and related activities set the stage for change and collaboration. The Learning Support Needs report confirmed the direction: focus on the user.

By 1998 it was obvious that there was a need to improve the space and service on campus devoted to student learning. IR and IT were in alignment in their concentration on the user and the user's learning needs. Information literacy instruction became a key element of the library's endeavours. The librarians began to successfully promote information literacy instruction to faculty. Instruction occurred more frequently but the librarians were limited by the inadequate facilities for instruction on campus and, more specifically, in the library. Information technology instruction for students did not exist. Students acquired the skills they needed sporadically and randomly.

When the Alberta government implemented a grant programme for technology initiatives, the library was in a situation to take advantage. It would not have been as ready to present the proposal for funding if it had not been on the continuous track of researching learner needs related to both the physical environment and service delivery. Furthermore, by the library keeping the major stakeholders on campus (administration, faculty and students) informed throughout the pre-planning process, they were able to lend significant support to the project when the funding opportunity became available.

The planning process

The three phases to our planning process were concept development, design and implementation.

Concept development phase: What was unique or useful about our process?

Because of their common interests and previous collaborations, IR and IT collaborated from the beginning on the new project. The directors of both IR and IT participated in the conceptualization and visioning processes. Such collaboration and support was a major element of our success. Primary stakeholders need to participate from the beginning of the planning process to ensure success. We wanted as many interests as possible represented at the table. We were inclusive during our concept development phase. Representatives from various units across campus attended the concept development meetings. The discussions originally centred on what 'we' or in some cases 'I' wanted. The real turn-around in the visioning came when the focus turned to what the user wanted and needed. Planning became clearer and less political when the user became the touchstone.

A planning document is vital to making a vision come alive. We used the following vision, mission and outcomes from the plan as our guide:

Our vision: To provide the space, technology and expertise needed to support the scholarly use of information resources and act as the focal point for information services.
Our mission: To be the core facility for the provision of information resources and information technology for scholars at the University of Calgary.

The *outcomes* on which we based our plan were clear and user focused and would allow users to:

* acquire information literacy and information technology skill
* acquire information resources
* acquire help
* access various spaces/technology to complete the work.

Design phase: Acquisition and dissemination of information

One of our first steps was to identify best practice sites and conduct site visits. A team of three visited existing information commons facilities at the University of Toronto, Purdue University and the University of Southern California. These visits helped us see the influence of design on service; it helped us understand what could work for us and what would not work. This aspect of planning should not be downplayed. Most significantly at this point we hired a project manager. The manager's responsibility was to concentrate on communication, effective consultation and decision making.

The communication strategy for the Information Commons project was to:

* create an internal strategy for primary internal stakeholders directly involved in the implementation of the project
* design an awareness campaign aimed at primary and secondary internal and external audiences (university community)

- develop a training programme for staff directly and indirectly involved in the service provision of the Information Commons (library and IT staff).

Other considerations in the planning process included hiring a good architect and design team to work with us to develop the design according to identified needs and outcomes. Our architects related well to the needs of the users. Their actions mirrored and enhanced our consistent focus on the user. Further information regarding the planning documents, communication plan, press releases and photographs are available on the Information Commons website at www.ucalgary.ca/IR/infocommons/.

Implementation phase: Preparing staff and space

During implementation, and as a result of following the communication plan, all the stakeholders (IR and IT) were involved and informed. The result was ownership. The stakeholders understood the vision and mission and anticipated the outcomes.

The new Information Commons Service Desk would be the main reference desk for the library as well as the main technical assistance desk. In addition to continuing to provide reference service from the service desk, the library staff would also provide basic technical assistance. Technical staff (student assistants and technical specialists) would be available to answer more complicated and/or lengthy requests, in addition to providing basic orientation to the library resources. The user would perceive an integrated service. To successfully implement this service design, library and IT staff were taught their new skills prior to the opening of the Information Commons.

Service design and delivery

The goals of our plan formed the basis of our service design and delivery. The elements of our plan include expertise, instruction, space, technology and access. The unique element of our service delivery plan is the nature of the collaboration between IT and IR.

Expertise

It takes a great mix of information specialists and technology specialists to meet the learning and information needs of our users. The information specialists provide reference assistance, informal one-on-one instruction during the reference transaction and in-depth reference, as well as basic technical assistance. Student assistants, called *navigators*, provide assistance and informal instruction with technology problems. Technical specialists provide back-up for more complex problems.

Instruction model

Because there is no required core curriculum in IT or information literacy, we developed a model of instruction that gives students the opportunity to develop these core skills. Instruction and training specialists from IR and IT work together and/or separately with the students and faculty to bring information literacy and information technology literacy to the users.

Technology instruction sessions are regularly scheduled throughout the fall and winter terms primarily in the Information Commons. Students attend on a drop-in basis. Information literacy instruction is provided in response to a faculty member's request as part of the specific course instruction. General information literacy instruction is also a part of the model. We offer courses on basic and advanced internet searching, and library research, outside of the course-based instruction, on a drop-in basis. General instruction is an alternative way of offering literacy instruction for those students who may not encounter a course-based opportunity. Attendees tend to be older, returning, undergraduate or graduate students.

Because information literacy skills acquisition is not part of the curriculum, promotion of the instruction is key to awareness and good response. Our course-based instruction is promoted between librarian or IT instructor and course instructor/faculty member. We also actively promote all of our non-course-based instruction, both IT and information literacy on the web at www.ucalgary.ca/InformationCommons/freetrain.html.

At our peak instruction times we have offered over 30 hours of instruction per week in each of the Information Commons classrooms. This is a mix of course-based, productivity (i.e. software) and general instruction.

Space

Our focus is on creating the self-sufficient learner fully capable of using the technology, and of accessing and assessing information. Our design promotes and facilitates formal and informal learning. We designed the facility so that instruction and collaborative learning could take place throughout. The service desk facilitates one-on-one assistance. The layout and design features promote group work and learning. For example, the workstations' unique curved design accommodates one to four users at a time; collaborative workrooms invite groups to work together in quiet business-like rooms. The design is purposefully flexible and fluid. Students choose what works for them.

The formal learning occurs in the Information Commons classrooms which are fully wired for video and data projection. The state-of-the-art classrooms are used for hands-on information literacy and productivity instruction. When not being used for instruction, the classrooms are open for student use.

Because the space itself is welcoming, open and safe with colourful walls, windows and glass, carpeting and artwork, the Information Commons has become a social centre as well as a learning centre. It is a place to be on campus. We have accomplished our goal of attracting students to the Commons to learn.

Technology

Having reliable and functional technology is an important factor for the users. We have the best publicly available PCs on campus – all with the same general download, Microsoft Office 2000, all with internet access. There are five networked printers and one colour printer. Technology support is always available from the IT staff who provide the one-on-one assistance for software and printer problems and the library staff who provide the hardware support, and is available to view online at www.ucalgary.ca/informationcommons/software. html.

Access

To foster learning and to allow for maximum use of our facility, users have access to the Information Commons 24/5 during fall and winter terms. Not only is the Commons open, but it is always staffed so that the user can always get assistance when needed. In Winter 2001 access was extended to 24/7 during the last month of the term. Response to the initiative was positive. It is not uncommon to see 40–50 students working at their computers in the early morning hours, and, during the final month of the term, this number can double. Access, good technology and assistance provide a level playing field for the users. All have the same opportunity to succeed.

Collaboration

Once we developed a vision of the facility and the service, the key question became how would IR and IT collaborate? The collaboration has been worked out over time. IR initially brought staffing, facility and equipment. IT brought equipment and technical expertise. As noted previously, the significance of having the right people at the table to make the decisions cannot be downplayed. It makes co-operation and collaboration easier.

Integration and collaboration remain ongoing. One key method is through membership and participation in an operational committee called the ICOPS (Information Commons Operations Team). ICOPS membership is made up of representatives from all stakeholder groups in the Commons. The Head of the Information Commons chairs this committee. The IT staff who work at the Commons report to IT. Additionally, IT and IR share the cost for the student technical assistants. The Information Commons is a complex organizational unit with a diversity of interests, priorities and resources.

Having a common goal and common process helps overcome the organizational and cultural differences. IR and IT remain flexible in their sharing of resources and services. Ultimately, we are successful because we created the place, we put the right people into the place, and we focus on the service.

Results of the service model

All of our activity measures indicate that the essential aspects of our service, including the instruction, are being well utilized (see www.ucalgary.ca/informationcommons/facts.html). We know, for example, that our reference questions have increased 12% during the first two years of operation. This is contrary to the trend at most academic libraries where the number of questions is decreasing. We believe that there are at least two factors influencing this trend: good service – our users tell us that we do a great job of providing excellent service and, there are more users in the library than ever before. On an average day there can be at least 5000 users coming and going through the Commons.

Table 13.1 *Activity measures before and after creation of the Information Commons*

Activity	1998/9	1999/00	2000/1	Change, %
Library reference queries	48,043	59,742	53,959	12
Computer/technology queries	N/A	18,360	20,101	100
Information literacy attendance	4,920	10,873	12,204	148

The most significant increase has been in the number of course-specific information literacy instruction sessions, a result of an ever-increasing emphasis on integrating information literacy with course instruction and the availability of the Information Commons classrooms. Over 3200 students have attended the productivity courses in two years. The instructors monitor attendance and user feedback and as a result have increased the number and variety of courses during that same time period. In the last two terms, for example, we have added intermediate courses in Word, PowerPoint and Excel as well as Netscape

Composer. Instruction is based on what is available on the desktop for the students to use in the Information Commons.

Maintaining contact with users helps keep the user perspective front and centre in service delivery. A feedback survey has been posted on the library web page since the Commons opened and is available to view at www.ucalgary.ca/informationcommons/feedback.html. The latest results indicate that the users are very satisfied with our service, facility and assistance. They are not as happy with waiting in line to use a computer or book a collaborative workroom. That they sometimes have to do so is a reflection of the high level of use of the Commons.

It is primarily from the users' comments that we really receive the full understanding of what they value about the Information Commons. The following comments are representative of students' views:

> The Information Commons is a terrific idea. It is great to have staff available to help with assignments and computer difficulties when I would normally be frustrated at home. P.S. I think that the courses that are being put on (Library skills and productivity) are outstanding. Thank you.

> I was stuck on my computer science assignment as I missed two weeks of lab as I was ill. I thought I would fail it, but a [student navigator] at the info desk spent his time in explaining to me the concepts and helping me through my problems . . . every time he came to help me he never showed any signs of frustration whatsoever . . . very kind and caring individual. I finally finished my assignment and I think I will get an A. Thanks.

Learning

The main result to focus on is: is the student learning? The answer, we believe, is a resounding yes. We believe that the students' learning opportunities are better because our service is integrated. Course-based instruction, general instruction and information technology instruction activity continue to increase. An increase in information literacy instruction has heightened the awareness of library resources. The result is increased use of those resources – circulation activity, database activity and question activity have increased. More students are engaged in the learning process in the Information Commons as a result of hands-on instruction, good access to resources and help when they need it.

The key to any successful initiative is flexibility, responsiveness and innovation. We continue to develop new ways to integrate our service. The next wave of instruction is likely to focus on the integration of information literacy and information technology to meet the learner's needs in a more immediate way. The following story is illustrative of this trend.

Normally, information literacy instruction is one event within a course as arranged between the librarian and the faculty member. Productivity instruction can occur outside of the classroom on a drop-in basis or within a course. More and more, however, the skills instructors and the faculty member are beginning to realize that the best results for the learner occur when instruction is integrated so that the learner learns where and when there is an immediate need to know. To discuss how integrated instruction affects the faculty member and the learner I went to talk to an instructor to get her feedback on an example in her course. Her students had received combined instruction from three instructors: how to find the information, from a librarian; how to use Excel to organize the information, from an IT instructor; and techniques, purpose and rationale of organizing and presenting information, from the course instructor. Following are her comments:

> What the library does I used to do. I moved to the library because of the good instruction facilities. Previously, I sent the students to go and learn as best they could. The instruction coming from the Commons is able to meet a timed need – during lecture time and facilitates what I do. The skills have improved for the students. Students know now what to ask – they know what they need to know exists. I am there to step in – to make a point about the instruction.

This example of integrated instruction would have been more difficult to create without the Commons being in existence. The librarian and the IT instructors work side by side. The extension in collaboration was a natural next step. This model of instruction is new for us. It speaks to the need for continuous efforts in integrated instruction aimed at supporting learning.

Conclusion

The Information Commons at the University of Calgary is an integrated service facility designed to support the learning needs of the user. Information Resources and Information Technologies began their collaborative relationship with a vision of creating a unique service environment where the user is able to acquire new skills and have access to information and help when they need it, in an environment that is creative, stimulating and welcoming. Success has come through paying attention to the planning process, the user and the people who provide the service. The collaboration never ends. We have many challenges ahead. How will we keep ahead of the crest in instruction? What future skills will the instructors as well as the learners need? How can we continue to engage the learner in acquiring new skills? How will advances in technology affect the space, the service and the user? Sustainability is also a real issue. It is vital to the success of the learner to continuously improve the facility, technology and service. And finally, what will the future hold for the further integration of IR and IT? One thing, however, is sure: we will find ways to sustain that which we have created. If we keep to the lessons we have learned so far, no doubt we will continue to meet and exceed users' needs and expectations.

References

Kearns, J. and Scharnau, K. (1999) *Learning Support Needs: what University of Calgary students need to be more effective learners*, University of Calgary. Available at www.ucalgary.ca/library/plans/learning needs/summary.html.

Library of the Future Task Force (1998) *Library of the Future Task Force: accelerating the Transformation of Information Resources final report*, University of Calgary. Available at www.ucalgary.ca/library/lftf/finalreport.

Library Task Force (1997) *Final Report*, University of Calgary. Available at www.ucalgary.ca/library/ltf/report.

Technology Task Force (1997) *Technology Integration Plan*, University of Calgary. Available at www.ucalgary.ca/~ispage/TIP.

14

One size fits all?
The Iliad experience

Susanne Hodges and Gareth J. Johnson

Introduction

The effective use of information underpins all aspects of academic life. Students are being encouraged to carry out work that requires independent research and to produce assignments using a wide variety of information resources. Yet many students are ill equipped for such work. They may possess comprehensive IT (information technology) skills but lack the ability to handle and evaluate a wide range of information. This chapter details the initiation, evolution of and challenges faced by the University of York information literacy programme, Iliad (Information Literacy in All Departments). It considers the benefits of providing a generic rather than subject-based programme and aims to provide useful information for those wishing to set up a similar programme in higher educational institutions.

The underlying ethos of Iliad for University (the programme includes a more advanced strand called Iliad for Work, with which this paper is not concerned) has remained unchanged for the past six years. However, it can be extremely challenging to provide a programme to suit all levels of ability and knowledge, given that students arrive with varying skills levels. Over the years, Iliad has had to tackle a number of issues, namely:

* how to provide an introductory generic information literacy course while still challenging those students who possess some basic information literacy skills
* how to increase the complexity of content but remain true to Iliad's underlying philosophy of bringing all students up to a baseline of IT and information literacy competency

- how to address a gradual increase in average baseline student skills
- how to address an increase in transferable skills training within academic departments
- how to address developments in online educational environments.

At the end of 2001 the programme was reviewed and the question asked, Do we still need a generic foundation information literacy programme?

Background information

In the early 1990s University of York staff in the Computing Service and Library became aware that many incoming students had problems with information handling and with the use of IT tools. In 1994 an Information Literacy Course Designer was appointed. Her brief was to research, design and develop materials for a course that would teach information-handling skills, including retrieving, processing and presenting information in its many forms. She was to report to a steering group consisting of the Computing Service Director and Head of User Services, subject librarians, Director of the York Award Programme (York's transferable skills award) and a student representative. The programme was to be aimed primarily at undergraduates but would be available to postgraduates, as required. For marketing purposes it was promoted as Iliad. The stated aim of the programme was to enable students to become proficient in retrieving, processing and presenting information in its many forms. The objectives were to provide students with basic, transferable information-handling skills to enable them to be more effective in their studies and to provide an awareness of the potential implications of continuing developments in information technology to prepare students for future employment. These aims and objectives are maintained to this day.

After discussions had taken place with academic staff in a wide variety of departments, a standard, generic 12-hour programme was designed. An assessment was designed and a University-validated certificate was to be awarded for successful completion of this. A workbook and tutor-led approach was chosen to best facilitate self-paced learning. In addition the programme was offered via two routes – a taught course or self-study. The self-study route was targeted at those students who felt more confident with IT but still wanted additional skills.

The programme was piloted on a compulsory basis in the History, Chemistry and Economics departments in the autumn term 1995, with 300 participants taught in single subject groups. The following year the programme was launched University wide. It was financed through a variety of routes including sponsorship from Arthur Andersen Consulting, a negotiated deal with York College of Further and Higher Education and support from the University. In recent years this sponsorship and funding has been lost and students now pay £15.50 to take the programme, with the Computing Service funding any shortfall.

In 1998 the Iliad for Work programme was launched. This consists of a menu of courses – Database Systems, Design of Web Pages and Office Skills. In 2000 Designing Computer Graphics was added. Like Iliad for University, Iliad for Work courses are assessed and a certificate is awarded. The Iliad for Work programme is a much smaller initiative and has not suffered the challenges that have beset Iliad for University.

The Iliad for University programme

In September of each year incoming students are sent a registration leaflet which includes a list of questions, such as do you know how to save files on to a networked file storage? If they answer no to more than two questions, they are advised to participate. Sending registration leaflets to home addresses has proved to be an effective marketing strategy. In addition, Iliad is promoted in some departments during induction week. The extent to which some departments actively encourage students to take the programme varies.

The content and level of the programme is constantly reviewed and major updating takes place as a result of technological changes, e.g. the change from the Corel Suite to Microsoft Office. The original format of the programme has remained unchanged but has been reduced to eight hours, consisting of four two-hour units: Computing at York, Researching and Evaluating Information Sources, Word Processing for Academic Purposes and Presenting Information Using a Computer. All units are generic except the Researching and Evaluating Information Sources session, which contains subject-specific examples. This workbook is written by the Iliad Liaison Librarian, with subject examples provided by the appropriate subject librarians, who deliver this session free of charge. Tutors for the other three sessions are bought in and are from a variety of backgrounds, e.g. postgraduates, junior lecturers, adult education teachers.

Each session is supported by workbooks which contain worked examples that gradually increase in complexity. Students are advised to omit sections with which they are familiar and to concentrate on new areas. For the duration of the programme, a weekly help session is provided and students may also call at the Iliad office or, if appropriate, the Library Enquiry Desk for help and advice. Student feedback has resulted in exercises and the assessment being reformulated to make them more relevant to students' current course work. Originally, students were given subject-related topics to research and evaluate for the assessment. Now they are encouraged to take a topic of their own choice relevant to their current studies.

A University-validated certificate is awarded for successful completion. Students may also gain points toward the transferable skills qualification, the York Award. The assessment, which is optional, requires that students describe and critically evaluate their strategy for researching a topic of their choice and includes citation of references for books, journals and web pages. Presentation of work using a word-processor is also marked. Assessments are marked by tutors, with students having to fulfil eight out of ten key criteria.

Delivery and participation

The programme runs from Week Three to Six of the ten-week autumn term. A Computing Service classroom is block booked for four weeks and the two-hour sessions run back to back from 9.15 to 5.15, Monday to Friday. Students tend to be taught in mixed-subject groups but some departments block this, making it easier to tailor sessions to specific-subject interests. Some departments make different arrangements with Iliad. For instance, the Archaeology Department purchases Iliad materials and delivers the programme itself. Other departments, such as Psychology, provide their own courses, taught by departmental staff, based partly or entirely on Iliad materials. A further option is for departments to take parts of Iliad and build them into their own transferable skills modules. Several departments, such as Biology, run skills modules that overlap with the content of the Iliad programme.

Overall, there has been a slight decrease in the percentage uptake. Around 600 students signed up for Iliad in 2001–2, which represented almost a third of the intake. If numbers of students from the departments that buy into Iliad are included, coverage was nearer to 50%. Because of resource levels (mainly availability of computing rooms) it would be difficult to accommodate more in the taught sessions. However, all students are able to take the materials for self-study.

The course is evaluated by means of feedback sheets filled in at the end of the course. Additionally students are invited to take part in focus group discussions. Iliad tutors meet after the course to share comments and exchange observations. In this way a complete picture of the course's strengths and weaknesses can be built up to inform the course's development and evolution.

Iliad staff consists of the Information Literacy Course Manager, who deals with strategic planning, day-to-day administration, creating and producing course materials, booking tutors and booking demonstrators. A half-time assistant provides clerical help. The Course Manager reports to the Iliad Steering Group and to the Coordinating Group for Supplementary Programmes. The latter Group reports to the University's Teaching Committee. Any major changes in course materials have to be approved by the Teaching Committee. The programme has faced several challenges over the past few years and, as a result, a review was carried out at the end of 2001. The review was conducted and written by Debra Fayter, former Iliad Programme Manager, University of York.

The major challenge has been how to provide a foundation information literacy course that still challenges more IT-competent – but less confident – students. With the increasing level of IT teaching in schools it was felt that the numbers of participants might fall dramatically. There has been a slight decrease in numbers but generally they remain at around 600 – which, as the numbers of incoming students have risen, means that the overall percentage of uptake has dropped. Feedback has shown that many students still have a low level of experience and a self-perceived need for skills – last year a traditional student admitted that she had never used the internet before. There may have been a gradual increase in average baseline skills but there are many non-traditional students who have few or no skills. Moreover student self-perception is often flawed and a student may be competent at IT but have few information literacy skills.

Not all students complete the course and this needs to be addressed. It could be that the course is too easy – feedback showed that 20% of those who completed the course felt that it was. Conversely, this still means that the course enjoys an 80% satisfaction rating. Despite some students finding the course too easy, 20% overall regularly fail the assessment.

Another challenge has been that only a small number of students complete the assessment which, importantly, is designed to make students reflect upon their information literacy skills. This is to be partly addressed in future by embedding the assessment as a task in the Word Processing for Academic Purposes session. Those who then wish to gain the certificate may develop their work to hand in.

Over the years there has grown a clear tension between three separate groups of students: those with few or no skills, those with competency but who want to know about the University of York network and those who only need bits of the programme. The recent review attempted to address this issue and its findings will be discussed later in this chapter.

The nominal fee is not thought to dissuade students from signing up. However, charging does mean that the programme cannot be advertised as 'key' or 'fundamental' to university study.

Generic or subject-based?

At York there has been a rise in departmental subject-based skills training. As discussed earlier, some departments have developed their courses using Iliad materials. However, other departments have developed their own skills modules, with no reference to Iliad, and some departments provide no skills training at all. There are concerns here over duplication of work, not to mention equal educational opportunities issues. There have been problems with overlapping materials and some students have resented paying for Iliad when their department provides such training free. However other students have commented that they were glad to have Iliad to take them along at a more sustainable pace.

The advantages of offering Iliad as a separate information literacy programme are:

- Students can choose to attend Iliad sessions that fit in with their timetables.
- Students work at their own pace through the workbooks and have support from help sessions, the Library Enquiry Desk or the Iliad office, if necessary.
- It gives students an opportunity to work outside their departments and to meet other students.
- Iliad provides a safety-net for students. The learning environment is supportive and separate from the department, so students feel less inhibited about asking basic questions.
- There is currently no alternative virtual learning environment at York to deliver such a programme. Also a virtual learning environment is not seen to be appropriate for an introductory course as the staff and student interaction is seen to be beneficial for students, allowing them to build up confidence and feel comfortable using different technologies.
- Departments may pick up part or all of the course materials and fit them into their own teaching.

Disadvantages include:

- The programme could be by-passed by students seeing it as non-compulsory and non-academic, or by students who do not recognize their own skills gaps.
- There is some overlap with departmental teaching.
- The quality of teaching if provided by departmental staff, as opposed to the usual Iliad tutors, could be variable.
- It can be difficult to get the right person on to the right course.

The future

The recent review of Iliad made the following recommendations:

* Alongside the main programme, each module should also be offered separately, so that those students who have specific skills gaps can select individual units according to need.
* A rolling programme to run all year round should be initiated.
* A closer dialogue with departments should be instigated, to clarify the role of Iliad in departmental teaching.
* The emphasis should be on information literacy skills rather than information technology skills. This would encourage students not to race through the workbooks and would ensure that they saw the relevance of the course to their studies.

At a strategic level, it is essential that the programme gains University acceptance, is fully integrated into the University structure and is seen as a core service. A collaborative and integrated approach to curriculum design and delivery must be encouraged, based on close co-operation between the Computing Service, Library, departments, and career and transferable skills programmes. On a practical level, ensuring availability of appropriate teaching rooms and facilities for producing printed materials, etc. is fundamental.

It is essential that generic information literacy skills required during the degree programme be highlighted as part of a Teaching and Learning strategy at an institutional, faculty and departmental level. The information thus gleaned should be used by the course provider, who should develop a range of effective broad brush and short courses that are part of a rolling programme.

It is important that a departmental contact is established. Departments should also ensure that students are directed to appropriate skills training courses. It is worth noting here that Iliad has been significantly instrumental in aiding departments at York to score highly in the Learning Support section of Subject Review.

Finding appropriate accreditation can be difficult but is necessary to make the programme appeal to students.

Finally, it is essential that the programme is branded and marketed effectively.

Conclusion

Clearly the original need for the Iliad programme still exists, both for some traditional students ('before I came to university I'd never used the internet'), for overseas/non-traditional students and for those with computing experience but not at university standard. However, a 'one size' course is no longer viable in that it cannot meet either departmental or individual students' changing information literacy needs. Nonetheless a large amount of generic material is still of value to students, provided enough contextual learning material is embedded within the course.

We may not have it exactly right at York but many students are very grateful that the programme is available. The student alternative prospectus in 2000 wrote of Iliad:

> If you come to York go on this course. Iliad trains you how to use the network and some of its programs and is vital to your success at the University. Communication is increasingly done by email and most tutors expect word processed essays, so for a mere eight hours of teaching you can benefit a great deal. This is a genuine student view and everyone who didn't do this course doesn't know how valuable it could have been.

Note: Parts of this paper are based on the Big Blue project report on Iliad. To see the full report visit www.leeds.ac.uk/bigblue/.

15

Promoting content – achieving learning goals

Ruth Stubbings and Alison McNab

Introduction

Library users in HE (higher education) institutions have greater access to electronic information than at any previous time. Although some students are quick to grasp the opportunities that this has opened up, for others it has created barriers and confusion (Kirby et al., 1998). The challenge for information professionals in academic libraries is to ensure that both students and academic staff can use electronic information effectively. This chapter discusses why barriers may exist in the delivery and take-up of IST (information skills training) sessions and how libraries can overcome them.

Barriers to successful IST

Herring (1997) believes that the growth of electronic information has led to changes in student learning and has created the need for good study skills, including information searching. The majority of library staff would agree with this and would argue that the need to provide guidance in the use of electronic resources, and to develop critical thinking skills, has never been greater. However this is at a time when modularity has made it more difficult to embed information skills training into the curriculum, there has been a growth in the diversity of student backgrounds, and students' attitudes to information has changed. Thus it can be difficult to provide IST and motivate students to attend or actively take part in training sessions.

Research projects in the UK such as JUSTEIS (JISC Usage Surveys: Trends in Electronic Information Service) (Rowley, 2000) and IMPEL (Ray and Day, 1998) feel that major barriers to the effective use of electronic information are time and information retrieval skills. The JUSTEIS project goes on to recommend that academic librarians should take a more active role in the promotion of electronic information and deliver more IST. The IMPEL project states that IST should be embedded into curriculum and delivered at time of need. 'If students are not encouraged to use electronic resources by their tutors, and information skills training occurs outside of the curriculum, students will be less likely to make use of electronic resources for academic purposes.' This is wise advice, but during the 1990s most HE institutions moved to semesters and modularity. For many libraries this had a major impact on the IST that they offered, as fewer academics were prepared to put time aside in their modules for what they considered to be non-core activities. Thus it has become more difficult to embed IST into academic programmes because of the reluctance of academic staff.

In addition, many universities have begun to widen access to their courses. This means that the student population is increasingly diverse in terms of age, academic achievement, IT (information technology) skills and information literacy. Despite there being a growth in IT competency, we would argue that the view expressed by Ray and Day (1998) – that there is a great difference between student capabilities – is still valid, perhaps even more so today. In nearly every class you will have IT 'experts' and 'beginners' – in fact 'beginners' today often need more guidance as they feel inadequate amongst all the 'experts'. Libraries therefore continue to find it difficult to pitch the content of their IST courses to their audience.

Linked to this is the change in student attitude towards information – a large proportion of students now feel very confident in finding information and do not see the need to attend IST courses. This is verified by survey work: Lubans (2000) discovered that students do not wish to attend training sessions on how to search for information, while an increased use and reliance of the web to support academic study was reported in 2001 (Cyberatlas, 2001). These same trends can be seen in the UK. In 2000 Loughborough University reviewed its induction procedures and student attitudes towards key skills. Gadd et al. (2001) discovered that 90% of the students surveyed felt that information skills were important, but that these skills would improve as a natural outcome of their degree. The JUSTEIS (Armstrong et al., 2001) and IMPEL (Ray and Day, 1998) projects confirmed that many students feel confident in their information-searching skills.

Most academic librarians, however, feel that students do not search the internet effectively or take the time to select appropriate resources. Feeling confident in using the internet and electronic databases is very different from being competent in searching them. For example, the JUSTEIS project (Rowley, 2000) found that, despite being heavily promoted, subject gateways were rarely used by academic staff and students. Pedley (2001) reviewed reports on searching strategies used on the internet and discovered that most web users type in short queries, rarely use Boolean operators and look at the first ten results they find.

Ray and Day (1998) and Lubans (1999) claim that students tend to develop information-gathering skills through trial and error and from their friends. JUSTEIS (Rowley, 2000) discovered that students often see their lecturers as the 'first point of contact' in relation to information gathering rather than the library, while D'Esposito and Gardner (1999) found the students they surveyed had not considered asking library staff for help. What does this all mean? Well, a large proportion of the student population tend not to realize that they lack knowledge concerning how to access quality resources and services and do not wish to take part in IST courses.

The Loughborough experience

Although it is recognized that it is better to embed IST into degree programmes (Walton and Edwards, 1998), as students then understand the relevance of information skills to their degree, the library has found it difficult to encourage this to take place. At Loughborough University, many academic librarians have found that only a small percentage of programmes (less than 10%) allow for the delivery of information skills in modules. Most of the customized IST delivered within a module is short in length (an hour or two) and the learning outcomes are often not formally assessed by either Library staff or academics. The good news is that this type of IST accounts for 62% of the IST delivered by the Library during 2000 and 2001, but as stated before it is to only a select number of students. To ensure that all students have equal access to IST librarians have developed training schedules that students can attend if they wish. 'Lunchtime in the Library' sessions were launched in 1996; they take place for an hour over lunchtime and outline how to find information in certain subject areas. 'DotM' (Database of the Month) training sessions, launched in 2000, last an hour and a half, with time for hands-on activities and concentrate on how to search particular databases. The DotM sessions have proved quite successful in terms of attendance and feedback from the participants. Why have they been successful? We believe it is because of the way the sessions are designed, delivered and advertised.

Herring (1997) argues that 'students expect the same standard of teaching from librarians as they do from lecturers'. Loughborough University librarians believe this to be true. All academic librarians (with subject liaison responsibilities) at Loughborough University conduct IST sessions. The academic librarians are encouraged to develop their presentation and teaching skills by attending training programmes run by the Library and the Staff Development

Department. Two of the academic librarians are members of the Institute of Learning and Teaching. A subset of these staff form the IST Group which provides strategic leadership and reviews IST activities. For example each year they produce guidelines on how to develop and deliver IST. All of this experience was drawn together when the Library was planning the introduction of the DotM training sessions. The IST Group spent a considerable amount of time discussing the aims of the sessions, the audience, presenters, delivery methods and how the courses should be evaluated.

The aim of the DotM training sessions was to ensure that the databases the library purchased were well utilized, both in terms of how they were searched and in how often they were searched. After a lot of discussions it was agreed that the main audience for the courses would most probably be undergraduate and postgraduate students. Academic staff would be encouraged to attend the sessions, but it was recognized that possibly only a few would because of time constraints and other commitments. Both library staff and publishers were invited to deliver the training sessions.

The next stage was to develop a training schedule and develop guidance for the presenters. The IST group deliberately chose to focus on databases that were new or were being under utilized. This meant there was varied attendance, but on average 15 participants (some courses have been very popular with over 40 people registering, while others have only attracted ten).

Using learning outcomes

Beard and Hartley (1984) advise that you should plan your teaching based on learning outcomes. To assist all presenters a general set of learning outcomes were developed. At the end of the session students will be able to:

- access the databases through the Library's web pages and/or the Library's network
- search the database by combining keywords
- select appropriate references and mark them
- save/print/e-mail the results of their searches
- find out whether the references are in stock in the Library.

As mentioned earlier, DotM sessions are delivered either by Library staff or by the publishers of the databases. All presenters are given a copy of the learning outcomes above and can amend them to suit their presenting styles, the content of the databases and the needs of the participants. To help students understand the training sessions it is important to communicate the learning outcomes to the students (Race and Brown, 1993). Some of the presenters negotiate the learning outcomes with the participants at the beginning of a class.

Activities and materials

Following Beard and Hartley's (1984) advice the IST group decided to include a variety of activities in the 90-minute DotM sessions. Typically the training sessions tend to be divided into three: a presentation, a demonstration and hands-on activities. It is hoped that the variety of activity will help to renew the students' interest (Brown and Atkins, 1988). Although presenters can adapt this, a strong request for at least half an hour (if not longer) for hands-on activities is made as Cox (1995) and Kirby et al. (1998) suggest this is good practice. In addition, feedback from participants shows this part of the session is the most popular. During the hands-on part of the course, presenters attempt to speak to each participant to provide individualized assistance.

Supporting material is provided by print handouts on the day (these are either Library or publisher guides on how to search an individual database) and activity sheets if the presenter believes these are appropriate. Copies of the supporting material are also placed on the University's electronic learning environment, LEARN, and are linked to from the Library web pages that advertise the training sessions.

Promotion, administration and evaluation

As stated earlier, motivating staff and students to attend and participate in library courses is hard work. DotM training sessions are advertised by both the Library and the University's Staff Development unit using a variety of means. Staff Development includes the sessions on their print and electronic schedules delivered to all University staff. The Library advertises to staff and students through print flyers and posters (placed in the Library and departments), the Library's web pages and e-mail. All try to be upbeat and informal. To date the most successful method of advertising is through e-mails to the staff and student notice boards, plus e-mails directly to particular cohorts of students a week before a session is due to run. Some academics are 'champions' of the Library and will draw courses to the attention of the students, which will be reflected in the attendance of a number of students from the same degree programme. This reflects JUSTEIS findings (Armstrong et al., 2001) that lecturers are influential in recommending sources and information activities to students.

Administration for the sessions is very efficient. Academic staff book their places on the course through Staff Development while students book a place through the Library administration assistant. Both send an e-mail accepting the booking. Two days before the course is due to run they send a courtesy reminder, outlining where the course is taking place and anything the participants are required to bring, such as their Athens passwords. The courtesy notice ensures a higher attendance rate. The administration assistant provides the presenter on the day of the session with a register of participants, evaluation sheets and any photocopying that was required. She also organizes directional signs to be placed strategically throughout the Library so that the training room is easier to find.

All the DotM sessions are formally evaluated through print questionnaires. Participants are asked to complete them at the end of each session, but they are also given the opportunity to take them away with them and return them in the internal mail. We generally obtain a high return of the questionnaires. The feedback is analysed both by individual presenters and by the IST Co-ordinator. The feedback is reviewed on a regular basis and used to inform the next training schedule. The majority of the feedback is positive and praises the presenters, the pitch of the talk and the opportunity for hands-on use of the databases. Negative feedback normally relates to technical matters such as the slowness of the network and the quality of the data projector.

Conclusion

This programme has resulted in a range of benefits for presenters, users and the Library service. The experience of working with clearly defined learning outcomes for DotM models good practice for Library staff and encourages them to adopt this in other IST courses that they develop. Participants are exposed to a variety of presenters (including some who work for information producers) but there is a consistency of approach and structure in the sessions. The evaluation of the courses and subsequent feedback into IST enables students to transfer their searching skills from one electronic resource to another. Finally, there is anecdotal evidence to support the view that advertising particular services through the DoTM sessions leads to an increased awareness of the product throughout the University, and encourages both those staff and students who do not actually attend the DotM sessions to investigate these services. For example after a DotM session on Compendex, the usage figures doubled from the preceding three months but also from the previous year's usage figures. Usage has continued to be higher than the equivalent months in the previous years.

In conclusion, we believe the DotM sessions are successful for the following reasons:

• All presenters understand the aims of the sessions.

- The learning outcomes are communicated to the students and in some cases negotiated with them.
- Time is set aside for hands-on use of the databases.
- The presenter often manages to speak to each participant and provide individual help and guidance.
- Good administrative support is provided to the presenters.
- Each course is heavily marketed through a variety of means.
- Each course is formally evaluated with feedback being incorporated into the training schedule.

References

Armstrong, C. et al. (2001) Low ICT Use by Students, *Library Association Record*, **103** (6), 358–9.

Beard, R. and Hartley, J. (1984) *Teaching and Learning in Higher Education*, 4th edn, London, PCP.

Brown, G. and Atkins, M. (1988) *Effective Teaching in Higher Education*, London, Routledge.

Cox, L. (1995) Fun Skills Sessions Got Them Hooked, *Library Association Record*, **97** (7), 384–5.

Cyberatlas (2001) *Internet Tops Library as Research Source for Students*, Cyberatlas. Available at http://cyberatlas.internet.com/markets/education/.

D'Esposito, J. E. and Gardner, R. M. (1999) University Students' Perceptions of the Internet: an exploratory study, *Journal of Academic Librarianship*, **26** (6), 456–61.

Gadd, E. A. et al. (2001) In with the New: reviewing library induction practices at Loughborough University, *New Library World*, **102** (1166/1167), 247–55.

Herring, J. (1997) Enabling Students to Search and Find, *Library Association Record*, **99** (5), 258–9.

Kirby, J. et al. (1998) *Empowering the Information User*, London, Library Association Publishing.

Lubans, J. (1999) *Students and the Internet*, Durham, NC, Duke University Library. Available at www.lib.duke.edu/lubans/docs/study3.html.

Lubans, J. (2000) *Study 4: Internet Use (February 2000) among 3rd Year Students at Duke University, Durham, North Carolina, USA*, Durham, Duke University Library. Available at www.lubans.org/study4b.html.

Pedley, P. (2001) Special Briefing: Information Overload and Information Literacy, *Managing Information*, **8** (6), 8.

Race, P. and Brown, S. (1993) *500 Tips for Tutors*, London, Kogan Page.

Ray, K. and Day, J. (1998) Student Attitudes towards Electronic Information Resources, *Information Research*, **4** (2). Available at http://informationr.net/ir/4-2/paper54.html.

Rowley, J. (2000) *JISC User Behaviour Monitoring & Evaluation Framework: first annual report*, Edge Hill, JISC. Available at www.jisc.ac.uk/pub00/m&e_rep1.html.

Walton, G. and Edwards, C. (1998) Information Technology and Learning to Learn, *The New Academic*, **7** (2), 3–8.

16

A tool for teaching e-literacy: the RDN Virtual Training Suite

Emma Place, Simon Price, Kate Sharp, Paul Smith and Tessa Griffiths

Introduction

As the internet becomes increasingly important as a resource for learning and teaching, students and lecturers will benefit from developing the skills required to use it to support their work. This chapter introduces the RDN (Resource Discovery Network) Virtual Training Suite (www.vts.rdn.ac.uk/), a free educational resource designed to help those in UK higher and further education to develop their internet information literacy (or e-literacy). It will describe how lecturers, librarians and IT (information technology) trainers can use this resource as a teaching tool to support subject curricula, library user education, student induction, staff development and training in IT key skills.

E-literacy in further and higher education

The potential of the internet to support education can only be met if people have the skills and inspiration to use it. Universities and colleges have their internet innovators but there are still a great many internet novices. Many lecturers will have spent a lifetime developing their information skills in the traditional information environment of the library, but may now feel the need to develop skills for the internet environment. Students may be familiar with using the internet at school or for recreation, but when they are new to further or higher education they will need to develop internet skills relevant to this level of study.

Information literacy is widely recognized as an essential skill for academic work in all subject disciplines. It enables people to recognize when they need information and to locate, evaluate and use relevant information for their work (ALA, 1989). It has long been taught in library user education and courses in study and research skills. As the internet increasingly becomes a major access point for information alongside the library, however, academics and students need to develop internet information skills – the ability to use networked information resources to support their learning and teaching. For a while there will be a skills gap in this area while the educational community becomes accustomed to new information-seeking behaviours that the internet makes possible. Staff development will be as necessary as training provision for students. For these reasons it seemed there was room for a national training resource, freely available for everyone via open learning on the web, that could help staff and students develop their e-literacy.

The RDN Virtual Training Suite

The RDN Virtual Training Suite is a free, national, public internet service funded by the UK Further and Higher Education Funding Councils, through the JISC (Joint Information Systems Committee, www.jisc.ac.uk/). It provides a set of 'teach yourself' tutorials on the web, each offering training in internet information skills for a specific academic subject. Over 50 tutorials are now available and there's a tutorial for most of the subjects taught in UK universities and colleges (see Figure 16.1 for a full list). The resource has been built collaboratively 'by the community for the community'. Subject specialists (lecturers and librarians) from over 50 universities, colleges, museums and research centres across the UK have authored and edited the tutorials, making them relevant to the needs of different subject communities.

The Virtual Training Suite has been embedded into one of JISC's larger national services, the Resource Discovery Network or RDN (www.rdn.ac.uk/), an internet search service designed to provide access to high-quality internet resources that can support learning, teaching and research. The tutorials in the Virtual Training Suite offer a taster of the many thousands of high-quality internet sites that can be found by using the RDN. The RDN hubs have played a major role in creating and updating the groups of tutorials:

- BIOME: the health and life sciences tutorials
- EEVL: the engineering tutorials
- HUMBUL: the humanities tutorials
- PSIGate: the physical science tutorials
- RDNC: the generic internet skills tutorial
- SOSIG: the social science tutorials.

Engineering and Mathematics (EEVL)
Internet Aviator
Internet Civil Engineer
Internet Electrical, Electronic &
    Communications Engineer
Internet for Health and Safety
Internet Materials Engineer
Internet Mathematician
Internet Mechanical Engineer
Internet Offshore Engineer
Internet Town and Country Planner

Health and Life Sciences (BIOME)
Internet for Agriculture, Food and
    Forestry
Internet for Allied Health
Internet Bioresearcher
Internet Medic
Internet for Nature
Internet for Nursing, Midwifery &
    Health Visiting
Internet Pharmacist
Internet Vet

Humanities (HUMBUL)
Internet for English
Internet for Historians
Internet for History & Philosophy of
    Science
Internet for Modern Languages
Internet Philosopher
Internet for Religious Studies
Internet Theologian

Physical Sciences (PSIgate)
Internet Chemist
Internet Earth Scientist
Internet Physicist

Reference (RDNC)
Internet Instructor

*Social Sciences, Business and Law
(SOSIG)*
Internet Anthropologist
Internet Business Manager
Internet for Development
Internet Economist
Internet for Education
Internet for European Studies
Internet Geographer
Internet for Government
Internet for Lawyers
Internet Politician
Internet Psychologist
Internet for Social Policy
Internet for Social Research Methods
Internet for Social Statistics
Internet Social Worker
Internet Sociologist
Internet for Women's Studies

Further Education
Internet for Art, Design and Media
Internet for Business Studies
Internet for Construction
Internet for Engineering (to include
    Motor Engineering)
Internet for Hairdressing and Beauty
Internet for Health and Social Care
Internet for Hospitality and Catering
Internet for Information and
    Communication Technology
Internet for Leisure, Sport and
    Recreation
Internet for Performing Arts
Internet for Travel and Tourism

Fig. 16.1   *Tutorials within the RDN Virtual Training Suite*

The Virtual Training Suite was built for the RDN by the ILRT (The Institute for Learning and Research Technology, www.ilrt.bris.ac.uk/) at the University of Bristol.

Learning objectives and tutorial structure

All the tutorials have the same aim: to enable the user to practise and develop internet information skills that can support learning, teaching and research in their subject. With this common aim, all the tutorials have the same basic structure and design, with four main sections (or chapters) that map directly on to the four main learning objectives. Each tutorial enables the user to:

- *Tour* key internet resources for the subject and then distinguish the different types of resources available on the internet, identify important resources for the subject and compile a personal list of links to internet sites relevant to their work
- *Discover* how to search the internet and then explain the differences between internet search tools (gateways, directories and search engines), identify internet search tools relevant to the subject, and develop effective techniques for internet searching
- *Review* and *judge* websites and then state why quality of information is an issue on the internet, critically evaluate information found on the internet, and avoid common pitfalls of internet use
- *Reflect* and *plan* to use the internet effectively for work and then summarize key internet information skills, and decide how to use the internet to support personal study, teaching or research.

Finishing all the sections takes around one to two hours, although users can choose to do one segment at a time over more than one sitting, or focus on the sections of most relevance to their work.

Features of the tutorials include simple step-by-step instruction on the web, interactive quizzes and exercises, a Links Basket (to collect a personal list of useful web links), a glossary of internet terms, a guide to citing websites, various print options (for notes or handouts), teaching resources, and free posters – to print and copy.

A teaching tool for lecturers, librarians and IT trainers

The tutorials can be used by staff and students for open learning, but they have also been designed as a tool for lecturers, librarians and trainers to use in their taught courses and VLEs (virtual learning environments). Deeper learning can be achieved when staff can offer guidance, context, feedback and ideally, formal assessment, at a local level.

More than 40 of the tutorials were designed primarily to support users in higher education. The subject approach and the skills covered comply with recommendations of the Quality Assurance Agency for Higher Education, which has included 'Information Retrieval Skills' and 'Information Technology Skills' as key transferable skills in their benchmark standards for the content of degree courses (QAA, 1999). The HE tutorials are being used as tools by lecturers who embed them into taught courses, librarians who use them in their information literacy training/courses, staff who teach research skills and study skills, in staff development programmes for lecturers, librarians and IT staff, and in open and distance learning.

Supplementary resources for teachers and trainers can be found in each tutorial. These include an introductory PowerPoint presentation, student workbook and handout and lesson plans. Teachers can use the print option to print the whole tutorial or specific chapters within it. These can then be used as slides or handouts.

Eleven of the tutorials have been designed specifically to meet the needs of students in further education. These tutorials have been carefully developed to map on to the relevant parts of the Key Skills Specifications for IT, as defined by the Qualifications Curriculum Authority (QCA, 2001). These tutorials have additional features including a 'Key Skills' section and subject-specific teaching packs that offer case study examples of how the tutorials can be incorporated into subject curricula for different courses at Levels 1–3 ranging from 'A' Level to GNVQ (General National Vocational Qualification) and AVCE (Advanced Vocational Certificate in Education) courses. The FE tutorials aim to be appropriate tools for developing Key Skills in IT within subject curricula, student induction programmes, staff development courses for lecturers, learning resource centre and IT support staff and ILRT (Institute for Learning and Research Technology) champions, and for embedding into VLEs and distance-learning courses. More teaching materials will become available in the future as we are currently working with practitioners to generate case study examples of how these tutorials can be effectively embedded into taught courses and VLEs.

Early evaluation

It is still early days for evaluating the impact of the RDN Virtual Training Suite. Some preliminary evidence is, however, available.

An independent academic evaluation of the usage and value of the Virtual Training Suite was completed in March 2001 (Amber, 2001). In terms of quantitative statistics, initial usage was encouragingly high. From March to

December 2000 there were over 43,000 log-ins to the site, with an average of 204 sessions per day. Interest in the future development of the project remained high as over 2000 people signed up to receive notification of the launch of the second phase of tutorials, implying that usage was likely to rise further in the future as more tutorials became available. Analysis of the online feedback forms completed between December 2000 and March 2001indicate that 25% of the users were librarians seeking material for inclusion in user education sessions, 14% lecturers, 11% undergraduates, 8% researchers and 10% postgraduates. The rest fell into other categories, such as school students. Fifty-six per cent of users classified themselves as independent learners. This shows that the tutorials are reaching a wide audience, representing all the categories of users for which they were intended. The majority of the respondents felt that they had learnt something from using the materials. They were seen to be a particularly useful starting point for internet novices.

A more recent qualitative and quantitative evaluation of the RDN as a whole was conducted in April 2002 (Coleman and Amber, 2002). The report states that:

> Many evaluation participants reported visiting the RDN to develop their Internet searching skills or to support their teaching and training in this area and accordingly, levels of VTS usage were very high. The Virtual Training Suite proved to be one of the most popular parts of the RDN, being perceived as a high quality and effective teaching and learning resource, and featuring the elements of interactivity that many evaluation participants sought in Internet resources.

Over 2000 e-mails from users have been received, providing qualitative feedback. User comments can be read on the website. Typical remarks include:

> Excellent choice of sources and commentary. It makes serious scholarly points very well and works at just the right level. I intend to embed this into my humanities information skills teaching (the Internet for English tutorial).
> (Academic Librarian, De Montfort University)

> What I liked most: You wrote it, so I don't have to! (Lecturer, University of Exeter)

> I was told by my university lecturer that it might be useful. I liked learning how to find academic information from the Web as opposed to popular info.
> (Postgraduate student, University of Liverpool)

> Thank you for sorting out the confusing world of the Internet.
> (Undergraduate student, University of Durham)

A great endorsement from the site occurred when Estelle Morris, the former UK Secretary of State for Education and Skills, selected the site as one of her top three educational websites.

The evaluation evidence strongly suggests that the Virtual Training Suite has met an immediate need, with high levels of usage and generally very positive feedback from large numbers of users. It will be interesting to monitor feedback over the next few years as more people get to hear about it and make their own assessment of its value. Will it be widely adopted as part of broader information literacy courses? What best practice for use of this resource will emerge? Will it be more popular as an open learning tool or as a teaching tool? Will staff prefer to develop their own e-literacy teaching tools rather than have an off-the-shelf product? Will it actually raise the level of e-literacy in UK further and higher education over time?

Future plans

We are frequently asked two questions about future plans for this project:

Will the tutorials be updated and maintained over time?

A stable curriculum for internet training is not possible in this ever-changing environment and clearly changes will need to be made to keep the tutorials current. The resource has been firmly embedded into the organizational structure of its parent service, the RDN, and will be maintained as part of this service. The ILRT and RDN hubs have assumed responsibility for the upkeep tutorials, with regular link checking and updating of subject content.

Are there plans for more tutorials?

Users sometimes ask if the Suite will be expanded and they have pointed out gaps in subject coverage, such as Music and Archaeology. One of the biggest demands has been for tutorials covering subjects taught within the further education sector. As a result of this feedback we will be building five new tutorials with JISC funding. We are also in discussion with the Learning and Teaching Support Network (www.ltsn.ac.uk/) LTSN centres, some of which are keen to develop new tutorials to fill subject gaps. ILRT is willing to talk to any organization interested in funding development of further tutorials.

Conclusion

As information for education is increasingly available via the internet we believe that e-literacy skills should form an essential part of any broader information literacy programme. They should also feature in taught courses and staff development programmes. There is an immediate need for training in this area as users try to make sense of the information landscape, which now includes the internet alongside the library and other sources. The web tutorials described in this paper are just one attempt to meet this need quickly and efficiently and we look forward to seeing what developments might be necessary in the next few years as universities and colleges work more within the internet learning landscape.

References

ALA (1989) *American Library Association Presidential Committee on Information Literacy: final report*. Available at www.ala.org/acrl/nili/ilit1st.html.

Amber, L. (2001) *Virtual Training Suite Evaluation Report*. Available at www.vts.rdn.ac.uk/evaluation.htm.

Coleman, P. and Amber, L. (2002) *The Resource Discovery Network Evaluation Report*. Available at www.rdn.ac.uk/publications/evaluation/evalreport02.pdf/.

QAA (1999) *Benchmarking Academic Standards*, The Quality Assurance Agency for Higher Education. Available at www.qaa.ac.uk/crntwork/benchmark/benchmarking.htm.

QCA (2001) *Qualifications Curriculum Authority – National Qualifications – Key Skills*. Available at www.qca.org.uk/nq/ks/main2.asp/.

17

A C&IT skills audit of staff and students

Juliette Pavey

Introduction

This chapter looks at the major audit of C&IT (computing and information technology) skills in learning and teaching of staff and students that was undertaken at the University of Durham to determine the current level of IT literacy of academic/academic-related staff and students. This audit led to the design of a C&IT skills inventory. The skills inventory is a description of the minimum C&IT skills expected of students and teaching staff that will enable them to enhance their learning and teaching.

Methodology

Students were questioned using a paper questionnaire during registration periods; the process of waiting in queues with nothing else to do was influential in providing a high response rate. Staff were targeted mainly through the web; however some paper questionnaires were distributed to gain an overall profile from those who might not necessarily use technology.

The audit was perception based, as tests were not carried out to determine actual levels of skill. The questionnaire asked the staff/students to rate their skills in using various types of software; then each type of software was broken down into specific skills ranging from none to the advanced. This was to ascertain whether participants possessed appropriate C&IT skills.

Descriptive statistics were produced for each question to gain an overall profile of skills. Further analysis was carried out and the factors of gender, age, campus and faculty were considered. For the purpose of the analysis the responses concerning the advanced level of skills for each type of software were used. ANOVA (analysis of variance) and t-tests were used to test the statistical significance of particular data sets.

Results overview (June 2000)

Results revealed (see Table 17.1) that a high percentage of students perceive themselves to have 'good' skills levels in using e-mail, a web browser, Windows and file management, and word-processing. In contrast a high percentage of staff perceive themselves to be 'advanced' users in using e-mail, a web browser, Windows and file management, and word-processing. Few students demonstrated, however, that they possessed advanced skills apart from word-processing. This is reiterated in a similar study carried out by JISC (Joint Information Systems Committee) which found the vast majority of staff are confident in the areas of Word and e-mail (JISC, 2001).

Cross-tabulations were generated for the exploration of various factors. Examples highlighting these relationships are shown in relation to gender and age.

Table 17.1 *Perceived skills levels for different types of software for staff and students*

Software	Skills level, %							
	None		Basic		Good		Advanced	
	Staff	Student	Staff	Student	Staff	Student	Staff	Student
E-mail	0.5	0.6	8.9	15.7	48.4	56.7	41.8	23.6
Web browser	1.6	1.7	15.6	19.7	30.6	54.6	36.3	20.4
Web authoring	53.3	50.2	25.7	24.8	13.4	15.7	6.9	5.1
Windows and file management	1.2	2.3	14.6	18.4	47.7	52.4	35.5	22.6
Word-processing	1.9	1.4	8.0	11.0	47.7	53.4	41.5	30.0
Spreadsheets	16.0	10.5	29.5	28.0	28.1	39.0	24.8	18.0
Presentation	28.3	29.8	26.4	28.4	28.5	26.5	16.0	11.0
Databases	38.5	37	28.5	32.1	19.3	19.3	12.7	7.3
Graphics	35.4	28.5	30.6	35.7	18.8	22.9	14.2	8.6

Results for staff

Regarding gender differences and the general confidence among staff in using computers, the test reveals a statistically significant relationship (see Table 17.2). The main difference lies in the responses in the 'very confident' category where males perceive themselves to be more confident computer users than females. However, the 'confident' category response by females is higher than that by males. Indeed, when the two categories 'confident' and 'very confident' are combined little difference is evident between gender and confidence.

Table 17.2   *Cross-tabulation between general confidence in using computers and gender (staff)*

Confidence level	Gender	
	Male, %	Female, %
No confidence	0.2	–
Little confidence	6.2	12.1
Confident	46.2	65.5
Very confident	46.6	22.4

In relation to age and confidence (see Table 17.3), a statistically significant value is gained. Differences do not, however, emerge between the youngest and oldest age categories. In the 'confident' category high percentages emerge fairly evenly across all age groups. However, on examination of the 'little confidence' category the highest percentages occur in the 60+ age group, but representation in the 20-age group is also fairly high. Therefore no generalizations can be made about age and confidence.

Table 17.3   *Cross-tabulation between general confidence and age (staff)*

Confidence level	Age group, %									
	≤20	21–25	26–30	31–35	36–40	41–45	46–50	51–55	56–60	60+
No confidence	–	3.1	–	–	–	–	–	–	–	–
Little confidence	10.0	3.1	–	6.8	8.2	2.6	11.9	12.3	8.6	25.0
Confident	45.0	37.5	54.9	43.8	47.5	63.2	49.2	48.2	65.7	60.0
Very confident	45.0	56.3	43.9	49.4	44.3	34.2	35.6	39.5	25.7	15.0

Results for students

Table 17.4   *Cross-tabulation between general confidence in using computers and gender (students)*

Confidence level	Gender	
	Male, %	Female, %
No confidence	0.8	1.0
Little confidence	12.0	21.1
Confident	55.6	64.7
Very confident	28.4	10.9

A statistically significant relationship between ratings in general confidence between the genders exists. Females responded highly to no/little confidence in comparison to males, although this is not a major difference. The main difference lies in the responses in the 'very confident' category: 28% of the males stated that they are very confident users in comparison with only 11% of females, demonstrating that males perceive themselves to be more confident computer users than females do.

Table 17.5   *Cross-tabulation between general confidence and age (students)*

| Confidence level | Age group, % | | | | | | | | | |
	≤20	21–25	26–30	31–35	36–40	41–45	46–50	51–55	56–60	60+
No confidence	0.8	1.0		2.5				9.1	6.3	
Little confidence	18.1	14.5	14.8	19.0	20.4	20.6	31.8	18.7	37.5	22.2
Confident	60.4	61.0	59.3	62.0	66.7	64.7	45.5	43.7	37.5	55.6
Very confident	18.1	21.0	22.2	12.7	9.3	14.7	9.1	25.0	12.5	22.2

In relation to age a statistically significant relationship between perceived levels of confidence in using computers and age is present. This is evident on examination of the 'confident' category where confidence is less between the age groups 46–60. An anomaly to this is in the 60+ age category where 55.6% feel themselves to be confident users. In general, results reveal that an increase in age shows a reduction in the level of confidence in using computers.

Staff–student comparisons

A comparison of staff and students revealed some interesting results. Prior to the study it was envisaged that the level of confidence and skills would be greater among students than staff. However, the results actually revealed greater confidence among staff. For general confidence in using computers 91% of staff perceive themselves to be either confident or very confident computer users in comparison with 79% of students. More staff responded in the 'very confident' category (40%) than did students (19%).

Students in the Sciences expressed a greater level of confidence, especially in the 'very confident' category, in comparison with students from the Arts and Social Sciences. Similarly staff responses from the Science and Service departments had high responses in the 'very confident' category. However, the response rate by scientists was higher than other faculties for both staff and students.

Factors affecting use of C&IT in teaching

Staff were asked to comment on various statements relating to the use of C&IT in learning and teaching and to say whether they agreed or disagreed with the statements. The statements related to whether greater use of C&IT in learning and teaching would be made with, for example, more lecture theatre equipment, time to learn new skills, more support and knowledge of how to find relevant materials. In general, staff either agreed or strongly agreed with the majority of these statements. Staff agreed strongly with the statement that they would use C&IT for teaching with more time to learn new skills (74%). We can equate this to a similar study carried out at Bristol University who discovered that only 37% of academic/academic-related staff felt that they had sufficient educational support and this was a limiting factor in their use of learning technologies (Jones, 2000). This corresponds to the Durham study, which found that 63% of staff agreed/strongly agreed with the statement that they would use more C&IT for learning and teaching if they had more support.

C&IT in learning and teaching

The questionnaire focused around the importance of being able to use various C&IT skills and their importance to learning and teaching, in order to identify gaps in training. This was highlighted most in a question that dealt with the use of the web for learning and teaching and where the greatest disparities between not having a skill, but expressing the importance of the skill to learning and teaching, occurred. The main areas identified as gaps in knowledge for staff were with using the web for interactive materials, assessment, feedback/evaluation, online discussion, learning environments and open/distance learning. A similar study carried out at Plymouth University revealed comparable results where the main requirements for training were in using the web, developing web pages and authoring materials (Bailey, 1996).

In terms of skills and their relation to learning and teaching the findings revealed a contradictory picture, with staff and students possessing high-level C&IT skills and high levels of confidence, but failing to acknowledge the importance of such skills to their learning and teaching. This is reiterated in a similar study by Jones (2000) who found that staff were confident and competent, with an interest or even an enthusiasm in technology, and with no problems of PC availability or internet access, but that they also, on the other hand, appear to be making little use of that technology to enhance or improve their main work activities – i.e. learning and teaching.

Comparison of results of first-year students entering the University between 2000 and 2001

One might have expected an increase in levels of C&IT skills between the two years because of such factors as the introduction of Key Skills into schools. However, overall, there was little difference between them. There was little contrast in request for training, overall training requests were reduced (9% reduction with regard to e-mail), but in general the figures stayed the same in the two years. There was a general increase in the use of the web and e-mail and significantly, there was an increase of 19% in participation in online discussion and 7% in online chat. We can equate this to the recent increase in virtual learning environments and managed learning environments in higher education over the past year.

Outcomes

The audit revealed significant results from which various recommendations have been made. The main outcome was to produce an inventory of skills, which is closely based on the questions used in the survey. This will be used to advise both staff and students of the range of C&IT skills that they should possess/develop and to encourage them to learn and train in those areas where skills need developing through appropriate training methods. Secondly, it is felt that the introduction of Key Skills into schools will bring changes in the levels of C&IT skills of students entering the University; therefore the audit and training provision will be informed by this and updated accordingly.

It was important to identify members of staff who revealed that they did not have a particular skill but felt it was needed for their teaching, and to consider how they might change this. Having identified those areas where skills are low one outcome could be to offer support and training (especially in those areas where confidence and level of skill are either 'none' or 'basic') for both staff and students in web authoring, presentation and graphical packages.

The emphasis of the audit was on the use of C&IT in learning and teaching, and therefore future work needs to focus in this area. It has been demonstrated that there is currently a gap between having particular C&IT skills and making them applicable and relevant to learning and teaching. In part this has been addressed through training in our learning environment, Blackboard. Teaching of the Blackboard software has included not only the general administrative training of adding course information but has addressed issues such as good practice with using discussion boards. Further projects have emerged with the focus of working with departments to develop innovative content to be delivered through DUO to provide students with an enhanced learning experience.

Future work will address this with workshops aimed towards bridging the gap between learning the technical skills and also identifying their pedagogical importance. This is highlighted in a study by Wiles et al. (2001) where academic staff failed to see the importance of generic skills training to their teaching practice. It was felt that academics would be more likely to participate if the pedagogical aspects of their own subject area were addressed by the staff training offered. This is particularly relevant to those identified from the audit that didn't have a particular skill but felt this skill was important to their learning and teaching.

It having been demonstrated that staff feel strongly about the limitations placed on their more extensive use of C&IT through such things as lack of support, equipment and knowledge, it will be important to address these issues, and to increase more effective and widespread use of C&IT in learning and teaching.

Finally, it will be important to link the audit more directly to the training programme so that staff/students on completion of the web-based survey are given direct feedback relating to their skills. This will provide them with information related to areas where their skills may be lacking, and direct them towards specific training programmes to encourage wider participation. Departments whose subject has C&IT integration need to be informed about their staff and student skills levels in order to integrate this information into their own training programmes.

To sum up, the main outcomes of the audits have been plans to do the following:

- To review the audit and inventory annually and update skills training accordingly, especially with the introduction of key skills to address changes.
- To carry out the skills audit as students enter the University and then again as they leave to gain a continual profile of skills, and to enable an evaluation of skills gained during their time at University.
- To encourage awareness of the skills inventory for all new members of staff through the University's Post Graduate Certificate in Education and others.
- To make the results of audit available to all departments to increase awareness of levels of skills.
- To identify subject-specific skills and inform departments.
- To target support and training in those areas identified in the audit and during completion of the audit to direct the student/member of staff to immediate feedback and recommended areas for development and training.
- To inform the University's Undergraduate Training Programme of the C&IT audit, report and inventory to feed into the current C&IT programme offered for undergraduate students.

• To encourage wider use of the University of Durham learning environment, DUO (Durham University Online), developed in Blackboard.

Conclusion

The initial aim of the audit was to determine the current level of C&IT skills of all students and academic/academic-related staff in the University. In general both staff and students within the University have a good C&IT skills base and perceive themselves to be confident computer users with staff being more confident than students. Areas of C&IT where skills need more development are web authoring, presentation, databases, and graphical packages. A study by TALiSMAN revealed that the majority of academic and research staff in Scottish higher education (80%) identified a need for training but felt that they did not have the time to undertake this training (Tomes and Higgison, 1998). This was evident in the results for the Durham study also where both staff and students, when asked to comment on whether such factors as provision of equipment, time, support, recognition and knowledge of where to go for advice/how to find materials would lead to their greater use of C&IT for learning and teaching, agreed or strongly agreed with the majority of statements.

It can be seen that the use of appropriate methods such as structured training and supporting the appropriate use of C&IT in learning and teaching in higher education will result in more effective use of these skills. Further information and links to the questionnaire, inventory and final report are available at www.dur.ac.uk/ITS/ltteam/skills/.

Acknowledgements

Thanks to SCAITS (Staff Communications and Information Technology Skills) and TALiSMAN (Teaching and Learning in Scottish Metropolitan Area Networks) whose questionnaires were used as a basis in the initial design of the audit.

References

Bailey, P. (1996) *Attitudes towards Using Learning Technologies Survey*. Technology Supported Learning Initiative, University of Plymouth. Available at http://sh.plym.ac.uk/eds/tsl/skiltext.htm.

JISC Regional Support Centre (2001) *Scottish Further Education Training Needs Analysis*. Available at www.rsc-ne-scotland.ac.uk/tna.

Jones, S. (2000) *The Disparity between the Willingness to Embrace – and the Actual Use of – Learning Technologies*, The University of Bristol Learning Technology Survey. Available at www.ltss.bris.ac.uk/interact21/in21p14.htm.

Tomes, N. and Higgison, C. (1998) *Analysis of the Training Needs of Academic and Research Staff in Scottish Higher Education*, TALISMAN (Teaching and Learning in Scottish Metropolitan Area Networks). Available at www.talisman.hw.ac.uk.

Wiles, K. et al. (2001) *Netculture: needs analysis survey of the staff development community supporting the application of C&IT in learning and teaching in Scottish higher education institutions*, © University of Abertay Dundee. Available at netculture.scotlib.ac.uk.

18

IT literacy: more learning, less cost

Deborah Walters, Debra Burhans, Barbara Sherman, Carl Alphonce and Helene Kershner

Introduction

Many British universities have an information technology literacy requirement but lack an information literacy requirement. At the University at Buffalo (State University of New York) there is no information technology requirement, but there is an information literacy graduation requirement that is met by students attending short courses given by librarians and filling out a workbook. This chapter discusses the redesign of a computer fluency course that is taken as an elective by students, and covers not only the standard information technology literacy topics, but gives students a deeper understanding of the basic principles of computing. The goal of the redesign was to use technology to enhance learning, while at the same time decreasing costs.

Early adopters of educational technology have found that most uses of technology to improve learning result in added costs both in terms of faculty time and in technology costs. For example, the development of the case-based ethics software at CMU (Carnegie Mellon University) (Cavalier, 2000) required a significant investment of faculty time to create a rich online environment. While many early adopters have willingly spent the time required to develop and mount technology-enhanced or online courses, this is not a model that scales for two reasons. First, while an early adopter may be willing to initially devote large amounts of time to their course, if the course continues to require significant additional effort, faculty members often find they are unable and/or unwilling to maintain that additional effort. Second, when other faculty members observe the amount of time invested by the early adopters, they can become even less willing to engage in such activity themselves.

Many early adopters have also found an increase in costs associated with the technology itself, hardware costs, maintenance costs, software costs, connectivity costs, etc. For example, the studio classrooms at RPI (Rensselaer Polytechnic Institute) (Wilson, 1996) and the Math Emporium at Virginia Tech (www.math. vt.edu/temp/emporium_presentation/) both required significant capital costs for buildings and equipment. Synchronous video-conferencing-style courses can be expensive in terms of building facilities and in terms of the recurring line charges. In addition, where students did not already have access to computers, the early adopters have had to deal with the costs of providing such access. These cost increases are especially problematic as the containment of rising costs is one of the top issues currently facing colleges and universities.

A computer fluency course was selected for the redesign as it is a topic where there already exists a variety of off-the-shelf e-learning material, so that the faculty would not have to spend lots of time creating their own materials. In addition, the redesign was embarked upon when the hardware, software, etc. was already available on campus, so that those costs would not be borne by the redesign project. The hypothesis being tested was whether under these conditions it would be possible to use technology to increase learning and decrease costs.

The course

Our redesign efforts focused on a four-credit-hour computer fluency course, CSE101 Computers, An Introduction. This course teaches both computing skills and fundamental computing concepts in both a lecture and a lab setting. In the pre-design course students met in a 50-minute lecture three times per week and in a hands-on laboratory for one two-hour block per week. While CSE101 was our focus, we approached the course redesign with the intention that the redesign tasks we employed should be transferable to other courses, regardless of whether or not they are computer science courses, or whether they are offered at our institution or elsewhere.

CSE101 serves non-majors students. While some of the students are familiar with and comfortable using computers, others are not. Indeed, some students have a great deal of apprehension about using computers. One challenge in teaching the course is to address the needs of both types of students.

Redesigning this course taught us that a computer fluency course presents some idiosyncratic challenges that may not be reflected in other courses. In particular we found that:

- The skills component of the course must be continually updated. The online version of one popular textbook is revised several times per semester.

The vendor-supplied software that supports or tests the skills component is also frequently released. Since undertaking this project there has been at least one software update every semester.

- Even though the conceptual material is more stable that the skills component, even this material changes much more rapidly than the conceptual material in other disciplines.

These factors mean that the e-learning materials must be re-evaluated and re-installed every semester.

We used the learning goals outlined in the report *Being Fluent with Information Technology* (NRC, 1999) as the basis for the course learning goals. Students who successfully complete this course:

- should be comfortable using computers
- should understand computers' basic operating principles
- should be able to adapt as technology changes
- should have the ability to critically analyse claims made about technology.

In short, students who successfully complete this course should be informed citizens of the technological world in which they live.

The redesign

Increasing student learning is by itself not an insurmountable task. If money were no object there are numerous ways in which one could imagine improving student learning. Our goal was to test the feasibility of using technology to increase student learning, while at the same time reducing costs. A general goal we had for our redesign plan was that it should be both sustainable and transferable. In other words, the redesign must cut costs in an ongoing fashion, without continuing large overhead costs (in terms of money or time). While we were clearly interested in finding a solution that worked for our particular course, we wanted our approach to include elements that could be applied successfully elsewhere.

Shift class time from lecture to lab

When we analysed the content of the course we realized that a significant amount of lecture time was devoted to teaching skills, something much better suited to a hands-on laboratory environment. There is evidence that students learn such topics more from the experiential, active learning during labs than from lectures in computer fluency courses (Davis, 1999). In the redesign plan we therefore shifted one hour from the lecture component of the course to the lab component. Students meet in lecture two hours per week rather than three, and meet in lab three hours per week rather than two. This resulted in a savings in faculty time of one hour per week of lecture time plus the associated preparation time. While this is not a recoverable cost to the institution (the faculty member is a salaried not hourly employee), the fact that classroom and lecture preparation time can be trimmed is a strong incentive to attempt a redesign. This time can be reinvested in other activities, such as more one-on-one interactions with students or more time for research.

But do the added weekly lab hours increase costs? The answer is 'no'. With two-hour lab sessions students were unable to complete their labs in the allotted time, and required extra time outside of their scheduled lab time to complete the assignments. While there was a lab assistant available, this extra time during open lab hours was unstructured. The lab assistant was available to answer questions, but was not guiding a class of students all working on the same assignment.

With the extra scheduled lab hour students have access to their lab assistant for one extra hour in a structured environment. The lab assistant is able to guide student through their work in a more effective manner. As a result students are generally able to complete their assignments within the lab period. This enabled us to reduce the number of open lab hours which more than compensated for the extra formal hours, thus reducing costs.

Although students probably spend the same amount of time in the lab they are more satisfied with the experience. Since they block off three hours of time for the lab when they register for the course they have the expectation that they will need to devote that amount of time to the labs in the course. Previously they felt they were spending extra time on the course, something they resented.

Since we were able to staff the lab for a smaller number of hours in total we realized a cost savings by increasing the number of scheduled lab hours and decreasing the number of open lab hours.

Lower ratios

Prior to redesign we staffed the lab with only one lab assistant for a lab with 28 students. Students expressed great frustration at the amount of time they needed to wait to get an answer. One consequence of this was that students were unable to finish their work within the allotted lab time, and made greater use of open lab hours as well as faculty and teaching assistants office hours. In the redesign two lab assistants were available in the lab. Student satisfaction increased as a result. Moreover, student reliance on open lab hours and office hours decreased.

Lab assistants

A very important component of the redesign was a change from using only GTAs (graduate teaching assistants) to using mostly ULAs (undergraduate learning assistants) to support the laboratory component of the course. The main motivations behind this change were:

- *Cost*: GTAs are very expensive. Each GTA is awarded a tuition waiver and a stipend (plus fringe benefits). ULAs are paid a flat hourly rate.
- *Skill set*: Our graduate students are primarily international, and it is rare that domestic graduate students are assigned to the low-level courses, since they generally have expertise required to support the upper-level courses. International graduate students are extremely bright and well educated, but have no experience with the USA undergraduate programme. For both undergraduate students and GTAs there is a significant culture and language shock when they meet in the classroom. Moreover, any highly specialized GTA, domestic or international, has forgotten what it is like to not understand the first thing about a computer. GTAs often become impatient with the student population in a computer fluency course. Since these students are often insecure about working with computers in the first place, this is a less than ideal situation.

ULAs are undergraduate students who have successfully completed the course, and who earned an A. These students, having gone through the course, know the material well, and understand the feelings of anxiety that the current students feel. They are therefore much more patient when interacting with this student population. Because the cost of GTAs is more than twice the cost of ULAs, we were able to hire enough ULAs to double the number of assistants in each lab section to staff each lab session. This enabled us to improve the learning environment for the students, while lowering the overall cost of course delivery.

Online skills training

Skills-training software trains students in the basics of using the operating system and the basic office suite software. There are two basic varieties – live-in-the-application and simulations. The former lets the student interact with the actual software product, observing the keystrokes and mouse clicks that the student is generating to determine whether or not a particular skill has been mastered. Simulations simulate the applications. An advantage of a simulation is that a student does not need to have the actual software installed to benefit from the training. Indeed, the students might have a different version (or no version) of the software installed. We found the skills-training e-learning materials to be quite mature. The software is often available on a CD-ROM that the students can use from home or in a public computing site. The reliability of the software was good, and students reported that they found it useful for learning.

Course management and online testing software

Integrated products to handle course list, grade entry, grade reporting to students, online testing, grading of quizzes/exams, etc. were explored for the redesigned course. Unfortunately, we were not able to find course management software that would interface directly with the online testing software available from the textbook publisher. The main problem was that it was not possible to have the online testing software enter the grades directly into the course management software. Another problem was that the course management software required the instructors to know in advance how many quizzes, exams and projects were to be part of the course.

Results

In general instructors reported that students were more satisfied with the course, and felt more comfortable and confident. In addition, the ULAs learned a great deal in the act of teaching, and they felt a more positive and powerful link to the department and the University. This was an unanticipated and very positive outcome.

Costs

With an enrolment of 426 students in the fall, this course cost $167 per student to deliver. Had we continued to teach the old way it would have cost us $249 per student. This represents a 33% drop in per-student cost. In terms of absolute dollars saved, this represents a savings of approximately $35,000 per semester.

Learning

Four measures were used to compare learning in the traditional and in the redesigned course: the amount of material covered, final course grades, pre-test and post-test scores, and attitudinal surveys given at the beginning and at the end of the semester. We collected baseline data in the traditional course during the semester before the redesign began (Spring 2000). The second set of data came from the first semester with the fully redesigned course (Spring 2001).

Material covered

The first measure indicated that learning increased in the redesigned course as compared to the traditional course since the professor reported being able to cover more material in the redesigned course.

Course guides

An analysis of the final grades for the course is another method for determining the relative learning in the traditional versus the redesigned course. Table 18.1 gives the results, which show that the completion rate (the percentage of students completing the course as opposed to withdrawing or resigning) was slightly higher in the redesigned course. There was also a slight increase in retention (the percentage of students earning a grade of C or higher). There was a larger increase in the percentage of students earning a grade of A- or higher. Finally, the mean grade earned in the course increased by a third of a letter grade, from a C+ to a B-. One potential weakness of a grade analysis assessment is that the professor assigning the grades is usually one of the researchers involved in a redesign project. Thus the professor's predisposition to believe that the redesign is an improvement might alter the grading. In this project, the professor was a part of the redesign team, but was not aware that the distribution of grades had changed.

Table 18.1   *Analysis of final grades in the courses*

	Completion	Retention	Very Good	Mean Grade
	F or higher	C or higher	A- or higher	
Traditional	91%	74%	37%	2.59
Redesigned	94%	78%	56%	2.90

Pre-test and post-test scores

The third measure of learning was more direct and used pre-test and post-tests. A set of questions from the final exam of the traditional course was selected to serve as a pre- and post-test. The questions were asked of the students in the redesigned course at the beginning of the semester and again at the end of the semester. Table 18.2 shows the results, and it can be seen that learning did occur in the redesigned course, as the percentage of correct answers increased from 30% to 60% during the course of the semester. While at the beginning of the semester some students could not correctly answer any of the questions, by the end of the course, no student answered fewer than 32% of the questions correctly. Similarly the maximum percentage correctly answered increased.

Table 18.2   *Pre-test and post-test scores*

	Correct, %	Min. correct, %	Max. correct, %
Traditional Post-test	69	21	88
Redesigned Pre-test	30	0	79
Redesigned Post-test	66	32	96

But did the learning increase in the redesigned course more than in the traditional course? Unfortunately, we did not give the pre-test during the traditional semester. If we were to assume that the same type of students were coming into the course with the same background each semester, then we could compare the post-test results of the two semesters. Under this assumption, there was slightly less learning occurring during the redesigned course. However, the next measure of learning calls this assumption into question.

Attitudinal surveys

The final measure of learning was a survey of student attitudes towards computing and their confidence in their computing skills. Since one of the goals of the course is to empower students in their use of technology, positive changes in student attitudes towards computing would be an indication that the course is successful in achieving this goal. The survey questions were answered using a four-point scale with one indicating the most positive response and four indicating the most negative response. Table 18.3 shows the results of the surveys and indicates that the survey results at the beginning of the course were different for the traditional and the redesigned courses. The survey results show that students entering the redesigned course were more confident and more empowered than the students from the previous year who were entering the traditional course.

Table 18.3   *Attitudinal survey results*

	Survey Average
Traditional – Before	2.90
Traditional – After	2.52
Redesigned – Before	2.44
Redesigned – After	2.46

For the traditional course the students' attitudes towards computing become more positive over the semester, as indicated by the decrease in the survey averages shown in Table 18.3. Students entering the redesigned course had more positive attitudes than those entering the traditional course. Interestingly, during the redesigned course student attitudes remained unchanged. This may have been because they were already more positive and thus we see a ceiling effect, or it may be because more material was covered in the redesigned course and thus as students learned more about the entire range of computing skills they found more areas where they were not experienced.

Conclusion

In terms of learning, three out of four measures indicate an increase in learning in the redesigned course versus the traditional course. More course material was covered during the redesigned course, the final letter grades were on average one-third of a letter grade higher, and students left the course with more positive attitudes towards computing. The fourth measure using pre- and post-tests of students' computing knowledge was inconclusive, as the pre-test was not given during the traditional course. These results suggest that is it possible to redesign certain courses to increase student learning.

It is also possible to reduce the cost to deliver at least certain courses. The greatest cost reduction potential lies in large-enrolment classes where fixed costs can be spread out over a larger number of students. Some savings are realized as actual dollar savings, while others are in an unrecoverable form such as faculty or staff time. Finally, and somewhat surprisingly, in the Buffalo case many of the cost-saving efforts actually improved the learning environment of students enrolled in the course, resulting in increased student satisfaction.

It should be noted that using online e-learning materials and/or course management software does not automatically result in cost savings. In fact, the cost savings seen in this course redesign came largely from using ULAs versus GTAs, which was only indirectly related to the use of technology. Yet the use of the e-learning materials may have contributed to the increases in learning.

Acknowledgements

This work was supported in part by a grant from the Pew Learning and Technology Program (www.center.rpi.edu/PewHome.html); see also University at Buffalo – Pew Collaboration at pew.cse.buffalo.edu/).

References

Cavalier, R. (2000) Cases, Narratives, and Interactive Multimedia, *Syllabus*, **13** (9), 20–2. Available at www.syllabus.com/mag.asp.

Davis, P. (1999) How Undergraduates Learn Computer Skills: results of a survey and focus group, *T.H.E. Journal*, **26** (9).

NRC, Committee on Information Technology Literacy, Computer Science and
    Telecommunications Board, Commission on Physical Sciences, Mathematics
    and Applications (1999) *Being Fluent with Information Technology*, Washington
    DC, National Academy Press.
Wilson, J. M. (1996) The CUPLE Physics Studio, *NLII ViewPoint*, **1** (1). Available at
    www.educause.edu/nlii/articles/wilson.html.

Part 4
Research perspectives

19

Creating effective information users

Sarah McNicol

Introduction

IT (information technology) strategies at both national and local levels often seem to be heavily concentrated on the provision of access to equipment and resources and this can lead to information literacy skills being overlooked (e.g. Office of the e-Envoy, 2001). This chapter looks at the work of 'Children, Access and Learning: Resource-based Learning and the Impacts of Environment and Learning Culture', a research project conducted by the Centre for Information Research at the University of Central England in Birmingham and funded by Resource: the Council for Museums, Archives and Libraries. The research team was anxious to investigate children's developing IT and information literacy skills to find out not just what types of resources – books, the internet, CD-ROMs, newspapers, and so forth – children used to help them to learn, but perhaps more importantly, what help other people gave them with resource-based learning projects.

Resource-based learning and individual learning

According to Beswick, 'Resource based learning is a term with a variety of meanings – essential to all however, is the assumption that the student will learn from his own direct confrontations, individually or in a group, with a learning resource or a set of learning resources or activities – rather than from conventional exposition by the teacher' (Beswick, 1977). Resource-based learning allows pupils to take greater control of their own learning and it is a model that fits within the concept of individual learning. The movement towards individualized or 'programmed' learning began in the 1960s, and the phrase has been revived by the present Government, which has stressed the importance of 'putting the learning needs of the individual pupils at the centre of everything we do' (Great Britain. DfES, 2001). In particular, recent developments in IT, such as Curriculum Online and ILS (integrated learning systems) have placed an increased emphasis on the needs of individual learners.

Children, access and learning

The Children, Access and Learning research project was carried out between March 2000 and September 2001 and involved one class of Year 7 (11–12-year-old) children in each of four case-study schools in England. Year 7 was chosen because, at this age, most children are developing an awareness of the process of learning itself and are gaining more independence, but still enjoy active parental involvement in their schooling. In each school, the children carried out a resource-based learning project, lasting approximately six weeks, which encouraged them to make use of resources in their school, home and local community. In two schools, the project formed part of the English curriculum; in another, it was taught as part of PHSE (Personal, Health and Social Education) and in the fourth within ICT (Information and Communications Technology). The projects also differed in terms of the degree of freedom children were allowed in both their choice of topic and format of the finished piece of work.

The schools were chosen to be representative of a wide range of types of school, geographical locations and socio-economic variables as indicated in Table 19.1.

In total, 94 families took part in the research. Data was collected via questionnaire surveys and interviews with parents, carers or guardians, interviews with children, weekly logs of resources children used in their resource-based learning projects, audits of resources available within the schools, teachers' assessments of the children's projects, interviews with teachers, head teachers, librarians and other school staff, and documents supplied by schools and local authorities.

In their interviews, children and parents mentioned a variety of ways in which people might help with homework. The most common included :

- motivation and encouragement
- making sure the Year 7 child had understood the task set
- helping the Year 7 child work through problems and to think of solutions
- teaching study skills, e.g. prioritizing, planning
- helping in using the computer or internet
- taking children to the library or going to the library for them.

Table 19.1 *Some of the variables indicating the differences between the schools and their localities*

School	Urban/ rural	Local ethnic minority, %	Local economic activity, %	Number of pupils (approx.)	Type of school	5 A*–C GCSE (2000), %	Special educational needs, %
School A	Inner city	23	75.7	1060	City technology college 11–18	77	19.4
School B	Semi-urban	1.27	82.0	1200	Community school 11–18	40	14.5
School C	Semi-rural	3.5	83.6	1800	Secondary 11–18	61	16.6
School D	Rural	0.5	74.8	600	Community school 11–16	58	34.6

It was interesting to note that, while children were often unsure of the most suitable learning resource to use to find the information they required, when it came to decisions about the most appropriate person to consult in order to complete a certain piece of work, their information skills were much more developed.

Within school, the most obvious source of help was the subject teacher; across the four schools, 53% of pupils discussed their project with the class teachers and in one school, the figure was 93%. However, some children had developed a close relationship with another teacher, often their form tutor, and clearly felt most comfortable asking this teacher for help, especially with more generic learning queries. Other individuals within the school mentioned by children included ICT co-ordinators and technicians, classroom assistants and school library staff. Valentine and Nelson (1988) have used the term 'sneaky teaching' to describe the type of help such individuals provide. A well resourced and effectively staffed school library open beyond the school day was identified by the research team as a key enabler to learning. It was interesting to note the different standards of library provision in the case-study schools. For example, the plentiful IT resources available at School A, a City Technology College, helped to compensate for the lack of provision in the homes of many of the children at this school. The library at School D was poorly resourced with few IT, or indeed, up-to-date printed resources, so here children were forced to make use of facilities elsewhere, in particular in the home.

Help at home

A recent MORI (Market & Opinion Research International) survey found that just over two-thirds of 12- to 16-year-olds rate their parents as 'the strongest learning influence in their lives' (Hammond and Gough, 2000). Academic research has also provided evidence that, 'the influence of the home and family background on a child's ability and achievement is at least as great as that of the school' (Wellington, 2001, 233). The findings of Children, Access and Learning support these assertions. Outside of school, it was clear that parents played an important role in learning: 57% of children claimed their mothers helped with homework and 44% mentioned fathers. The following are examples of children's comments: 'It's really important because they give better information. Internet and books, it's got its own language and sometimes I don't understand it, but when my parents explain, I understand it more'; 'If your mum and dad can explain it, you don't have to go to the teacher and you can go over and over it and spend as much time as you need on it.'

However, some parents were not able to help their children as much as they might have wished to for a number of reasons, including lack of time, work commitments and lack of confidence. Several said that they had helped when their children were younger, but did not felt they had the knowledge or skills, especially IT skills, to support them at secondary level. Typical comments included: 'Her schoolwork's a bit beyond us. We never did computers or anything like that'; '[her dad] feels really nervous about helping in case he gives her the wrong information . . . but I know he's desperate to help.'

A number of researchers (e.g. Cuckle, 1996) have suggested that good communication between home and school is a crucial element in enabling parents to help their children, especially for those who lack confidence in their own abilities. One of the enablers to learning identified by the Children, Access and Learning research was the need for effective communication between the home and school to provide parents with the knowledge and confidence to assist their children. Some parents felt they would be able to provide more effective help if they had more information about what their child was studying and what the school expected them to do at home. It was clear that each of the resource-based learning projects investigated placed different demands on parents. Many expressed concerns that their child may 'get left behind' because of a lack of access to resources or support. Conversely, other parents were reluctant to become involved in their child's learning, believing that education was, primarily, the responsibility of the school. Both these problems might, in fact, be overcome in a similar way. The evidence from the research suggested that, if children experience a lack of support from one source, they might be able to compensate by exploiting other options more fully. This process could be described as the creation of an individual learning network.

Individual learning networks

The concept of an individual learning network is illustrated in Figure 19.1. At its simplest level, within the home, an individual learning network might include parents, brothers, sisters or other relatives. Children found a variety of ways to expand their learning networks to include people outside their household, for example they might telephone, visit or e-mail friends or relatives who did not live with them when they needed help. Most children felt the need to be able to call on a number of people for help because they acknowledged that, like different resources, all individuals have their own strengths and weaknesses. Children, therefore, tended to link a particular person to one or more curriculum areas.

Personal learning directories

One of the research team's recommendations was that a tool should be developed to assist children in drawing up a list of the people they might call on for

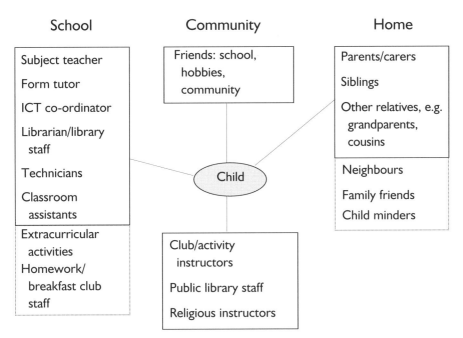

Fig. 19.1 *An individual learning network*

help with learning. As a follow-up to the main research project, this was piloted in one of the case-study schools. A personal learning directory proforma was designed to encourage each child to map individuals, such as parents, siblings, grandparents, other relatives, teachers, school and public librarians, club leaders, youth workers, religious instructors, friends and neighbours, against the type of help they might be able to provide. In terms of subject-specific help, this largely reinforced the findings of the main research project. For most school subjects, children were likely to rely on help from the teacher, plus a member of their family, most frequently a parent. However, while teachers were most usually featured as people who could help with specific subjects, parents were more frequently thought of as suitable people to assist with general study skills. Mothers were thought to have the widest range of skills: most children mentioned them as someone who could help explain and plan homework, revise, search for information, and organize visits. Fathers were thought to be most useful with planning homework, while siblings were most often consulted when searching for information. Grandparents, aunts, uncles and cousins also featured, often in relation to help with IT. Librarians were listed as people who could help children to search for information and to use the internet.

Help from friends

From both the main research project and this follow-up activity, it was clear that friends acted as an important source of help for many children, especially in the classroom or school library. However, children also worked with friends outside school, in each other's homes, public libraries or youth clubs, for example. One child said, 'I do my homework in the living room usually, but sometimes at friends'. 'I go to the Youth Club on Thursdays and do homework first with friends.' Friends were particularly likely to help with work involving IT. However, at this age, friends usually took second place, behind family members, as people who were likely to help with learning, but it might be hypothesized that, as children progress through secondary school and become more independent, both educationally and socially, their reliance on friends may increase, while the role of family members declines.

The research team suggested several ways in which children might effectively support each other, for example through study groups, which allow children to extend their learning network, giving them a wider circle of people to call on for assistance and advice. These can also improve awareness of learning resources and different learning techniques through shared experiences. A similar scheme is a 'buddy system', which pairs younger pupils with an older student. Building on the evidence that children appreciated help from an older sibling or friend who had already completed a similar piece of work, the

Children, Access and Learning report suggested that a buddy system could support those children who do not know any older pupils at their school.

Help within the community

Outside the environments of home and school, children identified resources within the local community that offered further opportunities to develop IT and information skills. Although the use of community resources was fairly limited for many of the Year 7 children, for example just less than one-third claimed to be regular public library users and only a few had ever made use of a homework or breakfast club, it is likely that, later in their secondary school careers, they may come to rely more heavily on resources beyond the home and school, through both necessity and inclination. The use of community resources depended, to a large extent, on the location of the school. At School D, which was in a rural area, there was very limited use of community resources, but at School A, located in an inner city, children had more regular and easy access to a wide range of resources such as public libraries, museums, homework clubs and religious organizations. However, in all localities, there was clearly scope for existing community facilities to be exploited more effectively.

Informal learning

This research suggests that teachers, librarians and other educators need to encourage all children to think of learning in its widest possible sense. While formal learning is generally recognizable, there is a danger that more informal learning opportunities within the home and community are often not exploited to the fullest. However, this type of learning is vital because it is frequently the most relevant to a child's everyday life. Coombs and Ahmed have defined informal learning as, 'The process by which every individual acquires and accumulates knowledge, skills, attitudes and insights from daily experiences and exposure to the environment – at home, at work, at play. . . . Generally informal education is unorganized, unsystematic and even unintentional at times, yet accounts for the great bulk of any person's total lifetime learning' (Coombs and Ahmed, 1974, 8).

The exploitation of learning opportunities in the home and community therefore helps to embed learning processes in a child's everyday life and may open up learning to those who are less readily motivated by formal study and educational institutions. The theory of situated learning is related to this concept as it views learning as a social process that involves participation in 'communities of practice', where expert knowledge can be gained from everyday experiences in the community or family (Lave and Wenger, 1991). The Children, Access and Learning project found evidence that a family or community tradition of visiting cultural institutions such as museums and libraries was one of the factors leading to more effective learning. Genuinely collaborative learning not only helps children to develop as independent learners, but also prepares them for the types of learning they will encounter later in their educational and working lives. Leadbeater is just one commentator who supports this view, arguing that, 'Schools and universities should become more like hubs of learning, within the community, capable of extending into the community. . . . More learning needs to be done at home, in offices and kitchens, in the contexts where knowledge is deployed to solve problems and add value to people's lives' (Leadbeater, 2000, 111–12).

Research recommendations

The research report recommended a number of ways in which the various agencies involved in children's learning might work together to facilitate the creation of children's learning networks. These included:

- the production of a database of resources available within the local area and within the region covering schools, libraries, museums, youth clubs, homework clubs and religious organizations
- a key person identified in all relevant bodies (for example, schools, religious organizations, libraries and museums) to facilitate communication between agencies
- public library satellites in community locations such as shops, community centres, leisure centres and health centres providing homework collections and internet access
- joint school/college and public libraries, sharing stock, IT facilities and staff
- mentoring schemes to support pupils who have limited access to IT facilities or poor IT skills
- online help from librarians to allow children access to library services from their homes and schools.

Conclusion

The Children, Access and Learning research found that certain learning activities were awarded a greater or lesser degree of importance in different families and communities. For some, learning was seen to be an activity that occurred solely at school, while for others, the skills gained through participation in hobbies or religious activities were most valuable. The attitudes of the community in which they live are likely to have an impact on the way in which children construct their individual learning networks and develops their IT and information literacy skills.

The clear message emerging from this research is that there is no single 'right' way for children to build up a network of people and resources to help them to learn and develop IT and information skills. For some, the family will be their main source of support, while others will rely more heavily on formal educators or, alternatively, on the help of friends. The overall pattern of a child's learning network will be determined by factors such as their personality, home circumstances and attitude towards learning, and will change and develop over time.

This research, therefore, suggests that children's information skills are often more sophisticated in relation to the selection of people who can help them than they are with regard to their choice of learning resources. Children are often unsure whether a book, internet site, CD-ROM or some other resource is best suited to their needs. However, even at a relatively young age, many children are able to construct complex individual learning networks, which they are able to exploit in a variety of ways depending on the type of learning they are doing and the amount and nature of the help they feel they need. This ability is rarely exploited by teachers, librarians and other educators. However, if children are to develop the higher-level information literacy skills needed to become independent learners, it is a strength that needs to be acknowledged, effectively harnessed and transferred from the selection of people to the selection of resources.

References

Beswick, N. (1977) *Resource Based Learning*, London, Heinemann.

Coombs, P. H. and Ahmed, M. (1974) *Attacking Rural Poverty. How non-formal education can help*, Baltimore, Johns Hopkins University Press.

Cuckle, P. (1996) Children Learning to Read: exploring home and school relationships, *British Educational Research Journal*, **22** (1), 17–32.

Great Britain. DfES (2001) *Professionalism and Trust – the future of teachers and teaching*, London, Department for Education and Skills.

Hammond, C. and Gough, M. (2000) *MORI Survey: A Note on Family Learning*. Available at www.learningbenefits.net/.

Lave, J. and Wenger, E. (1991) *Situated Learning: legitimate peripheral participation*, Cambridge, Cambridge University Press.

Leadbeater, C. (2000) *Living on Thin Air: the new economy*, London, Penguin.

Office of the e-Envoy (2001) *e-Economy*. Available at www.e-envoy.gov.uk/.

Valentine, P. and Nelson, B. (1988) *Sneaky Teaching: the role of the school librarian, teachers' and school librarians' perceptions*, Library and Information Research Report 63, London, British Library Research and Development Department.

Wellington, J. (2001) Exploring the Secret Garden: the growing importance of ICT in the home, *British Journal of Educational Technology*, **32** (2), 233–44.

20

Information literacy from the learner's perspective

Mark Hepworth

Introduction

Different approaches are evident in the literature on information literacy. Much of the work has focused on the processes and individual skills associated with information literacy (Doyle, 1992); Eisenberg and Berkowitz, 1990; SCONUL (Society of College, National and University Libraries), 1999). A high degree of consistency is apparent in terms of the identification of significant processes, which include how to:

- recognize information need
- distinguish ways of addressing the gap
- construct strategies for locating
- locate and access
- compare and evaluate
- organize
- synthesize and create (SCONUL, 1999).

Also provided are individual skills such as those identified by the ACRL (Association of College and Research Libraries). The ACRL website provides a detailed list of standards, performance indicators and outcome. For example, *Standard One: the Information Literate Student* determines the nature and extent of the information needed. The associated performance criterion is: the information-literate student defines and articulates the need for information. One of five outcomes: confers with instructors and participates in class discussions, peer workgroups, and electronic discussions to identify a research topic, or other information need (ACRL, 2000).

An underlying agenda of this work has been to identify processes and skills that can be taught and assessed. Bruce (1997), on the other hand, addresses information literacy from the objective of understanding what it means to learners. She identifies 'seven faces' of information literacy:

- the information technology conception
- the information sources conception
- the information process conception
- the information control conception
- the knowledge control conception
- the knowledge extension conception
- the wisdom conception.

Although there are similarities, a lack of correspondence exists between these two views. This raises the question of whether the widely accepted interpretation of information literacy is an abstraction that is disconnected from the learners' experience of information literacy. If this is the case then the 'teacher/trainer' should be aware that they are using abstract models to communicate information literacy and skills to learners. This could be important because learners may find it inherently difficult to relate to abstract learning material.

In this chapter, findings based on a study of 29 groups of part-time, Master's Information Studies, students in Singapore, using information systems and the university library, suggest that:

- The traditional information skills model for information retrieval describes the overall process but, in terms of practice, relates more to information seeking where queries are well defined and concern a known item rather than where queries are ill defined and concern an unfamiliar subject.
- Students, when exploring an unfamiliar area, experience the process in a common way and are confronted by distinct situations that need to be resolved.

It was possible to identify six such situations that students experienced. It is therefore suggested that these situations would provide a useful framework for teaching information retrieval where knowledge of the topic is minimal, because they correspond to the learner's experience.

Methodology

The sample included two groups of 58 and 60 students who were in their second year of study and were relatively knowledgeable about information retrieval and sources. They were chosen because they were involved in a task where they had to answer a question. To do so they needed to access information retrieval tools, such as the OPAC (online public access catalogue), the world wide web and online as well as CD-ROM databases, followed by finding material in the library. They provided an opportunity to study information-seeking and information-use experiences. They were split into groups of four or five. Each tutorial, over a period of six weeks, involved students both trying to retrieve and use information and also to collect data on their experience, interchanging between the role of respondent (answering the question) and researcher (collecting data on the experience).

Each group chose a topic to research from a list of 20 topics. The topics were broad and covered areas with which the students were not particularly familiar, such as 'What are the implications of the commoditization of information for information professionals in Singapore?' Students were first interviewed using a task analysis technique where they outlined how they thought they would undertake the project ('use the library', 'search CD-ROMs', 'define the topic'). They then came together in their groups and flowcharted the various steps they would take. This data gave an indication of how they thought they would conduct the task. To some extent this data did correspond to the traditional idea of the research/information skills models of which they had some knowledge and described a relatively linear path from defining the problem, identifying terms, to access, use and concluding report.

They then started to use information retrieval tools to help locate relevant information. Interaction with systems and useful and irrelevant information took place. While this was going on the respondents were asked to verbalize their thoughts and their behaviour was observed and recorded.

Findings

The information seeking and use process

As stated above, the students' own perception of the process and the accumulated data indicated similar broad processes that other authors have identified such as chaining (Ellis, 1989, 1993) or defining the problem (Kuhlthau, 1991). However, the process documented via the talk-through and observation was far less ordered and was highly iterative.

Each session lasted approximately one hour. Generally respondents conducted five to eight separate searches before identifying material that they perceived as relevant. Apparent success, i.e. finding highly relevant material, took a long time. This conforms to Spink, Bateman and Jansen's (1998) findings. Only seven searches, from the 29 groups, fell into the category of 'exactly what they wanted'. Generally the process documented via the talk-through/observation did not correspond to the student's perception of the process which was captured via the task analysis and group flowcharting. There was little evidence of students taking the measured approach they had outlined. In fact their descriptions proved to be an extreme simplification of what took place in practice which was quite iterative and apparently confused. Little evidence was found of students applying IR (information resources) methods they had been taught. A great deal of the respondents' efforts went into defining and understanding the subject domain and determining what might or might not be relevant to the question. This was probably because the respondents, despite having some knowledge of the topic domain, had relatively little knowledge of the specific subjects the research questions were about. Nevertheless, the extent of iteration and difficulty experienced by the students was surprising. This implies that either our previous conception of this process is simplistic or from the student's point of view the process is very complex. Perhaps, combining the two, we have radically simplified the process of knowledge generation and have underemphasized the process of recognizing and constructing boundaries around a new area of knowledge. Furthermore, the current artefacts that are supposed to be designed to help with this process (databases, online catalogues, etc.), in fact offer little assistance.

What did occur as respondents retrieved web pages, OPAC records, database records, headlines etc., and information, was that the students became clearer about the subject domain and what could be relevant or not relevant. In a sense the highly iterative and apparently ad hoc interaction seemed to serve the purpose of helping the respondent to draw boundaries around the subject domain and to identify possible paths that could be followed to identify relevant information as well as paths that should not. Respondents found this process frustrating and difficult.

Another reason for this iterative approach to searching was the respondents' reaction to perceived barriers. Examples of these barriers included error messages from the IR system, large numbers of hits, nil hits, and hits that were considered completely irrelevant. When situations such as these occurred respondents would tend to start a fresh search in the same IR system or choose another. Responses from the system were taken quite personally and met with a high degree of frustration. This may be partly because no explanation is offered by the IR systems as to what has gone wrong or how to correct the problem. In these situations there was little evidence of respondents analysing the problem and consciously refining the search strategy or using help systems to identify appropriate search techniques. Their frustration may also have been compounded by the fact that they had been taught that to find relevant information and answer the question quickly was efficient.

It is tempting to speculate that this apparent inefficient approach is in fact an effective way for the user to develop a cognitive map of the subject domain. This seems to be supported by the large number of quotes from the respondents that indicate the need to define the topic, and the problems associated with it, which re-occurred throughout the search process.

Implications for information literacy training

If one accepts the conclusion that, when the user is searching for information on an ill defined and unfamiliar subject, the processes of iterative interaction is useful, then training should reflect this. As noted above, the linear model of IR was not useful for the student. In fact the process of looking for information on an unfamiliar topic was frustrating for the students because they expected it to correspond to the question–match–retrieve–solution model. Students therefore needed to be taught to expect to browse, fail and gradually build a map of relevant and irrelevant information and places to find it. If students see the task as one that necessitates interaction with a broad range of sources and systems then they are more likely to exploit the situation successfully.

Six situations

As stated above, students, when exploring an unfamiliar area, experienced the process in a common way and were confronted by distinct situations that needed to be resolved. It was possible to identify six such situations that students experienced. These included:

- unsatisfactory results
- perceived errors
- relevant material found
- poor knowledge of artefacts
- lack of knowledge of the subject
- lack of knowledge of search techniques and system functionality.

These are not presented in any particular order and it would be hard to state that any one was definitely more significant than another. However Situation 5, 'lack of knowledge about the subject', did occur in more than half the search sessions. The labels for the scenarios were chosen to reflect, as closely as possible, the student's perception of the situation. Each situation is shown below, as an interaction between the environment (the information sources and systems), the psychological state of the person (i.e. their thoughts) and their behaviour (the actions they take).

Situation 1: Unsatisfactory result

A common scenario was that respondents retrieved results that were perceived to be unsatisfactory. This was the case when there were too many hits (what actually counted as too many varied between respondents), too few hits or irrelevant hits. These are common situations as documented by Shneiderman, Byrd and Croft (1997). This led to typical psychological responses (thinking processes) and behaviour as shown in Figure 20.1:

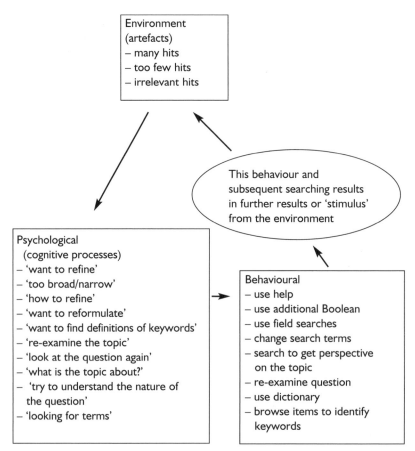

Fig. 20.1   *Situation 1: Unsatisfactory result*

Psychological responses can be seen to fall into two categories: looking for search techniques to narrow/broaden/refine the search and secondly, trying to understand the question including getting a better understanding of the subject domain and associated vocabulary. Behavioural responses included choosing specific techniques to change the relationship between search terms, or trying to find out how to do this, for example using the help system. Alternatively, the respondent revisited the question to try and generate new ideas about the topic or selected artefacts that might help with this process, such as a dictionary. Similarly browsing the text of retrieved items also served to try and clarify the topic (what is it about, what is relevant or irrelevant) and also to identify potentially useful search terms.

Situation 2: Perceived errors

Another common scenario was repeated error or inexplicable responses (these could be similar to those above, such as very high numbers of hits, but were interpreted in a more negative fashion, e.g. as that an error had occurred). This was accompanied by feelings of frustration and inadequacy. (See Figure 20.2.)

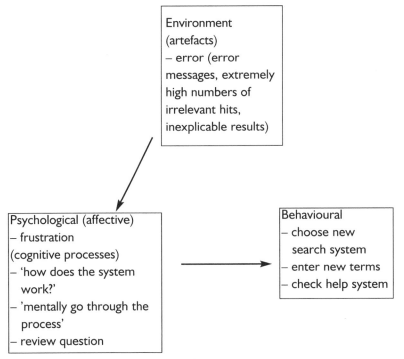

Fig. 20.2   *Situation 2: Perceived errors*

As commented earlier the process of searching was highly iterative, far more so than expected. On average respondents changed their search tool (search engine, OPAC, etc.) five times per search session. Choosing to search new systems seemed, from the researcher's point of view, illogical. Respondents in these situations were expected to spend more time reflecting on the process and developing search strategies that could be more effective. However, perhaps this apparent 'knee jerk' is in fact a rational strategy to cut one's losses and start searching 'fresh pastures' and should be seen as part of the wider process of orientating the respondent to the general subject domain and potential resources, as discussed earlier.

The lack of planning and the limited use of vocabulary corresponds with the findings of Spink, Bateman and Jansen's (1998) study on Excite searching, where the mean number of search terms was 3.34 and also later studies of over one million web queries (Spink et al., 2001) and those described in Jansen and Pooch's (2000) review of web-searching studies.

In this study, more often than not, search terms were limited to words or phrases found in the question. The following data resulted from observing the actions of the respondents. The vertical bar | indicates a fresh search.

– Information commodity | information + commodity | information services | information services + commodification | information commodity | commodification of information.
– User training + library resources | library user training | library instruction | library + computer + training + system | library + computer + training.

It was evident that the respondents did not find this an easy process and thinking of relevant terms was difficult. This may have been exacerbated by the fact the respondents were Singaporean, many of whom, despite studying in English throughout their education, generally prefer to use their mother tongue when talking to friends or family. However, the experience of teaching British students information retrieval shows similar problems occur with speakers of English as a first language. Other researchers have also identified the use of a limited range of vocabulary, for example in the USA and UK, Spink and Xu (2000) found that on average a query contained 2.21 terms when searching Excite and one in three had only one term. It may also be the case that if the searchers had been experts on these search topics then they would have had a broader range of vocabulary to draw on and a clearer idea of what they wanted as well as what was relevant and irrelevant.

Situation 3: 'Relevant material' found

Once materials were found that seemed to have relevance, further exploration took place. Features within the artefacts were then used to try and identify relevant material. For example, hypertext links to material with the same index terms were selected or links within or from a website were selected. Respondents also started to record elements such as call numbers and titles, and also to identify and note keywords and useful search terms, etc. Items such as headlines, texts, references and websites were perceived to be relevant when:

- they helped to answer the question
- they helped to explain what the topic was about
- items contained terms in the question
- items contained terms that could be useful
- items contained links to other potentially useful items.

Respondents did find it difficult to determine relevance. Comments such as 'not sure if relevant', 'seems relevant' were common. Respondents complained that in many cases headlines or bibliographic references were inadequate for judging relevance and that a summary or abstract would have been useful. See Figure 20.3 for a representation of these situations.

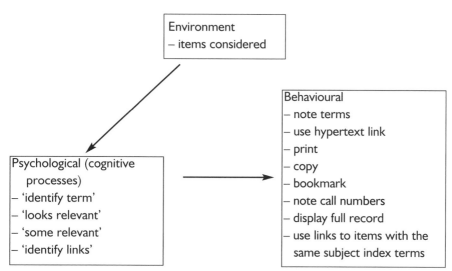

Fig. 20.3 *Situation 3: 'Relevant material' found*

Situation 4: Poor knowledge of artefacts

A fourth scenario was identified that reflected the respondents' lack of knowledge about the artefacts (databases, etc.) that would either help them locate documents or contained the full text of documents. It can be seen (Figure 20.4) that the respondent's strategy in this situation was a tendency to:

- try the artefact and see whether useful information was found
- choose the broadest collection of artefacts (sources) or, where possible,
- browse a list of sources.

Seldom was the latter strategy enabled by the system or services and when it was, insufficient information was provided to enable the respondent to make a well informed choice. Not knowing where to go for information is a familiar phenomenon and the poor performance of students in this area has been recognized (Allen, 1991; Seiden, Szymborski and Norelli, 1997).

Bearing in mind that the respondents were Information Studies students it was salutary to witness the difficulty they experienced in identifying useful electronic indexes or full-text sources. The respondents were generally unsuc-

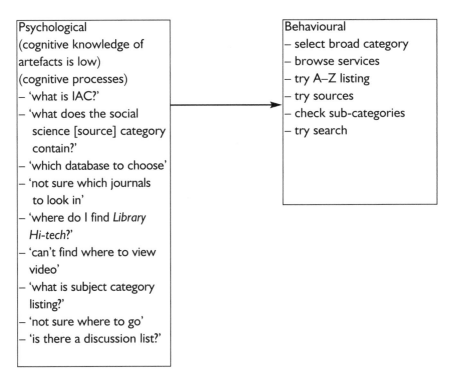

Fig. 20.4 *Situation 4: Poor knowledge of artefacts*

cessful in finding guidance that helped them to identify relevant sources. One of the attractions of the world wide web over other electronic information services is perhaps the fact that it appears to provide one window on to 'all' information; there is therefore no perceived necessity to choose particular artefacts that provide good coverage of specific topics.

Situation 5: Lack of knowledge of the subject

As stated earlier, respondents generally had little knowledge of the specific subject domain about which they were searching. This was reflected in their numerous statements such as 'What is the topic about?', 'Need to understand the topic', etc. and resulted in respondents referring back to the question, trying to identify relevant terms in the retrieved items, and in some cases the use of thesauri or dictionaries. Referring back to the question occurred throughout the search sequence and in 15 out of 29 search sessions. The following statements collected during observation/talk-through reflect the need for respondents to clarify the topic and the difficulty they experienced. Each statement falls under the psychological heading and indicates the thinking processes of the respondents. Because of the number of quotations they have not been represented in a figure. However, as before, the psychological data was associated with the behavioural data as shown below. Interaction with artefacts is indicated by reference to using OED or broadening the search, which implied using the search tools.

Psychological (cognitive processes) included: 'need to define concepts', 'no controlled vocabulary', 'must ask professor if on right track', 'what is the topic about?', 'remind myself of search topic', 'look at question and try to identify synonyms' [resulted in one phrase], 'identify terms' [resulted in two phrases], 'what is expected?' [resulted in one term], 'think about question', 'search not well defined', 'change words', 'must narrow', 'need to refine', 'try to define using OED' [unsuccessful], 'use all words from question', 'understand question', 'look for keywords related to the question', 'identify keywords from abstract', 'what is the question aiming at?', 'look at question again', 'title appears relevant but not', 'looking for terms on information services', 'take a broad start', 'not what I want', 'browse titles to see if additional terms to pick up', 'want an overview of different types of books available', 'didn't find right subject', [use Yahoo] 'to get more perspective on what commodification means'.

Behavioural responses included:

- referring back to the question
- using artefacts that help define and identify terms and subjects (such as OED – this only occurred in four cases but nevertheless has implications for the kind of help required)
- using techniques to broaden or narrow the search as a means to help identify relevant subject matter
- searching and browsing to identify terms and orientate themselves to the subject domain.

The cognitive processes can be seen to fall primarily into two categories: trying to identify relevant terminology and trying to understand what the search topic is about – both are obviously interrelated. These questions reflect a lack of knowledge about the subject domain and also the process whereby the individual orientates themselves to the topic and starts to build a mental map of the subject domain in terms of relevant concepts and relevant and irrelevant subject matter. This lack was not supported by any of the systems with which the respondents interacted.

Situation 6: Lack of knowledge of search techniques and system functionality

This situation (see Figure 20.5) identified inadequate thinking processes in terms of the students' ability to construct search strategies combined with a lack of knowledge of system functionality.

In general limited search functionality was used. In terms of Boolean logic the Boolean AND was the most common command (43 times out of 150 search strategies), proximity operators were only used once. The Boolean OR was used explicitly only twice. Parentheses were only used twice. Field searching was hardly used (keyword ten times, title three times). Truncation was only used eight times. For all respondents the most common strategy was to enter either a single term, several single terms or a phrase or phrases. Again these findings are supported by the work of Spink, Bateman and Jansen (1998) where little search syntax was evident and also in Spink et al. (2001) where a study of searching Excite discovered that only 5% of searches used any Boolean. However, it should be noted that in both studies the population was mixed and not solely made up of IS students where expectations in terms of search ability are higher.

Help systems were generally found useful when specific command syntax was needed but did not help with the need for more general strategies to help broaden or narrow the search. These findings, which show a lack of 'sophisticated' search commands and limited use of Boolean logic, echo the findings of other authors such as Ray and Day (1998), Spink and Xu (2000) and Rowley (2000).

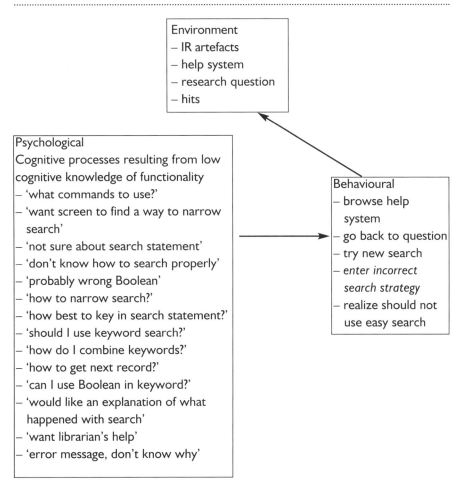

Fig. 20.5 *Situation 6: Lack of knowledge about search techniques and system functionality*

Implications for information literacy training

If these situations reflect the experience of learners when looking for information on an unfamiliar domain, then students should be taught to expect these situations and be given strategies to deal with them. Strategies should be tied to situations and not be conveyed in isolation. Trainers are likely to state that they already teach people how to do all of these things suggested below. However, they should question whether they actually link the advice to dealing with specific situations or whether IR skills are learnt in an abstract way. There is a big difference between saying here is the range of sources available or here is a list of commands which can be used, and saying which is useful in which situation.

Here are some examples:

Unsatisfactory results

Students should be encouraged to reformulate the search, refine the search and include other terms. They should also be asked to consider whether they are searching the correct source.

Perceived errors

Systematic use of the help system should be suggested. Many students (and other users) tend to blunder on rather than seek reference material that could help such as the help system, user guide, etc. The apparent 'simplicity' of the web and web search engines has to some extent given a false impression that IR should be simple and not require reference material. Alternatively, choosing a new search tool and using different search terms should also be suggested.

Relevant material found

Once relevant material has been found, students need to know how to capture material, whether simply cutting and pasting into suitably organized files or noting call numbers to follow up books or references for articles. This may seem obvious but it is not an aspect of the IR process that is generally made explicit, i.e. to capture data so that it can be used. Students should be encouraged to note down new terms that may be useful and to explore links between information such as subject headings that could be used to retrieve other related material.

Poor knowledge of artefacts

Knowing where to go for information has been a traditional skill of librarians. Students do not necessarily have any knowledge of the information landscape in their discipline, e.g. how or where information is published, and the information artefacts that can help to locate information, such as indexes. This knowledge needs to be conveyed.

Lack of knowledge of the subject

It is understandable that students have little knowledge of the subject they are studying, particularly in the first year. However the implications of this for IR are seldom made explicit. Students therefore need to be encouraged to break the question down into conceptual areas and what may or may not be related or relevant. The use of dictionaries, thesauri, encyclopedias and possibly newspaper and magazine sources (which could provide a good overview of a topic) that can help orientate the learner to the subject domain and identify search terms that may be useful should be seen as an integral part of the IR task. Browsing as wide a range of material to help build a conceptual map of the subject domain should be encouraged.

Lack of knowledge of search techniques and system functionality

Other authors, for example Rowley (2000), have noted the lack of students' knowledge of how these IR systems work and their functionality. Again students should be encouraged to take a systematic approach to cope with this situation. For example they should be encouraged to use the help systems, understand the structure of the IR system, appreciate the difference between easy and expert mode and be aware of the commands that are common to most IR systems, such as Boolean logic, proximity, truncation and field searching.

Conclusion

Information literacy is a broad and complex subject. It can be viewed in terms of abstract processes that can encompass all aspects of learning, or on a smaller scale in terms of the research process, or at the micro level in terms of moments of interaction with information systems. Identifying these processes can help to identify skills and evaluate performance. Alternatively, information literacy can be viewed from the perspective of the learner. In this case the researcher and teacher are concerned with identifying the critical situations experienced by the learner, understanding these situations from the learner's perspective, and using these situations to develop appropriate skills. Both approaches have their strengths and weaknesses. It is useful to know the range of commands and sources, the help system, etc., and this knowledge is currently conveyed by trainers. However it is a very different way of learning, and probably for many easier, to learn how to deal with specific situations. Learning is then contextualized, less abstract, and motivation is raised because learners can see the relevance of the training. They are then in a position to draw on appropriate strategies when specific situations are recognized.

The processes that have been identified by other authors ('distinguish ways of addressing the gap', etc.), as noted, do reflect key processes that learners need to be familiar with. However, in information-seeking situations, these processes apply more to the well defined question where people can think about their request and identify quickly key terms to look for and an appropriate strategy.

For example, when looking for a recommended book the learner enters the author's name in the author field or searches for the title in the title field. Specific situations and/or problems may need to be dealt with, for example knowing the correct format for the author's name, but it is a very different experience for the learner to use an IR system to try and identify material on, and learn about, a new topic. In the latter case, the learner needs to be able to deal with the situations identified above and also to be comfortable with a highly iterative process.

References

ACRL (2000) *Information Literacy Competencies Standards for Higher Education: standards, performance indicators and outcomes*, Chicago, ACRL. Available at www.ala.org/Content/NavigationMenu/ACRL/Standards_and_Guidelines/ Standards_and_Guidelines_by_Topic.htm.

Allen, B. (1991) Cognitive Research in Information Science: implications for design. In Williams, M. (ed.), *ARIST (Annual Review of Information Science and Technology)*, **26**, Medford, NJ, Learned Information, 3–37. Available at www.asis.org/Publications/bookstore/arist.html.

Bruce, C. (1997) *The Seven Faces of Information Literacy*, Adelaide, Auslib Press.

Doyle, C. (1992) *Final Report to the National Forum on Information Literacy*, ED351033, Syracuse, NY, ERIC Clearing House on Information Technology.

Eisenberg, M. and Berkowitz, R. (1990) *Information Problem Solving: the Big Six skills approach to library and information skills instruction*, Norwood, NJ, Ablex.

Ellis, D. (1989) A Behavioural Approach to Information Retrieval Design, *Journal of Documentation*, **45** (3), 171–212.

Ellis, D. (1993) Modelling the Information Seeking Patterns of Academic Researchers: a grounded theory approach, *Library Quarterly*, **63** (1), 469–86.

Jansen, B. and Pooch, U. (2000) A Review of Web Searching Studies and a Framework for Future Research, *Journal of the American Society for Information Science*, **53** (3), 235–46.

Kuhlthau, C. C. (1991) Inside the Search Process: information seeking from the user's perspective, *Journal of the American Society of Information Science*, **42** (5), 361–71.

Ray, K. and Day, J. (1998) Student Attitudes towards Electronic Information Resources, *Information Research*, **4** (2). Available at www.shef.ac.uk/~is/ publications/infres/paper54.html.

Rowley, J. (2000) JISC *User Behaviour Monitoring and Evaluation Framework: first annual report*, Edge Hill, JISC. Available at www.jisc.ac.uk/pub00/ m&e_repl.html.

SCONUL (1999) *Information Skills in Higher Education: a SCONUL position paper*, London, SCONUL. Available at www.sconul.ac.uk/publications/ publications.htm#2.

Seiden, P., Szymborski, K. and Norelli, B. (1997) *Undergraduate Students in the Digital Library: information seeking behavior in an heterogeneous environment.* Available at www.ala.org/acrl/paperhtm/c26.html.

Shneiderman, B., Byrd, D. and Croft, B. (1997) Clarifying Search: a user interface framework for test searches, *D-Lib Magazine*. Available at www.dlib.org/dlib/ january97/retrieval/01shneiderman.html.

Spink, A. and Xu, J. (2000) Selected Results from a Large Study of Web Searching: the Excite study, *Information Research*, **6** (1). Available at www.shef.ac.uk/~is/ publications/infres/paper90.html.

Spink, A., Bateman, J. and Jansen, B. (1998) Searching Heterogeneous Collections on the Web: behaviour of Excite users, *Information Research*, **4** (2). Available at http://informationr.net/ir/4-2/paper53.html.

Spink, A. et al. (2001) Searching the Web: the public and their queries, *Journal of the American Society of Information Science and Technology*, **52** (3), 226–34.

21

Schoolchildren searching the internet – teachers' perceptions

Andrew Madden, Nigel Ford, David Miller and Philippa Levy

Introduction

The continuing rapid development of ICT (information and communications technology) offers the 21st-century learner a growing range of information resources, many of which are accessible through the internet. Unfortunately, the volume of resources available on the internet, together with the variability in their quality, makes the internet a very confusing place to search. Although a great deal has been written on internet searching by adults however, surprisingly few studies have examined children's use of the internet and of search engines. This chapter discusses a project initiated by the University of Sheffield in collaboration with a secondary school to examine what can be done to fill this gap.

An unresearched area

In 1998, Schacter, Chung and Dorr observed that 'Children's information seeking and use of the internet are virtually unexplored areas'. This comment was echoed by Bilal two years later. Furthermore, it is hard to generalize from the few studies that do exist. Hsieh-Yee (2001), for example, summarizes eight studies of children's web search behaviour that took place in North America between 1997 and 2000. The ages investigated ranged from six to 15 years old, and the numbers of students in each study group varied considerably, with at least half of the studies involving fewer than ten students. Although it may seem surprising that there has been so little research, given the extent to which the internet affects modern life in the developed world, it should be remembered that the personal computer and the internet have become a widely accepted part of Western culture.

A recent phenomenon

The statistics in Table 21.1 show how rapidly access to computers and the internet has grown in the last decade. Clearly, such access was necessary before students could begin to search the internet. It was also necessary, however, that the internet should be available in a form that made it easy to search. Although it has been around for nearly 40 years, it was not until the release of the world wide web in 1991, followed by that of Mosaic (the first graphical browser) in 1993, that use of the internet became intuitive to anyone familiar with a Windows PC or Apple Mac (Berners-Lee, 1999).

Table 21.1 *Statistics indicating the levels of access to ICT and the internet in England and the USA*

Year	UK	USA
1991–2	21% of households in Britain had a home computer.[1]	22.7% of households in the US had a home computer.[3]
1993–4	The average secondary school in England had one micro computer per 10 students. Fewer than a third of these were capable of supporting a graphical environment.[2]	
1994		3% of instructional rooms in state schools had access to the internet.[4]
1998	Average of 8.7 students per computer in English schools. Two percent of school computers linked to the internet.[5]	51% of instructional rooms in state schools had access to the internet. One internet computer to 12 students.[4]
1999	Average of 27 internet computers per English secondary school.[5]	
2000		51% of households with a computer (41.5% with internet access)[3]
2001	>99% of English secondary schools connected, with an average of 108 online computers per school.[5] >75% of adults accessed the internet from their own home.[6]	

[1] Great Britain. Office for National Statistics (2001)
[2] Great Britain. Department for Education (1995)
[3] US Census Bureau (2000)
[4] National Centre for Education Statistics (2001)
[5] Great Britain. Department for Education and Skills (2001)
[6] National Statistics StatBase (2002)

The importance of the internet in education is now indisputable, and large-scale studies of the search habits of school children are now practicable. In November 2001, a three-year AHRB (Arts and Humanities Research Board)-funded project, 'Education for Evidence-based Citizenship: improving pupils' information seeking skills' was begun at the University of Sheffield. One of the questions the project seeks to address is: 'What tasks and activities do teachers require pupils to perform that (i) currently require or (ii) could potentially benefit from, effective internet information seeking and critical evaluative skills?' A preliminary attempt to answer these questions is presented below.

Focus of the project

The project is a collaboration between the University of Sheffield Department of Information Studies, and the City School in Sheffield. The City School is an 11–16 mixed community school with around 1500 pupils. According to the last Ofsted report (2001), 'The percentage of students known to be eligible for free school meals . . . is above the national average. Attainment on entry is below average. . . . The present percentage of pupils identified as having special educational needs . . . is also above the national average.' Despite these disadvantages, the report states that the school provides a satisfactory level of education. Among the things for which the school is commended are education in ICT and use of ICT to enhance learning across the curriculum. Not only does the school make good use of ICT, however; it also provides excellent access to ICT facilities. This access is increased by the fact that the school is home to one of the five City Learning Centres in Sheffield. It is not intended to suggest that this level of provision is representative of schools throughout the UK. Rather, as in the case of the study by Holloway, Valentine and Bingham (2000), because the intention of the project is to explore how children use ICT in the school setting, a school was chosen where student access is as free as possible.

Methods

In January and February 2002, a series of 20 semi-structured interviews was held in Sheffield. Eighteen of the interviewees were staff at City School, where interviews were held with two assistant head teachers, the senior learning mentor, the Special Educational Needs teacher, the library and learning centre manager, the co-ordinator of the scheme for gifted and talented students, the literacy co-ordinator, the ICT Key Stage 3 co-ordinator, the work experience and careers co-ordinator, the network manager, and subject leaders in English, Mathematics, Humanities, Science, Music, PE, ICT and Art. Additional interviews were held with Heads of Centres, Institute of Education at Manchester

Metropolitan University, and with the manager of Newfields City Learning Centre in Sheffield.

It was intended that the AHRB project would be based on action research. The scarcity of research to date into internet searching by children makes the experiences and observations of the interviewees particularly valuable. The themes identified will inform subsequent stages of this project.

The main purpose of these interviews was to learn, from the observations of people with relevant experience, how students search the internet. Nevertheless, in the course of the interviews, several other, related themes, emerged. These are discussed in the next few paragraphs.

Results: Internet concerns

The interviewees were all positive in their view of the internet as a pedagogic resource. Some concerns were raised, however. Three people explicitly expressed concerns about pornography, though others, more guardedly, referred to 'unsuitable', 'unsavoury' and 'undesirable' sites. In addition, two interviewees had worries about the risk of picking up viruses.

Other concerns related to aspects of accessibility: 'It's a very valuable resource – when it works . . . have problems with continuity of sites where we direct the kids to a site one day, go to the same site the following day and somebody's upgraded or something, it's unavailable'; 'I'm reaching a point where I reach a firewall and I can't get onto bits that are supposed to extend out of the site, and that is very frustrating.'

Results: Teaching with the internet

None of the interviewees had received formal training in using the internet. Mostly it had been 'picked up along the way'. Levels of experience varied considerably, from several years to a few months. One teacher claimed never to have used the internet. All the interviewees had, however, supervised classes of students using the internet. Many reported problems keeping the class 'on task', but all felt in control: 'More so than normal because it appeals so strongly to the pupils that you have less discipline problems in that situation than you have in the normal classroom situation.'

Some of those teachers who lacked confidence in their ability to use ICT were able to turn their lack of knowledge to an advantage:

> I always say at the beginning 'Look – I'm an old teacher – I don't know as much about computers as you – I know how they can be used, I know how they're useful, I know how important they are. You are part of a generation that is going through

school and through life, etc.' We do that. And that works very well. I've got the confidence to do that, and the brazenness to do it, and to harness it in a way.

When I first got these computers, I thought I was going to be really embarrassed by my lack of knowledge, but the kids haven't really been bothered at all by that. They've understood completely, and helped me, and that's been really, really nice actually, because they don't seem to think any less of me. But they've been very helpful to show off their skills, and teach me things. It's a two way thing, so that's been good.

Remarks from the teachers, and from the CLC (City Learning Centres) manager interviewed, suggested that classroom management skills were of far greater importance than ICT skills: 'It's very easy – if you're around a class of computers – [to see] who is actually on task and who isn't on task, so classroom management sorts that out'; 'I think it's a fantastic tool for the classroom – it brings everything in – but you have to be very, very careful. If you blink the kids can go and surf somewhere else, especially if the computers are turned away from you'; 'There is a real development need for teachers in managing an ICT facility for a class . . . I've seen teachers say "Go and search for this" and I see kids who look like they're off task to be frank. It tended not to work. It tends to create classroom management problems, 'cause kids end up all over the place.'

Results: A different resource for different students

One of the most positive themes to emerge was the extent to which the internet is of value in complementing traditional information resources that might present difficulties to some students: 'Some students appear to be able to read more effectively from a computer screen than from a book, and so have higher level computer reading skills than you would perhaps anticipate'; 'I think some kids actually find it easier to access information via computer than they do via say, maybe going to a book or going to the library'.

Interestingly, gender was less of an issue than might have been expected from studies such as Holloway, Valentine and Bingham (2000). Where it was raised, it was in the context of learning styles:

I think the boys particularly – it's much easier to direct them to art history with the computers. The girls will do what you've asked them to, 'cause they're very conscientious here. The lads . . . with the computer, they're much happier, much more at ease, much more comfortable than wading through a book – particularly those who have a struggle with literacy.

Some kids, especially girls, are quite good at looking at a book and writing it all down neatly, and they seem to remember that: but boys don't have that. Boys need to do and find out, and somehow having a mixture can work quite well.

Results: Factors limiting internet use

Despite their positive experiences with the internet, many of the teachers did not use it as extensively as they would have liked. The main problem they encountered was lack of time: 'We don't actually have the time on the courses that we run in school to . . . put students onto the internet, although we do use it for one of our projects'; 'There is an issue about time to search for and prepare learning with on-line resources.' This is being addressed in South Yorkshire, however, by an e-learning project which is 'providing time for teachers to produce materials and to seek resources and to develop those into learning packages'.

Another factor affecting usage appears to be the prescriptive nature of the National Curriculum: 'a lot of teachers come back to me and say . . . "why should I use the Internet?/I.T.? I can get my kids through the examinations – get the A to C's they need, they never need to touch a computer" '; 'In the situation that I'm in, having taught so long, I've got most of the kind of resources and materials that they need to process them through an examination.'

Results: Observations on internet searching

ICT training was provided to all Year 7 students, so none of the teachers encountered students who did not have the technical skills needed to search the internet. More problematic was the lack of skills needed to cope with the large number of hits that a search generated. Most interviewees were concerned about the quality of material retrieved, and its appropriateness to the students' level of education: 'The problem there is . . . actually sifting through what is relevant and what isn't relevant on the Internet. You can spend hours just looking for stuff and you will find complete nonsense'; 'It's got some problems – we have problems with the level of language on the Internet. Sometimes the language is too high for the kids – it can be inappropriate totally.'

Several of the teachers noted that students seemed to be drawn to pages by their appearance rather than their content: 'They like the sites that are colourful – that have got interaction, and the actual quality of the information in them may not be so relevant'; 'They tend to go for things with animation and colour.'

The teachers interviewed generally found that the students needed to be directed: 'I've learned from experience that they do need quite a lot of direction . . . and the ideal of allowing them freedom for independent research, doesn't always work as effectively. They need to possibly have more structure than I would have anticipated in the early days of using the Internet.'

The direction took one of two forms. Most commonly, students were provided with a list of appropriate URLs: 'We direct them to certain sites . . . rather than just using a free search.' More subtly, they were led by example:

> I've also been on the Internet myself previously and checked out one or two sites. Then I'll say to the class 'How about we use Google as a search engine . . .'. I'm always directing them to the sites I've already looked at. I'm not giving them [pre-selected sites, saying] 'You must use this site' . . . I'm guiding them to those sites so they're not tempted to put anything else in . . . you check their words in their searches . . . so it looks as if we're working together. Very sly.

Such direction tended to be aimed at younger students. There was a general perception that, as they got older, students became more discerning and could be given more freedom in their searching: 'We talk about are there any key indicators where the information's quality – particularly in Y10. Not in Y7 so much. It's difficult to introduce the concept of . . . what quality of information are you receiving. But in Y10 it's somewhat easier'; 'You change the use, so it becomes independent use when they're old and they can handle it – there's time, compared to directed use lower down the school.'

The internet was, not surprisingly, a widely used source of information for Key Stage 4 students researching their individual GCSE (General Certificate of Secondary Education) projects. In such circumstances, student searches would not, in general, be directed by teachers.

One of the key factors identified was the interaction between students. Teachers frequently noted the extent to which children helped each other in classes:

> There are students who find it difficult and haven't got computers at home, but there's always someone in the class willing to help them. They're very . . . very good at helping each other, and that's really nice.

> A couple of nights ago some youngsters . . . had to do some research on Emmeline Pankhurst, so they just clicked on Google, typed in Emmeline Pankhurst and . . . they came up with multiple references but they went for the first one that was what they wanted, and basically that's what they used for their source. But then someone else must have put something different in and they came up with just a slightly different one and they were all interested, because otherwise they were all getting the same reference . . . so they shared that information.

Where there is an efficient communications network, it seems only one student needs to do a successful search in order for the class to benefit. Students were considered by their teachers to be unimaginative and undiscerning in their searches; but in a community where news of a useful, an interesting, or an entertaining website can spread rapidly, such qualities do not need to be common: 'There's obviously currency in web sites, and they share information in that way.'; 'What tends to happen is someone discovers it and it goes round like wildfire'; 'Word of mouth . . . is quicker than any tannoy system.'

Conclusion

All the interviewees clearly appreciated the internet as a pedagogic tool, despite being well aware of its shortcomings. Its value in providing an alternative resource for students who struggled with traditional resources was widely recognized. Most teachers, however, felt that they had too little time to incorporate internet-based resources into their teaching, and that the narrowness of the National Curriculum acted as a disincentive. Younger students, it was felt, benefited from clear guidance when they searched the internet, though students clearly helped one another; and details of useful or interesting sites circulated rapidly.

Issues arising

The findings summarized in the paragraph above prompt two questions about the teaching of internet search skills in schools:

1   Although research in the area is limited, some studies have been done in which school children were asked to carry out finding tasks and searching tasks on the internet, and their levels of success were compared. According to Schacter, Chung and Dorr (1998), children performing finding tasks, to glean specific information such as 'What are the three types of crime that happen most in California' (Schacter, Chung and Dorr, 1998) proved less successful than children carrying out searching tasks, where more general information is sought (e.g. 'Find at least three pieces of information that will help you develop a plan to reduce crime in California'). At City School, teachers noted that Key Stage 3 students are less successful at searching than Key Stage 4 students. While student age may indeed be a factor, it may also be the case that the nature of the searches is different. Do teachers tend to set younger students the task of finding the answers to specific questions, while older children are engaged on more open searches of the type usually associated with project research? Although the findings of Bilal (2000,

2001) did not support the findings of Schacter, Chung and Dorr, the question still has relevance.

2 Usually, computer rooms follow traditional classroom design, with rows of computers on long benches, and all students facing the front. A common alternative is for 'islands' of tables, which seat three to four students: 'it means that the students are looking at each other and therefore there is an in-built tendency to talk to the person across from you: you can see their face.' Given the extent to which students appear to be helping and informing each other, should such designs be encouraged?

Future stages of this project will focus on the students themselves. It is to be hoped that the findings will help to answer these, and other, related questions.

References

Berners-Lee, T. (1999) *Weaving the Web*, London, Orion Publishing.

Bilal, D. (2000) Children's Use of the Yahooligans! Web Search Engine: I. Cognitive, physical, and affective behaviours on fact-based search tasks, *Journal of the American Society for Information Science*, **51** (7), 646–65.

Bilal, D. (2001) Children's Use of the Yahooligans! Web Search Engine: II.Cognitive and physical behaviours on research tasks, *Journal of the American Society for Information Science*, **52** (2) 19–136

Great Britain. Department for Education (1995) *Statistical Bulletin: survey of information technology in schools*, Issue 3/95. (Government Statistical Service).

Great Britain. Department for Education and Skills (2001) *Statistics of Education: Survey of Information and Communications Technology in Schools 2001*. Available at www.dfes.gov.uk/statistics/DB/SBU/b0296/sb09-2001.pdf/.

Great Britain. Office for National Statistics (2001) *Living in Britain: results from the 2000/01 General Household Survey*, HMSO. Available at www.statistics.gov.uk/lib2000/resources/fileAttachments/GHS2000.pdf [accessed 17 June 2003].

Holloway, S. L., Valentine, G. and Bingham, N. (2000) Institutionalising Technologies: masculinities, femininities, and the heterosexual economy of the IT classroom, *Environment and Planning A*, **32** (4), 617–33.

Hsieh-Yee, I. (2001) Research on Web Search Behaviour, *Library & Information Science Research*, **23** (2), 167–85.

National Centre for Education Statistics (2001) Available at http://nces.ed.gov/pubs2001/2001071.pdf.

National Statistics StatBase (2002) Available at www.statistics.gov.uk/statbase/.

Ofsted (2001) *The City School Sheffield. Report*, Available at www.ofsted.gov.uk/inspect/index.htm.

Schacter, J., Chung, G. K. and Dorr, A. (1998) Children's Internet Searching on Complex Problems: performance and process analyses, *Journal of the American Society for Information Science*, **49** (9), 840–9.

US Census Bureau (2000) *Home Computers and Internet Use in the United States.* Available at www.census.gov/prod/2001pubs/p23-207.pdf.

22

Attitudes of academics to the library's role in information literacy education

Claire McGuinness

Introduction

This chapter presents a section of the results from an ongoing PhD study, which explores the status of IL (information literacy) education within the context of third-level, undergraduate education in the Irish Republic. The study purports to build upon, and extend, prior research, which has been conducted into the nature of IL and its relationship to the educational process, although it is conducted not from the perspective of learners, but rather from the standpoint of those whose role it is to facilitate learning by others, in this case, academic lecturers. The topic is approached from an implementation viewpoint; IL is explored from the perspective of the often crowded world of the academic lecturer, in an attempt to understand the absence of IL programmes from most undergraduate curricula in the Irish Republic, although the focus is on two contrasting disciplines: Sociology, a research-based academic discipline, and Civil Engineering, a vocational discipline. This professional group has been chosen as the study sample for a number of reasons:

1 Lecturers exercise a great deal of autonomy over curriculum content, and for the most part decide what will be included in, and excluded from, their programmes. Thus, the place of IL education in undergraduate curricula depends primarily on their attitudes towards it. Equally, students are disinclined to engage in learning tasks that are not mandated by their lecturers, and not credit bearing.

2 Academics are perceived as the gatekeepers to undergraduate education; those seeking to implement IL education have no choice but to engage with them.

3   There has been relatively little written about academics' perceptions and attitudes towards IL and IL education – most of the literature on this topic is written 'by librarians for librarians' (Donnelly, 2000, 65) Much of the evidence thus far is anecdotal, pertaining to the experiences of individuals in different contexts. There has only been one major attempt to systematically investigate academics' attitudes in this context (Hardesty, 1991).

4   It is important to give voice to academics on this subject, since most of what is written, is from the LIS (Library and Information Services) perspective. By understanding how the academic environment appears to academics, we may gain valuable insight into the factors that constrain and enable the implementation of change, including IL education.

5   There is an assumption among LIS professionals that the integration of IL into teaching curricula is the optimum way to ensure that students become information literate. However, examples of successful initiatives are comparatively rare (although increasing), and non-existent in some contexts. Much IL education appears to consist of 'bolt-on' sessions, which closely resemble traditional BI (bibliographic instruction) – library tours, one-shot presentations, etc. The blame for this state of affairs is laid squarely on the shoulders of the academics, who are perceived to be loath to share their classrooms with others, including librarians.

Definition

While this research is not directly concerned with seeking a new definition for IL, it is essential to acknowledge the debate surrounding a viable working definition. The phenomenon has proven difficult to define; while the ALA (American Library Association) statement (1989) is the most commonly-referred-to definition, the meaning of the term continues to be disputed, and remains a 'vexed question' (Todd, 1999, 27). Some question whether the concept of IL actually describes something new, or whether it merely constitutes a repackaging of the concept known variously as bibliographic instruction, user education, library research, etc. While many of the proposed definitions posit IL as a set of skills and attributes that, once acquired, render an individual 'information literate', this approach has been criticized for its lack of contextual sensitivity, and assumption that skills are transferable across different situations. More recent approaches, such as Bruce's (1997), suggest that IL may be depicted as the relationship between individuals and information in a variety of contexts; she contends that individuals experience information use in unique ways, with conceptions focusing variously on differing aspects such as information technology, or information sources. Her 'Seven Faces' model is widely accepted as a significant forward step in our understanding of the individual experience of IL.

Teacher librarians – a question of status?

LIS professionals, in particular, have embraced the idea of IL education, and envisage a pivotal role for themselves in the process, with the resulting literature weighed heavily towards consideration of the teaching role of the academic librarian. The majority of papers are based on a key assumption, rarely challenged by LIS authors: namely, that library professionals are, by definition, the best qualified people to provide IL education, owing to their information expertise. Therefore, suggested strategies for how IL education should be delivered are fundamentally skewed towards the inclusion of librarians in key teaching positions, or as equal partners in collaborative initiatives with academic staff. In the literature, this assumption frequently results in expressions of frustration with academics, whom LIS professionals perceive to be indifferent to their efforts: 'Academic pariahs whom legitimate faculty may denigrate or merely tolerate, but do not generally completely embrace, librarians continue to wage an uphill battle for intellectual respect among colleagues in other departments' (Hauptman and Hill, 1990).

The present IL movement reflects an issue that is of fundamental concern to academic librarians, and relates to how they believe they are perceived by other segments of society. This is not a novel issue – during the 1970s, similar concerns ignited the debate concerning faculty status for librarians in the USA, and culminated in the publication of the ACRL (Association of College and Research Libraries) Joint Statement in 1974; this document was reaffirmed as recently as June 2001, which demonstrates the continuing relevance of this issue. The IL movement offers a framework for librarians to reassert their claims, and the issues are closely linked.

However, it is important, according to Breivik (1992), 'not to confuse the development of IL with library or bibliographic instruction' (10). She contends that these concepts are differentiated on the basis of their location within the general curriculum. While BI programmes are widespread, they are generally conceived of as 'bolt-on' courses, and 'discounted by students as an extrinsic part of the coursework' (Breivik, 1992). A key theme of the IL movement is 'curriculum integration' and relates to the notion that learning is facilitated most effectively when instruction is supplied at the point of need, e.g. when a particular research project has been set. This contrasts with 'traditional' BI methods, which are ostensibly unrelated to specific learning tasks, for example, library tours at the beginning of the undergraduate career. By contrast, suggested models for curriculum integration include credit courses in IL, or joint assignment setting by academic and library staff. Descriptions of actual IL initiatives in universities are increasingly available in the literature, and range from small-scale initiatives, to major curriculum restructuring. While some of these programmes appear successful, there is a sense that they are difficult to implement, with academic staff expressing little interest in getting involved, apart from occasional, enthusiastic, pro-library individuals.

This apparent lack of academic support, then, begs the question whether IL does, in fact, address a genuine need, or whether it is merely a flagship concern of LIS professionals, who are uncertain of their professional standing. This question remains largely unexplored. Where made, however, the arguments challenging librarian involvement in teaching are powerful; authors such as McCrank (1991), Foster (1993) and Boyce (1999) have questioned the motives behind the IL movement, concluding that IL is little more than an instrument of propaganda for LIS professionals, dissatisfied with their professional status. Other papers by Eadie (1990), Gorman (1991) and Pacey (1995) question the necessity of BI, arguing that the function of LIS professionals is not to teach, but rather to remove the barriers that prevent users from making effective use of the library. Smith (1997) suggests that, rather than attempting to fill a teaching role, a more effective strategy for librarians would be to train academic staff to provide IL education themselves. This contradicts much of what is written about teacher librarians. Acceptance of the above arguments has interesting implications for the future of IL; it suggests that, rather than treating academic staff as adversaries, and investing abundant energy into promoting themselves as teachers, LIS professionals should seek achievable ways to involve academics. A thorough understanding of the motivations and attitudes of academic staff in different contexts is a natural first step in this direction.

Although sparse, research that considers the position of academic teaching staff vis-à-vis IL education has appeared at intervals. Most empirical studies have sought to gauge academics' library-related attitudes, or attitudes towards BI. The most comprehensive study was carried out by Hardesty (1991), who developed and tested an attitude scale, the purpose of which was to: 'accurately describe the library-related educational attitudes of undergraduate faculty members'. Up to 20 other papers have also been identified by the researcher, the majority using large-scale questionnaire surveys to assess the attitudes and perceptions of academic staff. While results have been fairly consistent across different contexts, they do not necessarily provide in-depth understanding of the academic staff surveyed, and are mainly descriptive, focusing on, for instance, faculty preferences for particular BI instructional methods. Two studies have used interview data to supplement questionnaires (Dilmore, 1996; Leckie and Fullerton, 1999). The latter study, in particular, wished to explore: 'the factors involved in the why not? of the IL equation' (26), by conducting semi-structured interviews with academics in science and engineering faculties in two universities. The data gleaned from these interviews revealed a complexity of variables that influence the educational process in third-level institutions; these include, among others, class size, discipline, personal teaching philosophy, years of teaching and personal experiences learning to do library research, etc. The present study acknowledges the complex nature of the academic environment; academics are perceived not as deliberate adversaries, but rather as individuals operating under a different set of structures, whose perceptions do not necessarily align with those of librarians.

Rationale for study

The lack of integrated IL programmes in universities is attributed to reluctance on the part of academic staff, who are perceived as being in powerful positions in terms of designing the undergraduate curricula, and loath to share the classroom with library staff. A common argument in favour of collaboration is the notion that the two groups share a common goal – the areas of concern within higher education correlate strongly with the need for IL education; issues such as active learning, critical thinking and lifelong learning, characteristic of the modern paradigm of constructivist learning theory, seem to be coterminous with the concepts associated with IL education, based on the construction of individual meaning through effective information handling. If this is the case, then it would seem the obvious route to take is that of co-operation. The questions raised here are important ones: why is it that issues that are perceived as urgent by LIS professionals are not considered so by academics? And does this necessarily mean that one, or other, of the groups may be considered to be misguided or at fault?

The answers to these questions lie in determining how academics view IL, and how they perceive that it 'fits' within third-level education. It is possible that librarians and academics do not share a view of IL. They are working within different domains, although ostensibly within the same environment. Equally, understanding the other concerns and priorities that occupy academics' time in the current system may lead LIS researchers to qualify their assumptions about faculty recalcitrance toward IL education. Hardesty (1995) noted that LIS professionals might not have a clear picture of the variables that affect faculty opinions of BI, as a result of being socialized to their profession in a different way from academics. This study acknowledges these contentions, and attempts to address them in a systematic way.

Methodology

Data was gathered using a semi-structured interview approach, to allow participants to express their opinions and describe their experiences in their own words. A relatively fixed set of questions was designed, to allow comparisons to be drawn between participants and between sample groups, but a flexible, qualitative approach permits exploration of emerging themes. Analysis focuses on participants' descriptive accounts of their working environments, as well as the attitudes and perceptions underpinning their actions. In this way, the researcher develops an understanding of the structures under which they operate, and of the social relationships between organizational members, which influence the nature of change in the various institutions, and in the system as a whole. Interview topics focus on variables in the academic environment, and on the relationships between academic and library staff. This chapter focuses on the participant sample of 20 academic lecturers from the Sociology departments in five Irish universities, and addresses aspects of their perceptions of the library and library staff in their institutions.

Relationship between academics and library staff

Contact between the two groups appears infrequent, and centred on functional matters, related to the acquisition and deployment of physical information resources, such as book ordering or placing reading-list items on reserve. Positive comments about library staff by the academics relate to the perceived efficiency with which a requested item was located, purchased or made available by the librarians, or to participants' perceptions of the personal demeanour of the library staff – 'friendly', 'helpful', etc. Collaboration between the two groups, in teaching terms, does not exist in the way in which it is advocated in the literature; rather, librarians appear as service-providers to the academics, principally concerned with the management of information resources. In this context, the librarians' function is depicted as reactive, in that they deal with queries and problems as they arise, and as requested by the academic staff. Most participants claim to contact the library only when they identify a particular information need, or at particular times of the year, in order to ensure that information resources are in place. None of the participants discuss curriculum-related matters, such as course design or teaching strategy, with library staff, nor do they involve them directly in any of their courses. Participants speak of library staff only in relation to the needs they themselves have with regard to the library, as users of the service – they regard the library as the place where certain functions are carried out, but do not explicitly associate the library services with specific individuals. This is illustrated in the way in which participants use the words 'library', 'librarians' and 'library staff' interchangeably – as long as library requests are satisfied, who deals with them is of little consequence.

It is evident that participants spend little time reflecting on the nature of their relationship with library staff, as they are busy with other concerns. There is little evidence of formal contact, with participants engaging in interaction only when a particular need has been identified. Academics, unless serving as representatives on the Library Users' Committee, do not attend formal meetings with library staff. Frequently, participants act as intermediary between their students and the library, particularly when dealing with complaints about the library concerning lost or damaged books, or other similar matters.

'I don't know, I mean they are kind of regarded as functionaries, as people who dispense books and replace books' (SocA1).

Perception of teaching role of library staff

While the majority of participants (90%) in this study expressed the belief that library staff do, or could have, a teaching role in undergraduate education, their interpretations of what this role entails correlate closely with their overall perception of librarians as support staff. None of the participants involve librarians directly in any of their courses; there is no evidence that the two groups collaborate on anything other than the occasional classroom session or library tour. The majority of interactions between library and academic staff entail discussions about the physical resources that academic staff wish to obtain, either for personal use, or for teaching. There is evidence that the teaching carried out by library staff is of minor concern for most academics; for many, the research interview was the first time they had considered the matter.

While participants express interest in the idea of librarians providing instructional sessions, they seem reluctant, or unable, to carry the idea through to its conclusion. Some participants refer to lack of time and opportunity as the main barrier. Others have difficulty in seeing where library staff fit into the undergraduate teaching process, and offer explanations as to why this is. Some suggest that librarians lack the necessary subject expertise to be involved in undergraduate teaching. Familiarity with disciplinary conventions is one of the requirements for admittance into most academic disciplines. While librarians are perceived as experts in their own subject area, librarianship, academics do not consider that this qualifies them to become involved in teaching subject disciplines other than their own; they simply do not possess the requisite subject knowledge. In one case, the participant contends that it is librarians themselves who perceive that their teaching role differs from that of academics. She makes several points: First, that the library community does not actively encourage academic research among their members, and that this might be a factor in how librarians perceive themselves in relation to academics; second, that librarians may not conceive of themselves as teachers, but rather as facilitators, and as such, may be reluctant to become involved in teaching.

On the whole, participants' comments reveal that they do not believe that library staff currently play a significant teaching role in the university, and that they (lecturers) are uncertain about how this could be achieved. In terms of the type of instruction that library staff could provide, the majority of suggestions appear focused on traditional BI; namely, becoming familiar with the library, using print and computerized resources, navigating the web and other online resources, and above all, finding or locating information. Librarians are responsible for teaching library-based skills. Participants' descriptions are overwhelmingly resource based, and centred on the concept of guiding students in the use of the on-site tools. This takes place in a variety of formats, ranging from simple reference desk queries, to the library induction programme, to formal classroom sessions and demonstrations. 'I think that librarians often perceive quite strong territorial demarcation between themselves and academics, and I don't know how they feel about participating in academic courses. . . . I think probably they wouldn't see themselves as teachers, they'd see themselves as facilitators' (SocB2).

Responsibility for IL education?

When participants were asked who they believed had primary responsibility for ensuring that students become 'information literate', rather than automatically indicating the library staff, the responses were varied. While participants agree that library staff carry out a particular form of teaching, centred on accessing and using information resources, the question of who effectively retains control over the process reveals a different picture. In most cases, participants tended to view this as their own, or the department's, responsibility. While some referred to librarians' responsibility in this process, comments focus mainly on the overall teaching process, and the constraints experienced by participants in managing their own teaching programmes. IL education is perceived as merely one of a number of imperatives facing academic staff, and participants' responses pointed to a tendency on their part to assume that students were 'picking it up' in the course of their studies, possibly related to their own experiences as students. While they admit that students are expected to be self-sufficient in becoming information literate, they also believe that this is a strategy that is ineffective: 'they don't pick them up themselves' (SocE3). Rather, in view of the various constraints experienced at third level, participants feel they have little choice except to assume that students are somehow, albeit haphazardly, developing information skills. Lack of time and resources are commonly cited constraints; there is a sense that IL education is not a high priority for the participants, despite their views that it is a matter of importance.

Participants refer to tutorials, small-group sessions, research courses, essay assignments and dissertations as appropriate forums in which students might develop information skills, or in which instruction should be concentrated. Ostensibly, these are learning situations over which lecturers exercise considerable control, in terms of curriculum planning. When librarians are mentioned in this context, it is in a reactive sense, whereby they are requested by lecturers to come in and provide a single session for a class, a library tour, or demonstration of resources. It is clear that while the participants regard librarians as effective instructors of library skills, they do not perceive anything other than a peripheral teaching role for them.

Conclusion

Past studies have indicated that academics are often reluctant to 'share the classroom' with library staff. In this study, there appears to be a fundamental inconsistency between the perceptions academic staff have of the teaching role played by library staff, and their beliefs about where the responsibility for providing IL education lies. While the majority of participants agree that librarians are teachers – of library skills – they also believe that students do not receive adequate training in this area, and that this is as a result of their own inattention to the problem. 'It's not something that we systematically address . . . and we should, because we are increasingly aware of its importance' (SocC1).

Acknowledgements

The author gratefully acknowledges the support of the Government of Ireland Scholarship in the Humanities and Social Sciences in the pursuit of this research.

References

ACRL (2001) *Joint Statement on Faculty Status of College and University Librarians.* Approved June 26, 1972. Reaffirmed by ACRL Board, June 2001. Available at www.ala.org/Content/NavigationMenu/ACRL/Standards_and_Guidelines/ Joint_Statement_on_Faculty_Status_of_College_and_University_Librarians.htm.

ALA (1989) *Presidential Committee on Information Literacy*, Washington DC, American Library Association. Available at www.ala.org/Template.cfm?Section= Information_Literacy&Template=/TaggedPage/TaggedPageDisplay.cfm& TPLID=4&ContentID=403.

Boyce, S. (1999) Second thoughts about information literacy. In Booker, D. I. (ed.) *Concept, Challenge, Conundrum: from library skills to information literacy. Proceedings of the Fourth National Information Literacy Conference conducted by the University of South Australia Library and the Australian Library and Information Association Information Literacy and Special Interest Group, 3–5 December, Adelaide*, Adelaide, University of South Australia Library.

Breivik, P. S (1992) Education for the information age. In Farmer, D. W. and Mech, T. F. (eds), *Information Literacy: developing students as independent learners*, San Francisco, Jossey Bass.

Bruce, C. (1997) *The Seven Faces of Information Literacy*, Adelaide, Auslib Press.

Dilmore, D. H. (1996) Librarian/Faculty Interaction at Nine New England Colleges. *College & Research Libraries News*, **57**, 274–84.

Donnelly, K. (2000) Building the Learning Library: where do we start? In Bahr, A. H. (ed.), *Future Teaching Roles for Academic Librarians*, New York, Haworth Press, 39–75.

Eadie, T. (1990) Immodest Proposals: user instruction for students does not work, *Library Journal*, **115** (17), 42–5.

Foster, S. (1993) Information Literacy: some misgivings, *American Libraries*, **24** (4), 344, 346.

Gorman, M. (1991) Send for a Child of Four! Or creating the BI-less academic library, *Library Trends*, **39** (3), 354–62.

Hardesty, L. (1991) *Faculty and the Library: the undergraduate experience*, Norwood, NJ, Ablex.

Hardesty, L. (1995) Faculty Culture and Bibliographic Instruction: an exploratory analysis, *Library Trends*, **44** (2), 339–67.

Hauptman, R. and Hill, F. (1990) The Academic Librarian as Classroom Teacher. In Palmer Hall, H. and Byrd, C. (eds), *The Librarian in the University*, Metuchen, NJ, Scarecrow Press, 93–121.

Leckie, G. and Fullerton, A. (1999) IL in Science and Engineering Undergraduate Education: faculty attitudes and pedagogical practices, *College & Research Libraries*, **60** (1), 9–29.

McCrank, L. J. (1991) Information Literacy: a bogus bandwagon?, *Library Journal*, **116** (8), 38–42.

Pacey, P. (1995) Teaching User Education, Learning Information Skills: or towards the self-explanatory library, *New Review of Academic Librarianship*, **1**, 95–103.

Smith, R. (1997) *Philosophical Shift: teach the faculty to teach information literacy*. Paper presented at the Annual Conference of the Association of College & Research Libraries, Nashville, TN, 13 April 1997, available on ACRL website.

Todd, R. (1999) Information Literacy: concept, challenge and conundrum. In Booker, D. I. (ed.) *Concept, Challenge, Conundrum: from library skills to information literacy. Proceedings of the Fourth National Information Literacy Conference conducted by the University of South Australia Library and the Australian Library and Information Association Information Literacy and Special Interest Group, 3-5 December, Adelaide*, 25–34, Adelaide, University of South Australia Library.

23

The Big Blue project

Louise Makin

Introduction

This chapter looks at the JISC (Joint Information Systems Committee)-funded Big Blue project, jointly managed by the libraries at Manchester Metropolitan University and the University of Leeds, and established to audit current provision for information skills training across the UK higher and post-16[1] education sectors, identify instances of 'good practice' to form the basis of a series of case studies and make recommendations for the future. The completed work of the project, carried out between May 2001 and July 2002, can be found on the website www.leeds.ac.uk/bigblue/. Throughout the project the website was regularly updated in light of developments taking place within the sphere of information literacy. There are links to a number of resources including online information skills courses developed both in the UK and internationally, related projects and other resources such as competency standards and strategic plans. The site also contains all the outputs from the project including the full text of the literature review, bibliography, results of the online audit, taxonomy and the Information Skills Toolkit.

Literature review

There is a vast amount of literature available on information skills/literacy and as a result a decision was made to concentrate primarily on experiences in Australia and the USA as two of the most advanced countries in terms of information skills development. Given the remit of the project, the selected literature tended to be mainly concerned with the tertiary education sectors in the selected countries and was limited to material published in the last ten years, although some exceptions were made. There was markedly less published material available illustrating the UK experience than for the USA and Australia and that which was available was not always recent. The link between the development of skills and lifelong learning which particularly characterizes the Australian context is now being more explicitly stated within the UK, but a coherent strategy for achieving this has yet to be formulated.

The terminology used in the literature varies between information literacy in the USA and Australia and information skills in the UK. There is no one, clear, agreed definition of these terms but as both information literacy and information skills relate to the ability to locate, access, evaluate and use information they have therefore been used interchangeably during the project. The full text of the literature review and bibliographies of resources can be found on the project website, following the link under the heading 'Deliverables'.

Information skills audit

One of the project aims was to establish the current level of information skills provision within the higher and post-16 education sectors. This was achieved by means of a questionnaire distributed both electronically and in paper format to all higher and post-16 education institutions. The data requested was largely quantitative, to establish what was being delivered, to whom, by whom and by what means. The number of responses received in total was 278, representing 54% of HE (Higher Education) institutions and 36% of post-16. It was clear from the responses received that information skills are now becoming much more prominent. Almost 60% of institutions surveyed stated that information skills features in their institutional strategic plans and 88% of respondents stated that it was in their information services' strategic plans.

From the comments that were made some common themes emerged. These included the increased delivery of information skills training online and through VLEs (virtual learning environments). To balance these innovative developments many institutions are still experiencing difficulties such as ensuring student attendance, lack of collaboration with academic colleagues and establishing information skills as a priority at the institutional level.

Taxonomy

Information literacy is most often defined in terms of the attributes of an information-literate person. The taxonomy has been constructed from such lists drawn up by some key authors. Table 23.1 is an abridged version of that which appears on the project website. Areas of commonality in skills can be seen through the recurrence of certain terms, some of which have been highlighted. There are also key differences such as 'evaluates' and 'evaluates critically', which raises questions about the exact nature and depth of the skills to be acquired.

Table 23.1 *Taxonomy of information skills*

	Information skills competency standards		
Doyle (1992)	SCONUL (1999)	ACRL (2000)	CAUL (2000)
Recognizes the need for information	**Recognizes** a need for information	**Determines** the nature and extent of the information needed	**Recognizes** need for information and **determines** the nature and extent of information needed
Recognizes that accurate and complete information are basis for intelligent decision making			
Identifies potential sources of information	**Distinguishes** ways of addressing the information gap	**Accesses** needed information effectively and efficiently	**Accesses** needed information effectively and efficiently
Formulates questions based on information needs	**Constructs** strategies for locating information	**Evaluates** information and its sources **critically** and incorporates selected information into his or her knowledge base and value system	**Evaluates** information and sources **critically** and incorporates into knowledge base and value system
Develops successful search strategies			
Accesses sources of information including computer based and other technologies	**Locates** and **accesses** information		**Classifies, stores, manipulates** and **redrafts** information collected or generated

continued

Table 23.1 (continued)

	Information skills competency standards		
Doyle (1992)	SCONUL (1999)	ACRL (2000)	CAUL (2000)
Evaluates information	**Compares** and **evaluates** information obtained from different sources	Individually or as a member of a group, **uses** information effectively to accomplish a specific purpose	**Expands, reframes** or **creates new knowledge** by integrating prior knowledge and new understandings as an individual or member of a group
Organizes information for practical application	**Organizes, applies** and **communicates** information to others in ways appropriate to the situation	**Understands** many of the **economic, legal and social** issues surrounding information use, and accesses and uses information ethically and legally	**Understands cultural, economic, legal and social** issues surrounding information use and accesses and uses information ethically, legally and respectfully
Integrates new information into an existing body of knowledge	**Synthesizes** and **builds** on existing information, **contributing** to the creation of **new knowledge**		**Recognizes** that lifelong learning and participative citizenship require information literacy
Uses information in **critical thinking** and **problem solving**			

Model of the information-literate person and learning outcomes

Drawing from the taxonomy and other work carried out in defining information literacy, a model of an information-literate person has been devised. This comprises eight characteristics. An information-literate person:

- recognizes an information need
- addresses the information need
- retrieves the information
- evaluates the information critically
- adapts the information found to match information need
- organizes the information
- communicates the information
- reviews the process.

Work that has been carried out into performance indicators, in the form of the Information Literacy Standards from the Association of College and Research Libraries (ACRL, 2000) and the Council of Australian University Libraries (CAUL, 2000), is useful as it enables further depth to be added to such models as that outlined above. One of the project recommendations is that further work should be carried out in this area to produce a similar set of standards for the UK which should be endorsed by all relevant bodies. This would ensure some future degree of uniformity in graduate skills.

Post-16 model and toolkit

The post-16 model highlights the aspects of information skills found within the Key Skills framework at Levels 1–3. The Information Skills Toolkit takes this one step further by including information on how the statements can be interpreted in practice with examples from the project case studies. Comments from the Key Skills Support Programme are also included. The Toolkit's statements are taken directly from the Qualifications and Curriculum Authority's Key Skills specifications (as revised September 2000). The sections relating to information skills are included in the IT and communication skills components. It is hoped that the Post-16 Toolkit will assist staff in highlighting the need to integrate information skills training into the curriculum, as well as provide practical examples of how this can be achieved.

Case studies

A number of case studies have been carried out which illustrate instances of good practice in information skills provision. These were informed by features highlighted from US and Australian experiences in the literature review as well as from the findings of the audit. They have been included in the Toolkit in order to illustrate ways in which institutions approach various difficulties associated with developing an information skills programme.

The Information Skills Toolkit

The Information Skills Toolkit (see Figure 23.1) brings together some of the key deliverables that the Big Blue project has produced: case studies, literature reviews, links to websites and the results of the project's audit of information skills training in post-16 and higher education institutions in the UK. The Toolkit is intended to be a source of inspiration and practical support for institutions that are seeking to improve or implement information skills training, by providing examples from a variety of institutions from small colleges to large universities, plus the resources to capitalize on the ideas they will provide. The Toolkit is designed to be accessed via the web, although a printable version is available.

The Toolkit is divided into nine sections, each of which relates to a key feature of a successful information skills programme:

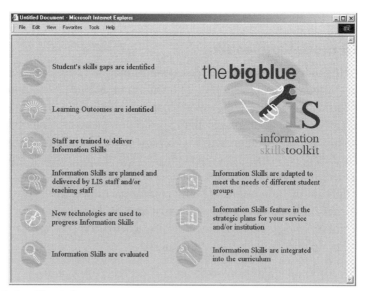

Fig. 23.1 *The Information Skills Toolkit*

- Learning Outcomes are Identified
- Information Skills are Integrated into the Curriculum
- Staff are Trained to Deliver Information Skills
- Information Skills are Evaluated
- New Technologies are Used to Progress Information Skills
- Student Skills Gaps are Identified
- Information Skills Feature in the Strategic Plans for Your Service and/or Institution
- Information Skills are Planned and Delivered by Teaching Staff and/or Library and Information Service Staff
- Information Skills are Adapted to Meet the Needs of Different Student Groups.

Each section contains an explanation of the aspect of information skills that it covers, plus findings from the audit, and links to relevant case studies and web resources. It is hoped that this will contextualize the different elements of information skills that the Toolkit identifies and provide realistic options for every kind of institution, backed up by real-life examples from the case studies.

The Toolkit's home page allows users to navigate the various sections. It is designed to resemble a 'manual'– reinforcing the idea that it is something that users can work from and use as a reference. Each 'button' is clickable and takes the user to the relevant section of the Toolkit. Figure 23.2 is a typical section from the Toolkit.

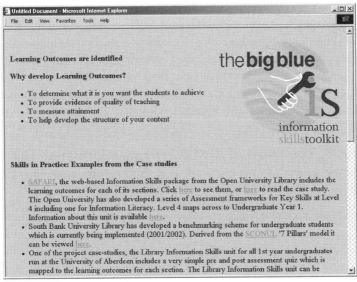

Fig. 23.2   *Typical section of the Toolkit*

From this page users can link to external websites and content on the project website. They can also navigate to subsequent pages and the homepage.

The following scenarios demonstrate how the project team anticipates that the Toolkit might be used.

Scenario 1: The Head of the LRC (Library/Learning Resource Centre) in a small post-16 college wants to develop learning outcomes, in order to focus information skills training

The Toolkit contains a section entitled 'Learning Outcomes are Identified'. This contains brief information on why learning outcomes are important and how to decide which outcomes are suitable for the student population. There are also links to online courses that include learning outcomes and links to institutions such as South Bank University and Southport College which demonstrate practical applications of Learning Outcomes and the impact they have on information skills training.

Scenario 2: A member of LRC staff who delivers information skills training wants to start evaluating the programme, or encouraging students to evaluate their skills

This user would turn to the section of the Toolkit entitled 'Information Skills are Evaluated'. This section includes an explanation of the value and importance of evaluation and the issues to consider when undertaking evaluation, such as deciding the type of data wanted and how it will be collected and processed. This section also lists less obvious benefits of evaluation, such as using positive evaluation to support funding bids or to embed information skills into the curriculum. Finally there is a link to a case study from the University of Aberdeen where pre- and post-self-assessment has been carried out to encourage students to track their progress and see the value of information skills.

Scenario 3: The Head of the LRC wants information skills to be recognized outside the service, e.g. by college managers and academic staff

This is a key challenge for many institutions, and an important first step in providing effective training that students will be motivated to attend and that can be embedded into the curriculum. The section of the Toolkit entitled 'Information Skills Feature in the Strategic Plans for Your Service and/or Institution' provides statistical information from the project's audit on what percentage of institutions currently have information skills in their service or college plans. There is a list of reasons to include information skills in such plans, suggesting that inclusion in LRC service plans can act as a springboard for inclusion in college plans. There is also a link to some characteristics developed by the ACRL which illustrate best practices of information skills programmes – a useful source of inspiration when demonstrating the value of information skills in a college plan.

Conclusion

The remit of the project has proved to be very wide ranging and as a result the project team has tried to produce information and resources applicable to a variety of situations and experiences. It is hoped that all the project outcomes will have contributed to this and that the website and the Toolkit in particular will provide a starting point in planning a new service or programme. It is also hoped they will be a resource that will be referred to again and again for support, ideas and motivation.

References

ACRL (2000) *Information Literacy Competency Standards for Higher Education: standards, performance indicators and outcomes*, Chicago, ACRL. Available at www.ala.org/Content/NavigationMenu/ACRL/Standards_and_Guidelines/Standards_and_Guidelines_by_Topic.htm.

CAUL (2000) *Information Literacy Standards*, 1st edn, Canberra, Council of Australian University Librarians. Available at www.caul.edu.au/caul-doc/InfoLitStandards2001.doc.

Doyle, C. (1992) *Final Report to the National Forum on Information Literacy*, Syracuse, NY, ERIC Clearing House on Information Technology. ED351033.

SCONUL (1999) *Information Skills in Higher Education: a SCONUL position paper*, London, SCONUL. Available at www.sconul.ac.uk/publications/publications.htm#2.

Notes

1   The term post-16 education refers to all non-compulsory education, other than higher education, which is available to those over the age of 16. This includes institutions such as sixth form and FE (further education) colleges.

2   The Qualifications and Curriculum Authority is responsible for standards in education and training in England and Wales. Their work includes maintaining and developing the school curriculum and associated assessments, and accrediting and monitoring qualifications in schools, colleges and at work. The Key Skills Qualification relates to skills in IT, communication and the application of number. Available at www.qca.org.uk.

24

Using information in the 5–14 curriculum in Scotland

Audrey Sutton

Introduction

The recognition that the 'information society' is the environment in which young people study, and will continue to work and study, was the background to a recent PhD research project carried out in conjunction with the Robert Gordon University in Aberdeen. The ability to use information, particularly through the use of ICT (information and communications technology), is now regarded as vital to lifelong learning and the ability to succeed in the knowledge society (SEED, 1999). In Scottish schools, the articulation of core skills within the Higher Still curriculum (covering the upper years of secondary education, ages approx. 14–18), with its emphasis on the use of ICT and the ability to learn independently, places further demands on staff and pupils to ensure that information-handling skills must be taken seriously and developed to the same extent as subject knowledge across the curriculum. The aims of the PhD project were to inform the current debate over the way in which teachers and librarians can combine the knowledge they have of how children learn, and how they use information, to respond to the challenge of preparing young adults to be fully and accurately informed by the information sources at their disposal.

In the UK, the conditions that will be created by a fully functioning National Grid for Learning (Great Britain. DfEE, 1997) and the opportunities that will be provided by the New Library: the People's Network initiative (LIC, 1997) will combine to offer students a range of information and learning choices that will be overwhelming unless their information-related skills are honed to allow them to make these choices well.

The current study centres around the need to examine the way in which pupils in the upper primary and lower secondary school find and use information for the purposes of their research in school, and to find ways in which teachers and librarians can assist them in this process. More specifically, it uses the context of the Scottish education system and examines the expected progression of students from Level D to Level E within the 5–14 strand of English Language, entitled Reading for Information (SOEID, 1991). The 5–14 curriculum is undertaken by all primary school pupils (Years 1–7) as well as all pupils in Years 1 and 2 of secondary education. The movement from primary to secondary education in Scotland takes places at around age 12. Curricular subject areas are defined within a number of strands. This is a challenging stage of skills development within the educational process, and concerns a number of areas of research such as cognitive development, reading research, information-seeking behaviour and motivation to learn.

The primary–secondary school transition involves the development of students from being able to collect and collate information, to being able to evaluate the usefulness of information for a particular purpose and to use it for a piece of personal research. The above strand concentrates on the reading of non-fiction material by students, and their ability to understand, assimilate and successfully use for their own purposes the information which they extract from their reading. The expected product is 'a piece of personal research' (SOEID, 1991, 39).

This stage of reading development is deemed to coincide with the transition from primary to secondary school of pupils within the 11–12 years age range, and is expected to take place by the end of Secondary Year 2 (S2) in secondary schools (SOEID, 1991). There are many problems associated with this expectation, not least the lack of guidance for staff involved in teaching this process, and the fact that this maturing of educational outlook is expected to occur across the primary–secondary divide. The author's return to school librarianship after a number of years highlighted the need for research, since the understanding of this area and the guidance available to staff had not appeared to develop in the intervening years. In fact, Simpson (1988) advocated a well planned and conceived transmission of learning skills through the existing curriculum in a way in which, she believes, the current curriculum planners have failed to do.

The educational area known as 'information skills' has already been the subject of a great deal of research; but literature searches have shown that there has been very little work done on the question of the development of these specific attainment targets in the context of 5–14 in Scotland. Moreover, little work has been done on combining knowledge of these skills with the literature on learning, which can illuminate our understanding of these skills.

Focus of research project

The central aim of the research was to find ways in which teachers and librarians could help pupils use information more effectively for their research purposes. This involved an examination of how students use information, i.e. how they progress from being able to collect and collate information to being able to use it in context to discuss, support and refute arguments, an issue that has long been the focus of attention for teachers and librarians.

It emerged, however, that this aim could not be achieved without the development of two complementary 'tools' that would allow this examination. In order to fully investigate how students use information for their own purposes, it became necessary to develop a terminology of information-related skills with which to discuss the issues with teaching staff and students. Secondly, the research then revealed the absence of a suitable method that could be used to adequately observe children engaged in this type of activity. A framework with which to carry out classroom observation in Scottish schools was therefore developed in response to this need. This chapter concentrates on the development of this framework of information-related activities, although the study had a wider focus.

Development of the Information Skills Framework

It became clear in the course of the research that it would be necessary to examine the student from two points of view: as a learner and as an information seeker. It would also be important to ascertain which skills are most important in the transitional process, i.e. which made most difference to the understanding and use of information, particularly at the Levels D–E transitional stage, where critical attitudes are expected to develop. This examination took two related and complementary forms – a theoretical critique of the documentation and literature related to the subject, and a practical analysis of learning activities based on classroom observation. It emerged that the focus of the study (skills at Level D and Level E) could not be studied in isolation, and it was therefore decided that a broader study of the skills across the 5–14 curriculum was necessary in order to contextualize the detailed area of study. This was achieved by an examination of information-related skills across the curriculum, with data being drawn from the 5–14 documentation and from related documents detailed in the study. Specification and examination of the range of key skills relevant to reading for information at Level D to Level E, focusing on the continuity, or lack of continuity, of the application of these skills, was also necessary.

The specific context for the project was that by Level D, the attainment target for reading for information is, 'to find, select, and collate information from more than one source' (SOEID, 1991, 17). This should be attained by P5–P6 (ages 9–11), but certainly by P7 (age 11–12). By Level E, the attainment target is, 'Apply the information acquired from a number of different sources for the purpose of a piece of personal research' (SOEID, 1991, 17). This is expected by P7–S1, but at the latest by S2 (ages 13–14).

The expectation that students will make the progression from being able to collect and collate information to being able to evaluate information and use it for their own purposes is a central part of the learning process. This expectation, and the subsequent setting of a specific attainment target in this field, and at this specific level, presupposes the existence of a clear strategy for the teaching and learning of these skills within 5–14. It also makes the assumption that all pupils have been taught that reading non-fiction requires a very different process from reading fiction, which is predominantly narrative in style and personal in content. The information about skills gained from the documentary analysis would inform subsequent classroom observation of pupils engaged in information-related tasks at Levels D and E.

However, an examination of the programmes of study and attainment targets within 5–14 English Language revealed an absence of information and guidance on the teaching and assessment of the skills and strategies that would eventually allow students to become critical readers. The attainment targets detail what should be achieved, but the means of achieving it is neglected. Moreover, clear definitions of skills were also absent. More serious, however (and this became clear in the researcher's discussion of the project with teaching staff and librarians), was the absence of a curricular framework that took overt cognisance of the developmental and cross-curricular links forged by information-handling activities. The absence of an awareness of the individual skills involved at each stage of the 5–14 curriculum, and their relationship to other strands and levels, meant that, in order to provide a sound basis for the research, an understanding of the underlying expectations in information-related teaching and learning had to be achieved.

It was initially proposed that this objective could be achieved by developing a checklist of skills expected at Levels D to E, based on documentary and literature analysis, and that these skills could be included in a database of cross-curricular skills that would provide a type of framework of information skills throughout and across the subject areas of 5–14. The theory that emerged from this documentary and literature analysis, including a database of 5–14 skills and an observation checklist, was to be used to inform a practical process of 'matching', whereby the individual skills identified would then be used as a basis for classroom observation. Students would be observed in information-related activities and their performances assessed according to the frequency and proficiency with which the student applied these skills. Important information about how and when individual skills and strategies were implemented would be learned from this observation.

However, several reservations emerged during this process. Firstly, definitions of, or examples of skills which were deemed to be 'critical' (in both senses of the word, i.e. 'crucial', and 'enabling critical attitudes to be adopted') did not emerge from the documents. Secondly, as the study progressed it emerged that the weakness of the above approach was that it pre-determined the results of the observation, in part a result of the observation checklist and schedule being based on the 5–14 documentation, thus simply accepting and reiterating the very system the project attempted to critically examine. For these reasons, this method was applied during Stage 1 of the classroom observation in one school and subsequently rejected. Elements of behaviour and attitudes, which were ignored by the checklist approach, had emerged during the classroom observation sessions and a new approach, and therefore new objectives, were necessary in order to take the additional data into account.

The previous phases of the research project were concerned with developing methodologies to find a language with which to describe the skills used in information-related work in the course of the 5–14 curriculum. However, the existence of a culture, researched and described by Bruton and Allan (1996), whereby teachers and pupils alike are reluctant, and in some cases unable, to describe the processes of reading and using information also emerged. They concluded that there seems to be a lack of language with which to discuss reading and reading development and that we must make our knowledge and lack of it explicit by sharing it. The checklist of skills that emerged did provide a useful terminology for the discussion of the skills being discussed, but did not prove to be a useful tool in the observation and investigation of what was actually happening in the classroom. Therefore, in order to avoid simply identifying yet another structure to be imposed on observed behaviour, as the checklist was doing, an alternative approach was taken, influenced by the ethnographic paradigm, though based on the positivist approach described above, to investigate what is real for young people as they read. This approach used a different method in an effort to achieve a more accurate picture of what actually takes place in the classroom during information-related activities.

The revised approach was also influenced by the literature relating to grounded theory methodology. While it would not have been appropriate to adopt a grounded theory approach at this stage of the research, nevertheless the debate relating to the need for a more open yet systematic approach to data analysis proved useful in the analysis of the data from the previous and ongoing classroom observation, in order to take into account any data that might not fit neatly into the structure imposed by the 5–14 checklist, thus developing a new approach to analysis of data. Subjectivity threatened to undermine this phase of the research, and as a result the work of Bloom (Bloom and Krathwohl, 1956) and Nahl (1993) was used to contribute to the data analysis. The intrinsic aim of this project was to examine how critical attitudes to information can be encouraged to develop in late primary/early secondary children. The influences on this process can either be educational or more personal (emotional, effect of background, or learning styles to name a few examples). In order, therefore, to explore this phenomenon from a new approach, while taking cognizance of research already done in this field, it was decided to apply elements of the separate yet complementary taxonomies of Bloom (Bloom and Krathwhol, 1956) (educational/cognitive) and Nahl (1993) (affective, cognitive, sensorimotor model of the information search process). Thus, a new framework (i.e. other than those examined in the literature, which were rejected as being developed by other authors for different situations) emerged for observing and studying children engaged in the information-seeking and -using process.

The Information Skills Framework

There were two contexts in which the researcher essentially required to examine what students did during the information-related process. The first was an educational context, and to this, Bloom's taxonomy levels of 'knowledge, comprehension, application, analysis, synthesis and evaluation' were applied. This taxonomy clarifies and objectifies the work done in Stage 1 of the research process, where the development of the skills database and consequently the skills checklist attempted to enumerate and classify the types of skills that were deemed to be observable in children throughout 5–14. Bloom's work could have been used from the outset, but this would have undermined the desire of the researcher to investigate the nature and incidence of information-related skills from as many points of view as possible, and to understand the foundations of the work of Bloom and other information skills experts. The devising of the checklist achieved this aim.

The second was a more wide-ranging context, to which Nahl's reinterpretation of Kulthau's six-stage model of the information search process was applied, including the standard components of the behavioural domain: affective (feelings), cognitive (decisions) and sensorimotor (actions) aspects of behaviour. This model was redefined for the purposes of the current study, and synthesized with the educational perspectives suggested by Bloom, in order to provide a practical model to analyse observed information skills behaviour in school-age children.

A combination of relevant properties of the elements of these models was applied to the observation data in order to proceed with coding of data. Thus, ironically, a new framework emerged for observing and studying children engaged in the information-seeking and -using process, which was tested over the remaining period of the study. Although this dependence on a model had hitherto been avoided, the development of the new framework was dependent on the researcher's observations rather than relying on one that already existed and may not have been relevant in the curricular context.

The stages of each procedure (i.e. that of Bloom – knowledge, comprehension, application, analysis, synthesis and evaluation – and that of Nahl – initiation, selection, exploration, formulation, collection, presentation) do represent developments (not necessarily chronological) in the individual advance towards the successful use of information for a required task. In the new framework developed during this study, these steps have been brought together and used to devise notional 'stages' of this progression to enable the observer to have an holistic picture of the information-seeking and -using process. This hypothetical framework of 'equivalent progressive steps' has therefore been developed from the elements present in information-related behaviour from both the point of view of students as learners, as Bloom's process suggests, and from the point of view of students as information seekers, as Nahl suggests (Nahl, 1993, 1996 and 1998).

This hypothetical framework assumes a development in the processes used by pupils in both of the above domains, although not a chronological one. It differs from the traditional information skills frameworks in that:

- it emerged from information gained from documentary analysis and classroom observation, rather than from theory
- it recognizes that information use is not simply a cognitive operation, but depends also on activities related to the affective and sensorimotor domains
- it incorporates examples of skills that are relevant to each level of the 5–14 curriculum, making it useful throughout all stages of the curriculum.

The observed behaviours were then analysed against this framework in order to define where the concentration of information-seeking and -using behaviours lie, and consequently where the weaknesses in the application of these skills can be observed. It must be stressed that although the framework is presented as incorporating progressive and chronological stages, this is only for ease of presentation and analysis – the skills within each stages were observed and analysed in their own contexts within the classroom and were coded according to individual categories within the framework, not as part of any predetermined progression. This revision of method took place during a second stage of classroom observation, in a second school. However, the qualitative method of data collection used throughout the practical data-gathering sessions, including those carried out in the first round of classroom observation, consisting mainly of taped conversations and activities and field notes, provided a rich bank of data that could be analysed according to the revised method.

Thus, and finally, to achieve the main aim of the study, which was to effectively investigate how pupils can become critical of information at Levels D and E, this framework was used as a tool to analyse the data collected from the observation of pupils engaged in information-related work in classroom settings. Figure 24.1 shows an example of the Information Skills Framework. The framework accepts the totality of the information-seeking processes as described by Kulthau (1991) and Nahl (1993), refines it for, and later applies it and tests it in, the context of the Scottish educational system, attempts to show the breadth of behaviours that come into play during the process, and allows the onlooker to make use of the more readily identifiable affective and sensorimotor demonstrations of skills and to assess the cognitive behaviours and skills in terms of educational objectives.

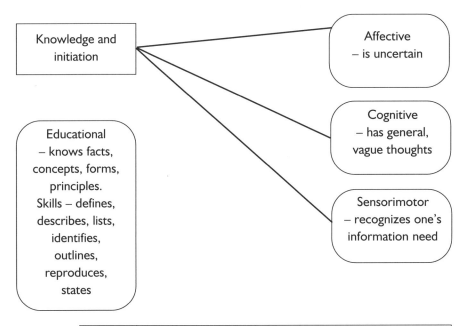

Fig. 24.1 *Information Skills Framework Stage 1*

Conclusion

The analysis (using the framework) of qualitative and quantitative data (gathered from classroom observations and interviews) revealed a number of factors that were crucial to the development of critical attitudes to information. Selection of task/topic by pupils was important (teacher-defined tasks were often inappropriate or not fully enough planned). Hepworth (1998) found that one of the information-related weaknesses of the students in his study was their lack of ability to 'define the problem' within a task. The limitations of the task and the inability of students to revise research questions and procedures is related to this – if a pupil was adhering to a task set by the teacher, pupils who were applying critical skills often recognized the need to change focus or direction, by which time it was often too late to achieve a new goal. The importance of the 'synthesis' stage of learning process became apparent – this is where the pupils found that the 'hard bits' occurred and success here was vital. Related to this was the observation of a concentration of skills in 'safe' areas such as collection and presentation, where little analysis of information was necessary. The use of deep and surface approaches to teaching the topics and the skills also made a difference, as did the use of metacognition, where pupils were taught to reflect at every stage and to keep diaries of their progress. The findings of Loranger (1994, 347) were pertinent: 'Although the unsuccessful students were generally less efficient in their use of learning strategies, they were satisfied with their academic performance. That is, the unsuccessful students perceived themselves as successful learners, lacking self-knowledge of their inefficient strategy use.' Finally, it became clear that unrealistic expectations of the levels pupils would achieve contributed to their apparent failure to achieve targets, which in turn was related to the absence of assessment guidance in these stands in the curriculum.

The framework was tested at Levels D and E of the Scottish curriculum. Wider testing is now necessary to develop the framework further and to compare findings at different stages of the curriculum or in different classroom settings.

References

Bloom, B. S. and Krathwohl, D. R. (1956) *Taxonomy of Educational Objectives Handbook I: Cognitive Domain*, New York, Longmans, Green.

Bruton, A. and Allan, J. (1996) Teaching and Developing Reading in the Secondary School, *SCRE Newsletter*, **59**, (Autumn). Available at www.scre.ac.uk/rie/nl59/nl59allanbruton.html.

Great Britain. DfEE (1997) *Connecting the Learning Society: The Government's consultation paper on the National Grid for Learning*, London, Department for Education and Employment.

Hepworth, M. (1998) A Study of Undergraduate Information Literacy and Skills: the inclusion of information literacy and skills in the undergraduate curriculum. In *Proceedings of the 65th IFLA Council and General Conference, Bangkok, Thailand, August 20–August 28, 1999*. Available at www.ifla.org/IV/ifla65/papers/107-124e.htm.

Kuhlthau, C. C. (1991) Inside the Search Process: information seeking from the user's perspective, *Journal of the American Society for Information Science*, **42** (5), 361–71.

LIC (1997) *New Library: The People's Network*, London, Library and Information Commission.

Loranger, A. L. (1994) The Study Strategies of Successful and Unsuccessful High School Students, *Journal of Reading Behaviour*, 1994, **26** (4).

Nahl, D. (1993) *How to Create User-Friendly, Affective Point-of-use Instructions, and its Effects on Search Behavior and Self-Confidence*, PhD dissertation, University of Hawaii. Available at www2.hawaii.edu/~nahl/articles.html.

Nahl, D. (1996) Affective Monitoring of Internet Learners: perceived self-efficacy and success. In *Global Complexity: information, chaos and control. Proceedings of the 59th ASIS Annual Meeting*, 33 Baltimore, MD, October 20–25, 1996, 100–9, Silver Spring, MD, ASIS.

Nahl, D. (1998) Learning the Internet and the Structure of Information Behavior, *Journal of the American Society for Information Science*, **49** (11), 1017–23.

SEED (1999) *Communities: change through learning*, Report of a Working Group on the Future of Community Education, Edinburgh, Scottish Executive Education Department.

Simpson, M. (1988) Improving Learning in Schools – What Do We Know? A cognitive perspective, *Scottish Educational Review*, **20** (1), (May).

SOEID (Scottish Office Education and Industry Department) (1991) *Guidelines on the Curriculum: English Language 5–14*, Edinburgh, HMSO.

25

Infonauts: transcultural issues in information societies

Nader Naghshineh

Cyberspace is a completely spatialized visualization of all information in global information processing systems, along pathways provided by present and future communications networks, enabling full copresence and interaction of multiple users, allowing input and output from and to the full human sensorium, permitting simulations of real and virtual realities, remote data collection and control through telepresence, and total integration and intercommunication with a full range of intelligent products and environments in real space.

(M. Novak, *Liquid Architectures in Cyberspace*, 1991)

Introduction

I sometimes shudder at my age when I gauge it against the technological tools I have used and discarded in the past 25 years. Hand-operated mechanical computation machines, slide-rules, calculators, punch cards, mag-tapes, memory cards, ZX-80 Sinclair, Commodore, PC-Junior, my Intel-based computer, and now the ubiquitous PDA. I wonder how many IT literati and information professionals hold such private museum pieces? But how much, I wonder, does it affect my status as a citizen of the much-vaunted global information society? When I sit behind my desk, I have more information at my fingertips than all my past ancestors put together. Yet this does not make me feel smarter or omniscient. As more and more information sources are brought to my attention via the internet, learning to handle containment rather than access may be the challenge. There is often a desire for a mix of specificity and serendipity. And then there is the question of privacy while online.

I found out early that while I could design and implement an information service according to given standards, there seemed always to be a cultural issue that manifested itself unannounced. The performance seemed to be linked to the cultural make-up of both the information advisory staff as well as the users themselves. And this really made me think whether this concept of an information society is really as globalized as the informatization of our life? In addition, there seems to be a challenge to what some call monocultural orientation where the individual is taken to be a member of only one culture. The realities of the 21st century seem to indicate that the explosion in informatization of the society has caused us to search for an identity that stretches across several cultures (see Keio University, www.sfc.keio.ac.jp/lt/en/gaiyou.html).

Such considerations drove me to an eight-month sabbatical field study on the impact of culture on information-seeking behaviour (supported by ISIS Research Grant 78-0229, April–November 1999).

Information down the ages

My study enabled me to trace the historical operational roots behind the information society. It seems to me that the concept has experienced several rebirths over the past two millennia (Naghshineh, 1999). Twenty-five centuries ago, the Persian Empire had established a management information system based on a unified code, a dependable line of communication and the pony express. The Achamaenians had effectively established the first information society of the ancient world well within the limits of their technological prowess (Naghshineh, 1998). In *The Victorian Internet*, Standgate (1998) observes the impact of telegraph networks on society. The reaction of people towards this new technology was strangely like the one we are observing now regarding the internet. Close observation reveals similar shifts in information-seeking behaviour concerning every communication and media breakthrough, from telephone, to marconigrams, radio, television and personal mobile devices. Each has entailed a redefinition of our info-sphere, our privacy, the web of relations through which we receive and impart knowledge. And yet none has achieved its promise. There is much hype about the global information society, but if you compare the projections for 20 years hence with how it actually was 2500 years ago, the difference is marginal conceptually speaking (see Figure 25.1). The two are operationally different only if we narrow our definition to the primary impact of technology as an instrument of control rather than instrument of emancipation. In fact the very perception of information, whether as an instrument of control or liberation, is culturally driven.

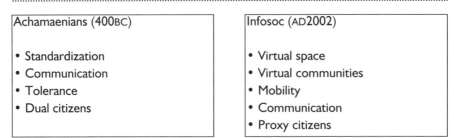

Achamaenians (400BC)	Infosoc (AD2002)
• Standardization • Communication • Tolerance • Dual citizens	• Virtual space • Virtual communities • Mobility • Communication • Proxy citizens

Fig. 25.1   *From cuneiforms to bits and bytes*

Our global society is fast becoming divided into *technos*, people versed in the manipulation and utilization of technology, and *tech-nots*, those who are at the fringes wondering why things are happening so fast. Many blame the information explosion. I do not believe so, for the reason that there has been an information explosion associated with every technological revolution.

Information and cultural background

I believe that we are being limited too much by the concept of the information society as professed by the developed countries. In fact, there may be a multiversity of information societies given different cultural backgrounds. The real question is how these societies make up the quilted global information society.

In the drive towards progress in information handling, we have neglected to pay attention to a crucial component, man himself. One thing I have learned in the classes I have taught is the fact that not all cultures lend themselves equally to the appreciation of information technology. Information is a force that we are not consciously aware of and yet it binds us to varying degrees. It is the force that we seldom acknowledge in our interactions, and our perception of which is to a large degree dependent on cultural upbringing. And perhaps that is why there seems to be an obstacle in the way of establishing a universally effective IT and information literacy programme.

In any form of courses intended for IT literacy or education, one needs to be sensitized to the cultural issues. We have been told that soon we would be living in virtual worlds of our making, worlds where we would define our virtual relationships with those others who are sailing the seas of information. In our lifetime we would see the transformation of PCs into virtual machines, our portals to the domains of our choosing. Yet the web is not augmenting minds that have been brought up in different cultural settings.

We have to explore this central question, whether attention to issues of a transcultural or even multicultural nature could contribute to a successful IT literacy programme? Does it necessarily follow that, having the ability to shape existing societies into information societies, we have to do it?

A case in point is Iran. Without doubt, the internet could be touted as a shining example of how a society has embraced and developed a technology ahead of its government. Yet the central issue remains, would an Iranian infonaut navigate like, say, an American one? How would we measure the performance? We have a choice of diversity in harmony or a homogenized combination. The latter seems to be the thrust of most IT literacy education. Yet I personally believe in the former. We need to develop a vision for an IT literacy programme within the context of the culture that is targeted to reap its benefit. Iran is a mosaic of various ethnic groups, rich and vibrant in their cultural heritage. One would need to find a Rosetta stone to convey the central concepts in instructing IT literacy. Most often we try to mould the students into stereotypes of IT literati.

In 1998, while on secondment to the Iran Scientific Documentation and Information Services (IRANDOC), I came to realize that there are three barriers to a successful culturo-centric IT literacy programme that aims to impart basic, universally acknowledged information skills. These barriers are personal, social and environmental. All three are strongly affected by cultural and linguistic backgrounds, as well as affecting the information-seeking behaviour in the six key areas of initiation, selection, exploration, formulation, collection and presentation offered in Kulthau's Information-Seeking Process model (Kulthau, 1991). If we probe deeper we will find that national cultures become important because of the combination of power reach, degree of dubiety evasion, degree of collectivism/individualism, gender-specific values and finally view of life. Culture does shape the means by which the circumstances of life are decided – consumption, production and distribution of material and immaterial goods and finally the individual's ideas in the societal debate on what is good, true or useful. I tried to address this issue.

The Dadeh–Navard concept

I at first moved towards defining a culturo-centric IT and information literacy programme. On paper it promised to better prepare the students for the acquisition, assimilation and indigenization of such training. In practice it proved to provide a more effective imparting of skills, better concept internalization, and a better chance of acceptance as well as deployment. The principles are the same, whether you are dealing with academics or businessmen.

This is why the concept known as *Dadeh Navard* (roughly speaking, Infonaut) seems to be promising. Based roughly on the information counsellor developed by the Iranian Military in the 1980s as well as borrowing elements from the information gatekeepers of the 1970s, a Dadeh Navard not only bridges the cultural barriers, but also serves as an agent of change within a target population. To be successful they must provide an active disintermediation, help the target population to develop new identities, identify and define new information assets, help the target population to define dynamic relationships among information assets and in short establish new and effective *Dadeh-Sepehrs* (Info-Spheres). This may ensure a basic level of universal information tradecraft among culturally diverse groupings.

To some the role of active disintermediation seems to be a contradiction in terms. It sounds as if the Dadeh Navard would really work to make themselves redundant. But this is exactly what an infonaut does, teaching how to fish instead of catching the fish. Skill enhancement occurs in direct correlation with the average IT skills of the target population.

The Dadeh-Navard concept also points out the necessity for any successful IT literacy or information fluency programme to address the following three key areas:

1 *Knowledge generation, identification and dissemination*: Books, tapes, films, maps, diskettes are all but media, and the functional aspects of knowledge have essentially remained unchanged. The student should be taught to treat these materials as forms for a function. The student should learn to understand the background processes leading to generation of knowledge, identify them and examine various modes of dissemination.
2 *Sociology, psychology and communication*: As members of a service sector, students should be furnished with the tools that will enable them to better serve the community that has a demand for an information service. This directly correlates with value perception, and thus engenders community support of library activities.
3 *Technology and management*: This section was the most difficult to design. It does not necessarily focus inordinately on computers, but rather on how technology facilitates library activity. Students should not be trained in any specific technology per se, but rather given the basic tools to be able to better identify and adapt the best technology to the task at hand. The same goes for management – activities such as resource sharing fall under the purview of management techniques.

Conclusion

I believe we need to address the issue of whether, in designing a curriculum, there are indeed factors that span cultures, and thus can be more readily accepted. At the moment an experiment is taking place, in which IT literacy materials available online to students of the University of Glasgow, Scotland, are also being offered to students of the University of Teheran. The results of the comparison of students' experiences and learning will directly address the issues I have raised. It is my contention that this is the real challenge in teaching – to impart knowledge in a creative and attractive way and let it establish its own pathways within a culture.

Acknowledgements

I would like to use this opportunity to express my gratitude to many individuals who supported me in my research. A special note of thanks goes to the University of Teheran, both the Chancellor and International Office, for providing the necessary funding at a crucial time. But more than most, I would like to thank the Wild Bunch of the Iranian informatics scene, without whose support, creativity and boundless energy, I would have never been able to make this study.

References

Kulthau, C. C. (1991) Inside the Search Process: information seeking from the user's perspective, *Journal of the American Society for Information Science*, **42** (5), 361–71.

Naghshineh, N. (1998) The Force of Change: libraries as a social instrument: a concise case study of Iran, *Library Review*, **47** (4), 225–9.

Naghshineh, N. (1999) Impact of Transculturalism in Information Seeking Styles and the Role of Information Gatekeeper Concept. Paper delivered at Vienna, VA. Unpublished.

Standgate, T. (1998) *The Victorian Internet*, London, Orion Books.

Index